TERRARUM

No Longer on the Map

"The Cartographer at work," German engraving of 1598.

No Longer

DISCOVERING PLACES

Raymond H. Ramsay

on the *Map*

THAT NEVER WERE

NEW YORK / THE VIKING PRESS

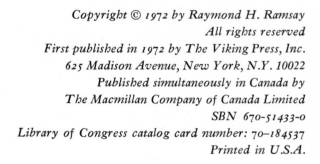

Dedicated to my grandfather
WILLIAM LENOX RAMSAY 1861–1940
who sparked and furthered my early interest
in history and geography

Acknowledgments

This book is the result of many years of reading and note-taking rather than of a particular research project. My interests have always been primarily history and geography, but they have ranged over a considerable number of other topics as well, and I hope to have succeeded here in adding some illumination to the subject by bringing in relevant information from sources perhaps not familiar to the specialist scholar.

The reader may notice that I have leaned rather heavily on a certain few sources as reference. This is unavoidable in dealing with a topic where the available literature is scanty, but it is also desirable since most of these sources are now long out-of-print and not generally available. Those of a scholarly bent may find my documentation somewhat sparse, but this is inherent in the nature of the material, for to a large extent the maps themselves are the primary sources. The illustrations are intended to serve as a substitute for more copious annotations—a substitute that some readers perhaps will find more interesting. I have used footnotes (indicated by asterisks) for explanatory or ancillary material, and endnotes (indicated by numerals) for the citing of sources.

Probably no one but those listed therein ever reads through the acknowledgments section of a preface, but I urge the reader to do so, since otherwise some of my debts of gratitude will go unpaid. I must thank B. Walter Hauck, of the University of California (Berkeley), for his invaluable assistance in the linguistic area; W. Bruce Buchanan for equally invaluable financial aid; and Kit Reinert for practical help of other sorts. Josephine Austin, Michael Makowski, and Betty Pollock read the manuscript and were most helpful and encouraging. And these friends must be mentioned for their valuable interest, and help of one kind or another: Jane Augustus, Yvette Gagnon, Henri Gaines, Frank Galland, Jean Hochberg, Elmer Lindstrom, Richard O'Connor, Larry Ross, Albert and Jacqueline Ruby, Max Scherr, the late R. C. Tabb, and especially my father, Henry H. Ramsay. Not to mention my landlord, John Arthur Gustafson, who patiently put up with my "letting things slide" while I devoted all of my time to the book.

And my special thanks to the late Dr. John Kirtland Wright, who was head of the American Geographical Society. He read the work in manuscript and was a severe but most friendly and encouraging critic. I cannot stress too strongly how much the final form of the book owes to the good Dr. Wright.

The same holds true for Dr. Ernest S. Dodge, Director of the Peabody Museum, Salem, Massachusetts, a distinguished writer on historical geography. He also read the manuscript and was most helpful and encouraging.

I should also like to express my thanks to the staff members of the Loan Department and Reference Department of the University of California (Berkeley), and to those of the Berkeley-Oakland Library Service System. I also wish to thank the young artist John C. Gustafson for his assistance in preparing the illustrations.

And special thanks to Barbara Burn, my editor at The Viking Press, whose help was instrumental in turning a somewhat choppy manuscript into something that I believe is worth your reading.

Berkeley, California
May 1971

Preface

Many places are no longer on the map.

New France, the Belgian Congo, Siberia, Dakota Territory, Courland, Western Reserve, Manji, and the Holy Roman Empire are only a few examples.*

But such regions lie outside the scope of this book. No mystery attaches to their having vanished from the map, because the names were political, not geographical. The territories have been given new names, or divided into smaller units or incorporated into larger ones, or simply reorganized on a different basis. Thus today they are "on the map" only in historical atlases or as unofficial popular names for loosely defined regions.

The Kingdom of El Dorado is quite a different case, as are the Strait of Anian, Norumbega, Grocland, and the Isle of Satanaxio. These are no longer on the map because they never existed—at least not in the form by which early geographers knew them. Then how did they come to be mapped at all? That is quite a story; in fact, quite a few stories.

Some of these originated in outright fraud while others were distortions of fact. Many arose from the misunderstanding of anything from the spelling of a word to the nature of the universe. Some were merely unnecessary duplications of islands located elsewhere; others

---

* These examples, and a number of others, will be described in more detail in Appendix I, page 243.

illustrate the danger of taking myths too literally. Some of them took a mighty grip on men's minds, and were potent factors in the working of history. A few, by pure coincidence, turned out to exist in reality.

Some of these stories have been told before, many times, but in several cases, recent information causes them to be seen in a new perspective. A few of them, I believe, are here being given their first connected presentation in a book intended for the general reader.

There is one point which should perhaps be cleared up right away. Everyone to whom I outlined my idea for this book seemed immediately to hit upon "Atlantis" as the classic instance of what I had in mind. Actually, Atlantis is entirely outside this study, because no Greek maps and only four or five Roman ones have come down to us, and none of them show it. Atlantis was supposed to have sunk some thousands of years before Plato propounded the tale, and the Egyptians, from whom Solon was supposed to have heard the tale that came down to Plato, did not make maps on such a scale as to take in the Atlantic Ocean and its islands. Atlantis, leaving aside questions of its actual existence, has never been on the map.*

This should suffice for a preface. The reader is welcomed aboard for a voyage to the lands of Nowhere, and an exploration of the devious channels leading to them.

---

* For present purposes we do not count maps made by modern students, showing their theoretical locations for the lost continent.

Contents

No Longer on the Map

CHAPTER 1.

El Dorado: Man and Myth

As the rising sun slants the long shadows of tall pines across the mountainsides, a bizarre procession follows the winding trail up the slope. At its head marches a group of nude men, intoning a high, wailing chant, their bodies smeared with red ocher in token of mourning. Next follow some one hundred men, dressed, in grotesque contrast to those in the lead, in full finery of gold and silver, trogon feathers, and jaguar skins. No wailing dirge for them; they march with brisk cheers, many of them playing merry tunes on flutes and pipes. The priests are there, in tall caps and long robes of black, and had a European been present, he would have been struck by the white crosses adorning their robes, a strange touch in this pagan setting. And at the rear, a group of richly bedecked nobles bear among them the weight of a litter, hung with gold discs, on which reclines a man as nude as those in the lead. He does not wear the red mud of mourning, however, but the bright gold of triumph. His body has been rubbed down with resin and powered with gold dust, and he gleams like a gilt idol in the morning light.

The trail halts at the edge of the mountaintop lake, in a spectacular setting circled by towering peaks, and here the march ends. The men at the rear bear their gilded burden aboard a large balsa raft, and row half a mile out to the center of the lake. Now the man on the litter becomes an active participant, by diving into the water and taking a quick swim to wash off his golden covering. At this point the men on the shore respond with song and cheer, and fling offerings of gold and jewels into the lake. The no-longer-gilded man boards the raft again and is rowed back to shore, and all those present return down the slope to the town for the feast and dance that will celebrate the installation of their new chief.

Such was the ceremony of El Hombre Dorado, the Gilded Man, as the Spaniards heard of it. By a strange trick of destiny, this occasional ritual of an unimportant Indian tribe in a remote corner of South America was to grow into a mighty geographic myth, add a term to every civilized language, and spawn a series of myths in its turn, some of which are not entirely dead even today.

By 1537, the Spaniards had looted Mexico and plundered Peru. This new world, discovered less than half-a-century before, had so far proved to be an amazing treasure house, reserved for them alone. If there was more to be had, they were eager to find it.

Sebastián de Belalcázar had established himself as a general of some importance by his conquest of Nicaragua before accompanying Pizarro on his invasion of Peru. Consequently he was detailed by Pizarro (who was not much of a field officer) to mop up the Peruvian forces that were still offering resistance in the north. It was near Quito, in modern Ecuador, that he finally defeated them; and it was there that an Indian told him of the land of Popayán, still farther north, and of its people, the Muysca, whose new chiefs were installed with the ceremony of the Gilded Man.

By now the Indians knew that the best way to get rid of the Spaniards was to pitch a good yarn, with plenty of gold in it and a location somewhere else. In this case the yarn happened to be true, but Belalcázar's Indian informant either did not know or failed to mention that it was also slightly outdated.

Belalcázar and a chosen party set out from Quito late in 1535,

Sebastián de Belalcázar.

heading northward, in search of this people who had gold to throw away. What happened from then on is not absolutely clear, because sources vary. But, roughly, it seems to be along these lines: before Belalcázar reached the Muysca country early in 1536, it had already been invaded and conquered by an expedition from the Caribbean coast to the north, headed by Hernán Pérez de Quesada. This venture had been disappointing from the treasure-hunting viewpoint, but had added another piece of land to the claims of the Spanish Crown. In any case, Belalcázar arrived only to find that he had been pre-empted.

And somewhere in the course of events, whether before Belalcázar's arrival or after, a third factor appeared—a free-lance German adventurer named Nicholas Federmann, who showed up on the scene in command of the remnants of a party that had set out from Venezuela some time before (some accounts say as much as five years earlier). So the land of El Dorado was now occupied by three mutu-

Sixteenth-century picture of Lake Guatavitá.

ally distrustful groups, who agreed to let the king of Spain settle their rival claims to it. In the end, Belalcázar was appointed governor of Popayán, now a state in southern Colombia.

The Muysca people, who practiced the quaint and gaudy custom of gilding their new chiefs in gold dust, were a branch of the Chibcha nation, and only a few years earlier they had been subjugated by the more powerful Bogotá Chibchas, who gave their name to the present capital of Colombia. Thus, by the time the Spaniards arrived, the ceremony of El Hombre Dorado was no longer in practice.

It did not take the Spaniards long to learn the true situation. The Muysca were now a conquered people with no chiefs of their own to install with gold offerings. They, and the Chibchas generally, mined no gold of their own, and had been getting what little they used for ritual purposes by trade with the Peruvians. And to make matters worse, Lake Guatavitá, the mountain tarn where the sacrifices had taken place, was over 400 feet deep and could not be worked by divers, so that the gold on its bottom was beyond recovery. The original El Dorado was a strictly nonpaying proposition, and by rights the legend should have died right then, to remain only a minor incident in the history of South America.

It is a mistake to contend, as some have, that the gold-hungry Spaniards kept the myth of El Dorado alive out of sheer will to believe, shuttling it round the map to new locations when it failed to turn up as charted. The conquistadores may have been gold-happy, but they were realists. It was about this time that Friar Marcos de Niza returned to Mexico with wild tales of the rich cities of Cíbola to the north, but when Coronado's expedition failed to find them they were simply written off, not assumed to be real but undiscovered (see Chapter 6). Similarly, in 1563, when Diego de Ybarra's report of discovering "a new Mexico" full of wealth for the taking proved false, the only geographical consequence was that the name "Nueva Mexico" was allowed to stand, as it still does, designating the present American state occupying that area. So the Spanish conquerors' usual attitude toward "bum steers" is clear enough. The continuing legend of El Dorado arose from unusual circumstances.

While the Bogotá Chibchas were conquering their Muysca cousins, the Tupinamba Indians on the faraway southeastern coast of Brazil were in a state of religious ferment. The details are obscure, but people were seeing visions and an apocalyptic mood was in the air. Then a prophet arose among them, summoning the nation to follow him westward to the paradise of their belief, the Land Without Evil. The trek that ensued took nine years. Thousands of Tupinambas toiled through the formidable waste of the Mato Grosso and over the high Andes, to end up finally at Chachapoyás in northern Peru in 1539.

The Spaniards avidly questioned these new arrivals from the unknown interior, and they learned much that helped to fill out the maps, information which proved useful in subsequent explorations. But in particular they asked, not without leading questions, about rich kingdoms and golden cities in the unexplored hinterlands, and the Tupinambas told them what they wanted to hear, or at least gave answers which the Spaniards interpreted in the most optimistic way. It is also possible that the semi-primitive Tupinambas, unacquainted with gold, interpreted the Spaniards' questions in terms of their own less grandiose concepts of wealth.[1]*

So El Dorado took on a new form, this time not as El Dorado the Gilded Man but El Dorado the Golden Land. The gaudy name seemed appropriate enough to be applied to whatever golden lands should be discovered.

The Tupinamba, having had their influence on the story, faded out of it. Some settled on the Peruvian coast, but most of them found that Spanish-held Peru fell somewhat short of the Land Without Evil, and they gradually straggled back to their homeland on the Brazilian coast, where Rio de Janeiro was later to arise. Many of them are still there, more or less in a state of mixed blood.

About 1530, when the Tupinamba migration was in progress, one of Cortes' former comrades in arms, Diego de Ordas, while traveling up the Orinoco, heard about an Indian nation rich in gold, located near a large lake in the vicinity of the Meta River. (It should be noted that this was several years before Belalcázar heard of El Hombre Dorado. The two stories are essentially unrelated, but they later became fused, as we shall see, because they both pointed to the same general area and because both involved a lake.) During the 1540s, however, Spanish explorers thoroughly combed the Meta River area of Colombia, as well as the adjoining uplands around Bogotá. They found no civilized Indians, no cities, and no gold.

The possibility that El Dorado was farther south, in the present Ecuador, had been dismissed when Gonzalo Pizarro, the much younger half brother of the conqueror of Peru, led an expedition out of Quito in 1539. This was before Belalcázar had returned and at about the time of the arrival of the Tupinambas in Peru, but whether either of these circumstances influenced the timing of the venture is not clear. In fact, while Gonzalo intended to keep an eye peeled for

---

* Superscript figures refer to the notes beginning on page 259.

Imaginative portrayal of the Amazons in combat.

the land of gold, his real objective was a region where cinnamon reportedly abounded. His party suffered terrific hardships in crossing the Andes, and did find a few trees with cinnamon bark (not enough to be profitable) but no sign of El Dorado. The party eventually split up: Gonzalo Pizarro returned to Peru (where he was put to death for treason a few years later), and his lieutenant, Francisco de Orellana, with some of the men of the expedition, headed out by boat down a mighty river which finally brought them to the Atlantic coast. During their trip downstream they had many clashes with Indians, and in their report of one such instance in which the women as well as the men took part in the fighting they bestowed the name "Amazon" on that river.

These investigations of northwestern South America can be said to have put an end to the "real" El Dorado—the direct outgrowths of the reported Muysca Indian ceremony. From this point on the myths take over.

The Spanish authorities can be blamed for keeping the myth of El Dorado alive. It served a useful purpose.

By the middle of the sixteenth century, the conquistador period of Spanish-American history was at an end. Towns and haciendas had been founded, a form of government had been established, and the regular Spanish Army now provided the needed protection. It was no longer the day of the military adventurer, but of the settler, the planter, the miner, the entrepreneur. Most of the riffraff who had done the initial conquering, however, were still around. They infested every civilized settlement: aging, unemployable ruffians who spent their time drinking, brawling, stealing, raising hell in general, and making life hazardous for all respectable women. When they caused too much trouble, it was always possible to round them up, put them under the command of an officer tough enough to handle them, and send them off into the wilds to search for El Dorado. It would keep them out of the way for a while and with any luck some of them wouldn't come back. And there was always the possibility that they might discover something.

Earlier, about 1541, the story of El Dorado had become attached to another region far from Bogotá and the Meta River. An expedition out of Venezuela led by a German, Philipp von Hutten, encountered and was defeated by the powerful Omagua Indians of southeastern Colombia. The impressive strength of this Omagua nation caused the accounts of its capital, first seen and described by von Hutten, to become wildly exaggerated, and by about 1558, the stage was set for the expedition that represented the final, inglorious dissipation of Spanish conquistadorism.

The leader of this ill-fated venture, Pedro de Urzúa or Ursúa), was definitely not the right man for the job: a green young officer, neither experienced nor hard-bitten enough to control the crew of roughnecks turned over to him. He planned to travel by stream, starting in Peru on the Río Huallaga, and sailing down to the

Marañon (which later joins the Ucayli to form the Amazon) and through the heart of South America to the Atlantic coast, searching on the way for any golden cities that were to be found, and keeping their ears open for any native reports of such cities.

Apparently the once-tough adventurers had gotten soft from living around the civilized towns, and they found it hard to adjust to the privations and monotony of jungle travel. They drifted downstream, finding no gold and becoming increasingly discouraged. A fight occurred, during which Urzúa's second-in-command was killed, and Urzúa ineptly handled the situation by promising the killers immunity if they would confess and, when they did so, by hanging them anyway. This was no way to establish authority with mean, dangerous men, and real trouble quickly shaped up.

The principal figure in all that ensued was a fiftyish gallows bird named Lope de Aguirre, whose previous career was distinguished only by his involvement in several attempted mutinies in Peru. He was, in fact, a good example of the sort of undesirable that these false expeditions were designed to keep away from the settlements. Aguirre became the leader of the malcontents, and headed up a plot to kill Urzúa. The murder was an act of revenge rather than a real insurrection, however, since the rebels immediately put another young officer of the regular Spanish Army, Fernando de Guzmán, into Urzúa's post as commander.

Though Guzmán was better liked by the men, he had the disadvantage of really believing in El Dorado, or at least in his duty to hunt for it. But the hardened old insurgent Aguirre had by now developed some ambitions of his own, ambitions of a more practical nature. He sparked another cabal, killed Guzmán, took command of the force himself, and proclaimed himself "General of the Marañon." The seedy ex-conquistadores now found themselves led by one of their own, a man who could handle them. They pressed on, searching not for El Dorado, but for a suitable part of the country in which to set up their own independent empire.

What course they followed is not clear. They may have followed the Amazon down to the Atlantic, but considering their final destination it seems more likely that they sailed down the Amazon only to its junction with the Río Negro, and then followed the Negro upstream to the Orinoco, and so out to the Caribbean. We do know what happened during the remainder of the journey: suspicions and hostility, cliques and cabals, fighting and disorder, indiscriminate murder of the Indians and of each other—a nightmare trek leaving a trail of blood.

Finally in 1561 the piratical band came into the Caribbean and hit upon the settled Island of Margarita ("The Pearl"), off the coast of Venezuela. The island was lightly garrisoned, and its conquest was easy. Aguirre had the governor and his officers put to death, and he ruled Margarita for a few months. He seems by now to have become a murderous psychotic, and his reign was a ghastly affair of constant treachery and bloodshed. Even Aguirre's casehardened followers found his excesses too much to stomach, and desertions occurred almost daily. Despite this, the mad conqueror attempted an invasion of Venezuela itself. The Spanish Army force opposing the invaders was considerably inferior in numbers, but Aguirre's men found themselves with no heart for the fight. They deserted him wholesale, the defending forces had an easy victory, and the gory life of Aguirre ended—appropriately—in battle.

This was the last officially organized Spanish search for El Dorado. In fact, there are indications that its gruesome outcome cast a shadow on the golden myth itself. The Spanish population of South America seems to have developed a feeling that the whole business of El Dorado was *desafortunado*—unlucky.

The cartographic situation cannot be explored satisfactorily at this point. The Spanish and Portuguese governments possess quantities of material, including maps, that was classified top secret during the great days of exploration, and that still has not been made available to scholars. It may include maps showing some tentative locations for the Land of El Dorado. One must remember that the quest for El Dorado was carried out by Spaniards in territory claimed by Spain, and during the sixteenth century it appears to have been an exclusively Spanish matter, little known to the rest of the world, and unlikely to be found on any but Spanish maps.* In any case, I have been unable to find "El Dorado" as such on any sixteenth-century maps. It existed in rumor and story, in reports and memoirs and histories, but apparently not in latitude and longitude. Another legend, however, that of Manoa, was soon to fuse with the El Dorado story, and this time it was to stand out fair and beckoning on the map.

Although the Aguirre fiasco officially discredited El Dorado, there were still some believers. One such was Antonio de Berreo, a solid citizen of Bogotá. In 1584, over twenty years after the Aguirre adventure, he set out into the Orinoco country in search of the elusive land of gold. He made two tries, the first fruitless, the second apparently to some purpose. Not that he found gold, but he did obtain some important information from the Indians. It seemed that the "El Dorado" the Spaniards had been seeking was actually named Manoa.

There was, de Berreo learned, a great lake called the Parima somewhere southeast of the Orinoco, and on its shore a gold-rich city called Manoa, the true original of the treasure-land that the Spaniards had been hopelessly chasing through the mountains and forests to the west. (We can now see how Diego de Ordas's 1530 report of a city of gold beside a lake becomes constitutive to the quest.) It appeared that the land of gold had finally been pinpointed. This was much too big a story to be followed up by a local adventurer in search of wealth. The king of Spain had to be informed.

Domingo de Vera, de Berreo's general manager, was dispatched to Spain to do the necessary organizing. This delay took time, allowing the rumors of El Dorado, which were previously confined to the Spanish dominions, to spread throughout Europe, and in the meantime de Berreo received an appointment as governor of the island of Trinidad. Finally, in 1595, de Vera sailed from Spain with several ships and a force of more than two thousand men, to trace the elusive El Dorado to its exact location. In the same year, Sir Walter Raleigh sailed from Plymouth on an expedition of his own, not yet related to de Vera's but soon to become so.

---

* For example, Antonio Galvano, the Portuguese historian, whose *Discoveries of the World* is inclusive up to about 1553, made no mention of El Dorado and apparently knew nothing about it.

De Vera's expedition met up with de Berreo at Trinidad, and proceeded without him to the Venezuelan coast where it struck out overland. Most of the men were greenhorns fresh out of Spain, not experienced junglemen like the conquistadores, and the hardships and hazards of the tropical wilderness soon finished off many of them. And the few who survived found nothing.

Raleigh's expedition swooped down upon Trinidad not long after de Vera had left. Raleigh plundered the city of San José (now Port of Spain), and took Governor de Berreo captive. Unlike Sir Francis Drake, who favored strong-arm methods, Raleigh had a policy of being a good jailer to his Spanish prisoners, and he could usually get them to talk. It was not long before de Berreo spouted all that he had heard and guessed about the great lake and the golden city, long referred to as El Dorado but now known by its true name of Manoa.

Raleigh sailed to the mouth of the Orinoco and there divided up his forces, leading some of his men in small boats up that great river. Before he had gone far, reports of an approaching Spanish fleet forced him to cancel the project and return to his own fleet, and thence to England. The following year, 1596, Raleigh was involved in the British attack on Cádiz, but he did send Laurence Keymis, one of his captains, to follow up his earlier effort. Just how far Keymis went, and what he actually saw or heard, is unknown, but he did bring back to England the story of a great inland lake (according to him, saline) called Parima. Keymis did not actually locate Manoa on this lake, but he said the lake was on the way to Manoa.[2]

This gave Raleigh all that he needed to write one of the classics of fabulous geography, *The Discovery of the Large, Rich, and Beautiful Empire of Guiana*, with a fulsome description of "that great and golden Citie, which the Spaniards call El Dorado, and the naturalls Manoa." The original Gilded Man had not been forgotten over the years, but the account had been altered. Raleigh related that it was the custom, when the Emperor of Guiana held a drunken carouse with his court favorites, for all the participants to strip, be "anoynted all over, with a kind of white balsamum," and coated with gold dust, by servants who blew it through hollow tubes, "until they be al shining from the foote to the head and that in this sort they sit drinking by twenties and hundreds and continue in drunkenes sometimes six and seven daies together." The original, occasional coronation ceremony had been expanded in the telling into a round of continuous homosexual orgies.

Another oddity which Raleigh located in this area (one unconnected with El Dorado) was the Ewaipanomas, the tribe of headless men. The legend of men who had no heads, and whose features were located in their chests, can be traced back to Pliny, who called them Blemmyae and located them in the African interior. Medieval geographers shuttled them all over the map, from Africa to Finland to northeast Asia, and finally to South America. The origin of this strange myth may have been in early Greek or Roman travelers' accounts of primitive ceremonial masks.[3]

From this point on, El Dorado fades away. The South American Spaniards made a few more halfhearted searches, and then became

Gilding a chief with gold dust, from Theodore de Bry.

Sir Walter Raleigh.

finally disillusioned with the whole idea. The outside world had never really swallowed the story, having developed a healthy skepticism about Spanish reports. (Sir Walter Raleigh was an outstanding exception.) Before the seventeenth century was out, "Manoa" was forgotten, and "El Dorado" had entered most Western European languages as a phrase meaning the unattainable quest.

Only one more search for Manoa is worth the telling. In 1616 Sir Walter Raleigh, now old and in bad grace and a prisoner in the Tower, managed to wangle another chance from King James I by trading on his supposed knowledge of the still-undiscovered city. He was allowed to outfit a new expedition, but because of James's policy of peaceful coexistence with Spain, could do so only on his guarantee that the route to Manoa would not encroach on Spanish territory.

On this voyage it became clear that Raleigh's luck had run out. His fleet was shattered by storms and many of his men died or deserted at every opportunity. Raleigh himself was stricken with tropical fever, and on his arrival he found a Spanish force opposing him. There was fighting, and it cost the life of Raleigh's beloved scapegrace elder son. In the end, this foray into Spanish territory caused the Spanish ambassador in England to demand Raleigh's punishment, and on his return the old treason charge that had landed him in the Tower was reactivated, and he was beheaded.

El Dorado was no more, but Lake Guatavitá, which had started the whole business, still remained. The Spaniards made a few unsuccessful attempts to drain it, but it was not until 1913 that an English expedition with modern equipment succeeded in pumping the lake dry and excavating its bottom. They found a few gold artifacts, but their booty belongs to archaeology rather than treasure hunting. The total value of the find was not even enough to cover the cost of the expedition. Does more treasure lie buried in the mud of centuries beneath the bed of the lake? It would be rash to assume that these investigators exhausted it completely. Still, it would be equally rash to assume, on the available evidence, that the Muysca Indians had practiced the ceremony of El Dorado for any great length of time, or that their golden offerings had ever been very numerous. Probably very little gold remains there to be discovered.

Manoa, the second El Dorado, first appeared on the map drawn by Raleigh in England in about 1596 for an unfinished and unpublished manuscript which is now in the British Museum.[4] Jodocus Hondius, a Dutch cartographer operating in England, apparently used it as the basis for his 1598 map of South America, the first published map to show Manoa. The mythical city's first appearance on the map outside England was in 1599, when the famed Flemish engraver Theodore de Bry published in Cologne his *America*, which included a detailed and highly imaginative map of Guiana apparently based on Raleigh's account rather than on Hondius. The map featured representations of the Amazons and the headless men, a curious animal apparently intended to be an armadillo, and "this sea called by the CANIBALES PARIME.* On the northwest shore of Parime [sic], stood "Manoa or Dorado . . . the greatest city in the world."

It is hard to determine exactly how long Manoa stayed on the map. The point is not too important, since early mapmakers had a notorious habit of copying each other, and thus often perpetuated the outmoded. I have in my possession two maps of South America, both undated but apparently of the early 1620s; the one by Willem Blaeu (a prominent commercial cartographer of that time) still shows "Manoa al Dorada" on "Parime Lacus," but the other by Michael Mercator (son of the famous Gerhardus Mercator) has dropped both lake and city.

Manoa-El Dorado was finished cartographically by the 1630s, but Lake Parima lingered on the maps throughout the eighteenth century, and was often shown as the source of the Orinoco. By 1802 Alexander von Humboldt had explored the entire Orinoco region and proved that there were no lakes there, although he admitted that the rivers in flood inundated so much territory that the rumor could have had a factual basis. Thenceforward, Lake Parima was no longer on the map.

El Dorado is now long dead, but its ghost still walks. The British public seems to have long had a tremendous curiosity about South America, the only continent where the British Empire never gained a hold to any extent, and which the British were never able to make their own. In modern times most South American myths and rumors are of British provenance, or find most of their acceptance in the British Isles. (They have their American adherents as well, but in the United States, South America tends rather to be regarded as "exotic" in the touristic sense.) This interest in Spanish America as an unknown land has been shared by such noteworthy British adventurers as Evan Bryant, W. H. Hudson, Cunninghame-Graham, and Julian Duguid. The notion of South America as a region where anything

---

* Not "cannibals" in our sense, but a corruption of the name Carib, which was the origin of the word "cannibal," possibly influenced by the Latin canis, "dog."

can happen has produced the dubious theories of Lewis Spence, the fantastic books of Harold Wilkins, and the famous lost Brazilian expedition of Colonel Fawcett—though that belongs outside of this study, since what Fawcett hoped to find was not lost Indian treasure cities but traces of Atlantean civilization. In general contemporary South American lost-city stories seem to find favor with the kind of people who also like flying saucers and lost continents. Such tales have no geographical significance, since serious geographers ignore them, and they do not appear on the maps. But the history of El Dorado would be incomplete without some note of its aftermath.

All reports of lost South American treasure are not necessarily

Section of Willem Blaeu map of about 1620, showing Lake Parime and Manoa al Dorada.

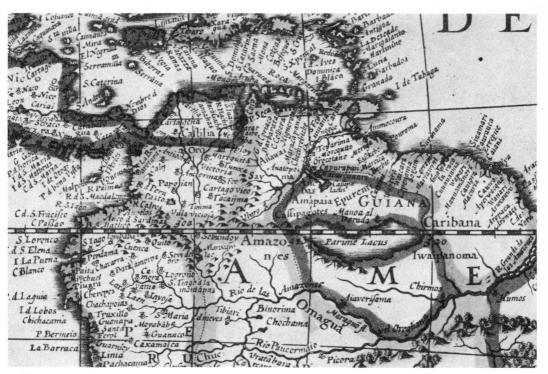

fabulous: there is, for example, the Gold Mine of the Martyrs somewhere in the central interior of Brazil. It was worked by certain Portuguese owners during the eighteenth century until their Indian slaves rebelled and killed them, and it has never been rediscovered. This seems to be a reasonably authentic lost-mine story, like many from our own American West. And it would be a mistake to read El Dorado into every rumor coming out of the South American wilderness. A continent in which considerable areas have remained unexplored until modern times would be bound to produce its yarns, even were there no precedent.

The tales that can be regarded as progeny of El Dorado have one distinguishing feature: a lost city (hopefully containing treasure) located alongside a lake, or some distinctive body of water, which serves as a landmark by which the city can be located. Of course there is nothing inherently improbable in this since people the world over have tended to build their towns by lakes and streams. The salient point is that every such rumor, from Lake Guatavitá to whatever is the most recent example of the genre, has followed the pattern of placing El Dorado and its descendants beside some sort of body of water.

There are, for example, rumors of a lost city somewhere along the Inca Way, the highway built by the Incas from Peru into the Amazon country, a few traces of which remain. The city, it is said, can be approached only by a vast staircase carved in the rock, above a cavern into which waters plunge to form a whirlpool.

But no purpose is served by a compilation of such stories. It must be admitted that the jungles of the Mato Grosso have not yet been so thoroughly explored that anyone can say with certainty—there are no lost cities in the area. Something corresponding physically to the El Dorado pattern could still possibly turn up, but those who take its reality for granted are strictly indulging in an act of faith.

The South American Secret City faith seems to reach its extreme point, though unrelated either to geography or to the history of El Dorado, in a certain contemporary Brazilian cult's belief in the city of Matatu-Araracuanga. It exists, hidden underground, somewhere in the Mato Grosso, and it is the abode of the Hidden Rulers of the World and home base of flying saucers sent out on reconnaissance flights to keep the world in order. So does the centuries-old merge with the ultramodern.

Terra Australis Quasi Cognita

There is, of course, a real southern continent, and it is becoming less and less unknown with almost every passing day. But this fact is irrelevant and immaterial to the present inquiry. Terra Australis would have made its way onto the maps in exactly the way that it did, even if the entire Antarctic region had turned out to be un-broken water.

Most geographical myths of the sort that we are here studying are of relatively recent vintage, products of late medieval times or of the Age of Discovery. But the Un-known Southern Land goes back well over two thousand years.

It might be too extreme to say that the ancient Greeks "knew" the world to be round. But they were aware of the reasons for supposing it to be so—including the non-scientific supposition that the sphere was the most "perfect" geometrical form—and they had arrived at a fairly ac-curate estimate of its circumference. The Greeks, as always, had a word for it. They distinguished between the *ge*, the terrestrial globe, and the *oikoumene*, the known world, "the world" in the sense that it was the scene of human affairs.

By about the Year One, the world the Greeks and Romans knew comprised Europe (exclusive of the far north), the Mediterranean area and its islands, the West African coast perhaps as far south as Sierra Leone, North Africa south to the Sahara, the Nile Valley at least south to the Sixth Cataract, the East African coast possibly as far south as Kenya, the Levant and Asia Minor, the Black Sea littoral, Arabia and Persia, Central Asia as far as the Syr Darya (or Jaxartes) River, India, and the Malay Peninsula. They had some hearsay knowledge of the vastness of Central Asia, and also of China, which they knew as Serica, the fabulous Land of Silk. In addition some off-shore islands were known: in the west the Canaries, possibly the Madeiras, the British Isles (including the Orkneys and possibly the Shetlands), and the mysterious Ultima Thule, possibly Iceland but more likely Scandinavia (the Shetlands also have been mentioned as a possibility; if it was Scandinavia there was some duplication, since Pliny mentioned an island to the north of Europe called "Scatinavia," populated by the "Helleviones"); in the east Socotra, the Maldives, Ceylon, the Nicobars and Andamans, Sumatra, and probably some few others of the Indonesian archipelago. In their belief the heat steadily increased as one journeyed south, till at the equator it became

A nineteenth-century reconstruction of the ancient Greek conception of oikoumene.

so fierce that no life could survive; hence they knew nothing of regions below the equator—officially at least, though there is evidence that a few equatorial crossings may have been made in classical times. And, despite the claims put forward by some enthusiasts, there is not the least solid evidence that those of Roman times knew anything of America.

The Greco-Roman geographers were well aware that their "known world" made up only about one quarter of the globe's surface, and they could not accept the thought that there might not be more. It offended their senses of logic and symmetry. Furthermore, there had to be nearly equal land masses in the other quarters for mere physical balance; otherwise, the world would not stay upright.

Today we know that the earth is held in position by the gravitational pull of the other celestial bodies, that what counts is the total mass of the world rather than its distribution; and that anyway there is no specific "up" in interstellar space. But for its time it was a quite cogent argument.

Krates of Mallos in the second century B.C. apparently was the first to work out a detailed theory of the counterbalancing land masses, which he named for their inhabitants, if any: the *Antoikoi* ("Opposite Men," whose land would have been in the position of Africa south of the equator), the *Antipodes* ("Opposite-Feet Men," who would have been in what is actually North America), and the *Antichthones* ("Those of the Opposite Land," this land corresponding to the actual South America). As for the *Antoikoi*, Krates believed that they might be Negroes. Homer, whom most Greek geographers took very seriously as a source, had spoken of the African people as "divided in twain," and Krates suggested that this might mean that more of them were living in the land south of the supposedly uninhabitable equator. The great geographer Strabo, a century and a half later, refused to accept this, and suggested instead that Homer had meant a division between the eastern and western peoples of Africa.

Once the existence of these lands was assumed, the possibility of voyaging to them had to be admitted. And this, plus poetic imagination, seem to be the origin of the many references in classical literature to "lands beyond the sea," which some have advanced as proving an unrecorded ancient discovery of America.

In the history of science, where new discoveries are constantly outmoding old conceptions, it often happens that a man is remembered primarily for being wrong, and his important work is forgotten. A prime case is that of the great Alexandrian Greek astronomer and geographer, Claudius Ptolemy, who today is known to the gen-

Map illustrating Krates of Mallos's conception of the world. Art work by John C. Gustafson.

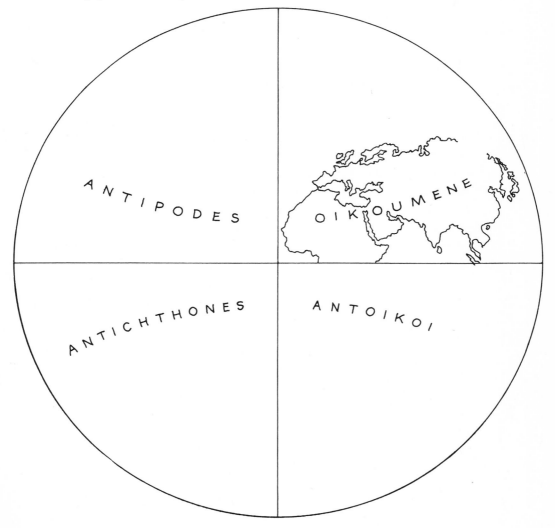

eral public only as the promulgator of the Ptolemaic theory that the sun and planets revolve round the earth. The truth is that Ptolemy was familiar with the idea that the earth might revolve round the sun, but he rejected it for lack of evidence, and quite rightly so, for his day. Ptolemy was a geographer, drawn to astronomy primarily because of the aid that star readings could provide in taking earthly bearings. His main interest was in means for determining distances and positions, and his work contributed much to the subsequent art of finding latitude and longitude.

All of this is by way of an apology for the fact that Claudius Ptolemy was as wrong about the southern continent as he was about the movement of the sun.

I pointed out in the introduction that no Greek maps have come down to us. There may be an exception to this, in the famed world map attributed to Ptolemy. In its present form it can be traced back only to the Ulm edition of Ptolemy published in 1482 (though new editions of Ptolemy with frankly modern maps had been coming out much earlier), but it was probably based on an earlier original that may have been authentic. And on it the coasts of both Africa and Malaya are shown descending south of the equator to merge with the coasts of Terra Australis, which then spreads off in both directions to girdle the entire southern extremity of the earth. This, in effect, makes the Indian Ocean a landlocked sea, and Africa simply a gigantic peninsula of the Southern Land.

Ptolemy was no doubt familiar with the story of an expedition under Phoenician leaders, sent out by an Egyptian Pharaoh of the seventh century B.C., which allegedly had circumnavigated Africa and proved that it did have a southern tip (Appendix V, page 252). But apparently he simply did not believe it. Herodotus, who recounted it, did not believe it either. Ptolemy preferred to accept a more modern and more scientific authority, the astronomer Hipparchus of the second century B.C. (the inventor of the theory of latitude and longitude), who had suggested that Africa and the Southern Land joined to make the Indian Ocean a landlocked sea like the Mediterranean.

In Hipparchus's day there was some reason for this notion, owing to the recent discovery of the land of Taprobane, south of India, which for all anyone knew might be a peninsula of the southern continent. But by Ptolemy's time Taprobane had been circumnavigated and proved to be the island known to the Romans as Serendip and to us as Ceylon. In centuries to follow, such was repeatedly to be the fate of reported outposts of Terra Australis.

This map of Ptolemy's, if authentic, features the first extant cartographic appearance of Terra Australis Incognita (for the benefit of the reader with small Latin, I should perhaps explain that my title for this chapter, which never was used in that form on the map, means the "Somewhat Known Southern Land"). Its second surviving mapping was made in the twelfth century by Muhammad al-Idrisi, an Arab geographer at the court of King Roger II of Sicily. For all practical purposes, Idrisi simply followed Ptolemy's scheme, and may have been familiar with his map, though in Idrisi's version the African coastlines, well known to Arab seamen, are much more accurately presented. Ptolemy's theories were not revived in Europe until the thirteenth century, and cartographers of the Middle Ages confined their efforts for the most part to the Europe-Asia-Africa land mass, without venturing into the unknown. In fact, in medieval Europe, there was a division of opinion as to whether Terra Australis existed at all.

It is a common mistake to suppose that medieval scholars believed the world to be flat, until Columbus (or someone of his period) advanced the radical idea of a spherical earth. No doubt the uneducated regarded it as flat; for that matter, they still do. In early medieval times a couple of geographers did introduce flat-earth theories, but they were Byzantines, not Western Europeans, and their ideas had little influence even among their contemporaries. Aristotle was the supreme scientific authority in medieval culture, and his acceptance of the rotundity of the earth was evidence enough, even without the evidence of the many Greek geographers whose work was well known (in Latin translation) to scholars of the High Gothic period. Geography as taught in all medieval universities assumed that the earth was a globe,* and the ceremonial orb that Holy Roman Emperors held on state occasions was regarded as a symbol of their claim to authority over the entire earth.

But it was no longer felt that the world required Terra Australis for the sake of mere balance. Christian ideas of cosmography, fortified by certain Biblical passages, assumed that an Almighty God could hold the earth in position regardless of the distribution of weight. Those medieval scientists who held out for the existence of Terra Australis based themselves on the Greek authorities. Those who disbelieved based their contentions on a more modern invention: the compass needle. Since it points north (of course, it points north *and* south, but its importance lay in the fact that it points more or less toward the polestar) they argued that it must be attracted by the heavier concentration of land in the northern hemisphere, or by the visibly greater number of stars in the northern sky.

There were theological questions as well, though less over the existence of a southern continent than over the question of its possible population. If Terra Australis were uninhabited, why had God been so wasteful of space? (But then, would it not have been equally wasteful if all that space were open water?) If it were inhabited, its people were presumably heathen, but how could the scriptural injunction to "go into all the world and preach the gospel" be carried out, since the impassable equatorial region lay between? (But if God did place unredeemed humans there, we are meant to preach to them, and a way must exist, which we have not yet found.)†

During the fifteenth century, the medieval scientists were proved right, at least in their contention that the equator could be crossed. The way to do so turned out to be absurdly simple: just sail across it. Prince Henry the Navigator of Portugal (who did no actual navigat-

---

* It was taught as a branch of geometry, in the quadrivium. Adam of Bremen was one of the few medieval scholars actually to use the word "geography."

† After the discovery of America, some theologians who had argued for an uninhabited Terra Australis contended that the Indians were not true humans but a race created by Satan for his own purposes. But this ran afoul of orthodox Catholic doctrine, which holds that God alone can create.

ing himself) sparked a crash program to explore the coast of Africa and discover the source of the rich alluvial gold of Guinea, and, if possible, a sea route to the Orient which would bypass the hostile Moslems who controlled the Mediterranean area. As Portuguese captains cautiously inched their way southward along the West African coast, they discovered lush vegetation and human inhabitants everywhere, and no sign of approaching a burnt-out equatorial zone where no life could exist. In 1472 three of these captains—Fernando Po, Lope Goncalves, and Ruy de Sequieiros—did cross the equator, with no ill effects whatsoever. Sixteen years later Bartholomeu Dias rounded the southern tip of Africa and found nothing but open water to the south, and the Ptolemaic concept of the southern continent was crushed for good.

This of course did not prove that no continent existed farther south. In fact, hardly had the centuries-old tenuous belief in *the* southern continent been disposed of than there arose a new general conviction of the existence of *a* southern continent, this time not as a mathematical abstraction or an article of faith in classical authority, but as a real piece of solid ground where a voyager could land. The crossing of the equator seemed to prove that a voyage thither was possible.

Then came 1492, and the discovery of lands to the west. Columbus to the end of his days believed, or would not let himself disbelieve, that he had actually reached the Orient by sailing west. But even before Columbus's death, Amerigo Vespucci had identified the discovery as a hitherto unknown territory, and it was on this basis that it became generally known outside Spain, resulting in the New World's receiving Amerigo's name. The general effect was electrifying. So much, for so long unknown, had been so suddenly and sensationally discovered. How much more might there not be? Terra Australis seemed definitely indicated. Call it coincidence, lucky guess, professional intuition, or whatever, but old Krates of Mallos had been justified. The *Antoikoi, Antipodes,* and *Antichthones* did exist. Certainly the wise Greeks must also have been right about the austral land mass.

Martin Waldseemüller's *Cosmographiae Introductio*, published at Saint-Lô, France, in 1507, was the source from which the name "America" was established, but Waldseemüller later changed his mind, gave Columbus credit for the discovery, and on a new map that he inserted in his 1513 edition he changed the name America (used only for the present South America) to Terra Incognita, the Unknown Land. The name of Terra Australis (Southern Land), traditionally applied to the hypothetical southern continent, soon became confused with this, hence "Terra Australis Incognita" appeared on world maps all through the sixteenth century and well into the seventeenth.[1] Some more optimistic cartographers preferred to call it Terra Australis Nondum Cognita, the "Not-Yet-Known Southern Land."

Vespucci's voyage of 1502, which took him south at least as far as the Falkland Islands, established the south-southwesterly slant of the eastern seaboard of South America, and geographers assumed that something similar obtained on the western side as well. They conceived of South America as roughly wedge-shaped, with a free southern tip, skirted not too far to the southward by the southern continent. This is well illustrated on a map published at Nuremberg in 1515 by Johannes Schöner, which apparently shows the Strait of

The 1507 Martin Waldseemüller map, drawn in gores, and showing (arrow at right) the first appearance of the name "America."

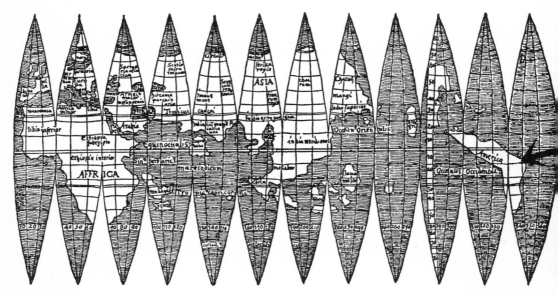

Section of the Schöner map of 1515, showing a strait below South America before the voyage of Magellan.

Magellan, four years before Magellan sailed.* Some historians[2] have speculated that Schöner may have had access to data brought back by some forgotten or unrecorded voyage of earlier date, but there is no real reason to assume this. The idea that South America had a tip was favored in geographical circles, though not accepted by all; and it was to search for this tip—and if it existed, to sail past it and search

---

* Antonio Pigafetta, the chronicler of the voyage, stated that Magellan expected to find the strait, so he may have been familiar with this map.

A probably imaginary likeness of Ferdinand Magellan.

for a westerly route to the Indies—that Ferdinand Magellan set forth in 1519.

He did find that conditions apparently conformed to Schöner: a narrow southern end to the continent, and a tortuous sea passage flanked to the south by a land of seemingly considerable extent. By night numerous fires could be seen along the southern coast. These were actually the campfires of nomadic Indians, but Magellan thought the fires to be volcanic, and named the land Tierra del Fuego, the Land of Fire. Neither Magellan nor his sailing companion, the Italian Antonio Pigafetta, who wrote the account of the voyage and drew a rough map of the strait, committed themselves to having discovered the Unknown Southern Land. But European geographers did make this assumption, and Tierra del Fuego became a fixture of Terra Australis, just below South America, for almost a century. Finally in 1616 the Dutch global navigator Willem Cornelius Schouten sailed round Tierra del Fuego to the south, discovered and named Cape Horn (after his birthplace, the town of Hoorn), and proved the Tierra to be an island. To the southwestward he sighted a coastline which he named Staaten Land, and thought might be a part of the southern continent, but which soon turned out to be a small island. From that time on, Terra Australis receded once more (it appears that Sir Francis Drake had previously rounded the Horn in 1577, but the details of his course are not clear).

In the meantime Terra Australis had cropped up elsewhere. In 1545 the Spanish voyager Iñigo Ortis de Retes had discovered a large island eastward of the East Indies, which by reason of its black-skinned frizzly-haired natives he named New Guinea. Could this be a northern promontory of the Unknown Land? For the next sixty years there was no reason not to suppose so.

Alvaro de Mendaña de Neyra sailed westward from Peru in 1567, searching for a possible continent in the Pacific vastness, though not specifically for Terra Australis. He did find islands, which he named the Solomons, apparently as a Biblical reference to the gold he hoped would turn up there. The voyage out, and the return, were hellish; and it was not until 1595 that he decided to do anything about his discovery. On his voyage back to the Solomons in that year he died, and his second-in-command, Pedro Fernandes de Quierós, a Portuguese, took over. He failed to find the islands, but he nevertheless returned to Europe and managed to impress both King Philip III of Spain and Pope Clement VIII with his wild speculative yarns about discoveries to be made in the Pacific, with endless gold and souls to be reaped. Finally in 1603 he was sent back with three ships to try again.

A couple of years later he was back in Spain, trying to impress the king with his fantastic account of the continent he had discovered and claimed for the Spanish crown. He had named it *Austrialia del Espíritu Santo*, and had formally laid the cornerstone for a city to be called New Jerusalem. The new continent, in his version, was larger than Europe and held more gold than Peru. In actuality, he had discovered the New Hebrides, and his *Austrialia* was merely one of them. Whether he was wildly jumping to conclusions in his report, or whether it was a deliberate attempt to bring back something good, is now beyond definition. In any case, Queirós's tales had no geographical effect. The Spanish authorities were most experienced in spotting mendacious mariners. They did not believe Queirós and did not release his report, and it did not become known until considerably later.

(The name of *Austrialia del Espíritu Santo* deserves a word. In Spanish it constitutes a pun, translatable either as "Southern Land of the Holy Spirit" or "Austrian Land of the Holy Spirit," the latter a reference to the Austrian origin of Spain's Habsburg rulers. It gave rise to the later name of "Australia," which means simply "Southern Land," and which was applied to an entirely different region.)

In his absence, Queirós left his lieutenant, Luis Vaez de Torres, in charge of the colony in *Austrialia*, but Torres considered himself deserted and shortly set sail for the Spanish-held Philippines. En route he passed south of New Guinea, and proved it to be an island, but did sight a coastline to the south. This too had no geographic impact, for it was allowed to die in the archives in Manila and was only rediscovered in the nineteenth century. The British then gave the name of Torres Strait to the stretch of sea between New Guinea and the northern peninsula of Queensland, for Torres had made the first known report by a European of the continent of Australia. The dis-

The Coppo world map of 1528, showing (1) Isola Verde (Greenland), and (2) the Isola Pocho Cognita.

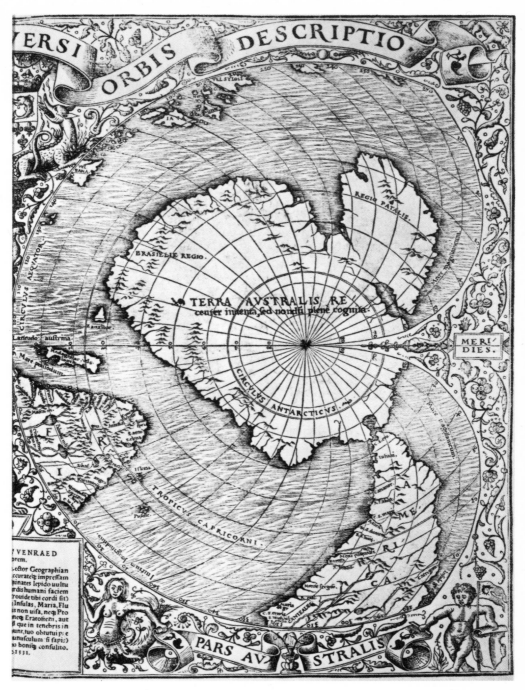

*Section of the Oronce Fine map, showing his concept of the un-
known southern continent, and its resemblance to the actual
Antarctica.*

covery that brought the region to the world's attention was the
Dutchman Dirck Hartog's glimpse of the western coast in 1613.

But the period when Terra Australis Incognita reigned on the
map in full glory had already begun. Early sixteenth-century repre-
sensations generally made the Unknown Land an unobtrusive oblong
at the bottom of the Southern Hemisphere, as on the badly drawn
1528 map by Piero Coppo, which places it due south of Africa and
calls it *isola pocho cognita* (the Little-Known Island). But this
changed in 1531, when Oronce Fine (or Orontius Fineus), a French
mathematician who drew the first French map of France, produced
a magnificent world map in two hemispheric polar projections, showing to full advantage the vast spread of the Southern Land, equipped
with capes and bays. It must be admitted that the outlines of his
southern continent, while vastly too large, are startlingly similar to
the actual coastlines of Antarctica as they are known today. From
this time on, *Incognita* seems more and more a misnomer, since it
would appear from the maps that a good deal was (believed to be)
known about the supposedly unknown continent, or at least about its
perimeter.

It was taken up next by the Fleming Gerhardus Mercator, remembered to this day for Mercator's Projection, a system for drawing world maps by treating the earth as a cylinder instead of a
sphere, which produces maximum distortion north and south of the
equator but remains in use because of its practicality for navigation.
On his famed and very influential world map of 1569, Mercator
turned Fine's handsome Terra Australis into a huge ungainly sprawl
across the bottom. Taking Tierra del Fuego as a starting point for
descriptive purposes, we can say that the continent is shown skirting
the tip of South America with a jagged coastline, then rising northward to make a concave curve beneath Africa, dropping southward
to produce a huge gulf far to the south of India. From there it zooms
northward in a huge promontory which almost touches Java, followed by a lesser one which falls short of the Tropic of Capricorn
and another huge one, which reaches just to the south of a fancifully
drawn New Guinea and then gradually tapers southward to meet
Tierra del Fuego.

*Gerhardus
Mercator.*

This map was followed up in 1571 by that of the even more influential Fleming Abraham Ortelius, whose *Theatrum Orbis Terrarum* of that year was the first world atlas. He copied Mercator's coastline for the southern continent, but added even more details. The Tierra del Fuego region was fitted out with a group of offshore islands redundantly called *Archipelago de las Islas* (the largest of them called Calis), with several capes, all individually named (Master's Cape, Cape of the Good Signal, Cape Desire, and Great Point), and with several rivers, one called the River of Islands and another Sweetest River (*Dolcissimo*). To the south of Africa he located the Land of Parrots (*Psittacorum regio*), which name he said, on no

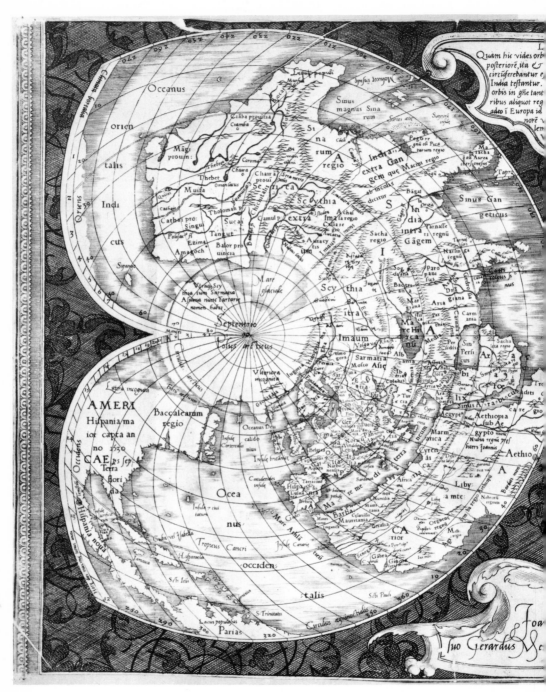

A Mercator map of 1538. (Courtesy of Rare Books Division, New York Public Library)

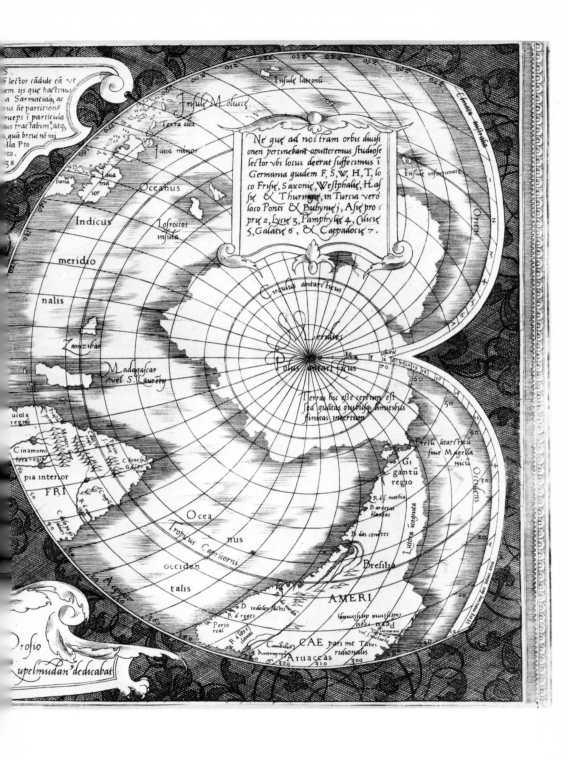

Abraham Ortelius.

particular authority, had been given it by the Portuguese.* On the great peninsula reaching northward toward Java he copied from Mercator three coastal areas called Lucach, Beach, and Maletur, as well as an offshore island tagged as Java Minor.

These names at least can be explained. They are out of Marco Polo. The great Venetian, describing China, spoke of a region to the

---

* The much-earlier Turkish Piri Reis map of 1513 (which shows South America joined to Terra Australis) places six-horned oxen in this same area and adds that "the Portuguese infidels have recorded it in their maps." Perhaps some tall stories of Portuguese provenance were floating around in the sixteenth century and influencing geography.

southward, which he himself did not visit, called Locac, where gold was found. Apparently he meant some part of Indo-China, and "Lucach" is simply a mislocation of Locac. "Beach" (pronounced *Bay*-ahk), described on the map as "gold-bearing province" (*provincia aurifera*), is apparently a bit of duplication, a copyist's error for Locac or Lucach, erroneously believed to be a separate region. Polo also mentioned Malaiur (Malaya), easily identified here as "Maletur." "Java Minor" may have had its origin in Sumatra, but was probably misplaced south of "Java Major" for the sake of symmetry.[3]

As for the transfer of Asiatic locales to the Southern Land, there seems no reasonable explanation. But the shifting of a remote place to the coast opposite was common in conjectural geography; we cannot explain it, only note it when it occurs. In Chapter 7 we will see it occur in the case of Anian, another location reported by Marco Polo.

The "Archipelago of Islands," the "Sweetest River," the various capes, the "Land of Parrots," and the rest, were apparently pure flights of fancy, though Ortelius undoubtedly had some sort of source from which he obtained them.

Thus was established the "Somewhat Unknown" Southern Land that was to make world maps bottom-heavy for close to a century to follow.

As mentioned before, Torres was the first European known to have reported sighting the coast of Australia (in 1606), but Dirck Hartog was the first whose report was published (in 1613) and so had an effect on geography. There are indications that there had been some previous awareness of its existence, at least among the Portuguese. It is recorded that by about 1540 Portuguese sailors knew of an area they called "Great Java" and thought to be a part of Terra Australis. And earlier, on Jorge Reinel's map of circa 1510, alleged to be the first Portuguese map of the Indian Ocean, there appeared a double line at about the location of the western Australian coast, a stylized device to indicate a coast sighted but not explored. Reports of these may have somewhat influenced concepts of Terra Australis, but nothing actually came of them.[4]

In the next period, the history of the search is part of the brave record of Dutch seafaring. Following their first sighting of the west Australian coast in 1613, the Dutch kept up an effort to find out more about it, as apparently the Portuguese had not. Various voyagers made landfalls on various parts of the coast, until it could be roughly pieced together. Concurrently with this, other Dutch skippers were probing along what is now known to be the east coast of Australia, but which these Hollanders considered as a southern continuation of New Guinea (Torres Strait, which separates Australia from New Guinea, was mistaken for a bay). And the Southern Land seemed to be there; the coastlines of the great peninsula of "Maletur" and "Beach" seemed to be shaping up, though considerably farther to the east than it was supposed to be. Exactly who originated the name "New Holland," and when, is not clear, but under the circumstances it was inevitable. These Dutch East Indiamen were not sure just what they had discovered—perhaps just another group of islands—but back home the cartographer Jodocus Hondius confidently mapped it as the *provincia aurifera* of Beach.

Then in 1629 Captain Francis Pelsart sailed from Batavia in Java with a small flotilla. Apparently he took some prospective colonists, or at least had something in mind for the exciting project of establishing the first European colony in the fabled Southern Land. His supercargo was one Jerome Cornelis, a former shady apothecary in Haarlem, who seems to have had some ideas of mutinying, seizing command, and going into piracy. But before he could take action, the expedition came to grief on the dangerous Abrolhos Islands (in Portuguese, the "Keep-Your-Eyes-Open Islands"), off West Australia.

Exactly what happened then is not clear; whether Pelsart took some of the party and sailed back to get help, or whether Cornelis held his mutiny on land and drove out Pelsart and those loyal to him. In any case Cornelis ended up in control. He killed some forty of the men to save water supplies, took over all the women for himself and his followers, and held a brief reign that was a succession of drunken orgies. He also killed several more of the men on suspicion of disloyalty to him, including the two ships' carpenters, and was thus unable to carry out his plan of salvaging material from the wrecks, building another ship, and becoming a pirate. When Captain Pelsart and his men unexpectedly returned, Cornelis was easily overthrown, and was summarily tried and hanged.[5]

Whether this discreditable incident had anything to do with it or not, the Dutch made no further efforts to colonize Australia (nor did the British until 1788). But they went on trying to discover more about it. There were no spectacular discoveries made by individual voyagers, but exploration progressed bit by bit, and by 1642 it was known that to the south of Cape Leeuwin the coast took a definite eastward trend. Was this the end of the land, or the beginning of a large bay? Anton Van Diemen, a governor of the Dutch East Indies, sent Captain Abel Janszoon Tasman to find out.

Tasman sailed down that western coast to Leeuwin, then southeasterly. For a long time no land was sighted to the northward, but eventually he came upon a considerable body of land stretching away to the north. He sailed round it on the southern side, and, not knowing whether it was an island or a peninsula of the Australian continent, named it Van Diemen's Land in honor of the governor. Actually it is a large island south of Australia, and the British later renamed it Tasmania in honor of its discoverer.

Section of the Hondius map of 1630, showing Beach Province.

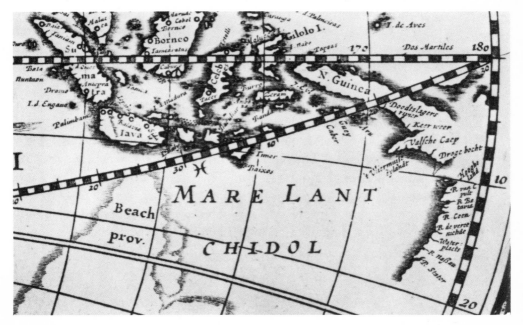

He continued southeastward, and about 1000 miles farther discovered a mountainous coast which he named New Zealand (it was the South Island of that group). Then he returned by a northerly course, discovering the Tongas and Fijis along the way. By sailing unobstructed for these thousands of miles south of Australia, he had proved it not to be part of any southern continent but an independent land mass. As for the coast called New Zealand, it might be part of Terra Australis Incognita, but he had found nothing to indicate it. This was in 1642.

Thereafter, for almost a century, the question of the Unknown Southern Land lay dormant. Cartographically, it began to drop off the maps. Not that it was regarded as nonexistent, but seventeenth-century geographers came to adopt a policy of mapping only the known, leaving unexplored areas blank and not trying to fill them in conjecturally. For example, the "New and Most Accurate [*sic*] Map of the Terrestrial Globe" (*Orbis Terrarum Nova et Accuratissima Tabula*) of Nicolas Visscher, undated but apparently of the 1660s, gives the outlines of Australia (except the east coast) with reasonable accuracy, as well as the southern end of Tasmania, and a rough indication of the known coast of New Zealand, but nothing at all of Terra Australis. The Antarctic polar projection on this same map is completely blank, except for showing the southern tip of South America with the island of Tierra del Fuego.

During this time in Europe the literary men took over the Unknown Land. It served them as Mars and Venus have served modern writers, as a locale where anything could happen—a locale for every sort of fantasy. One of these tales, which has become an English classic, is *Gulliver's Travels*, by Jonathan Swift. There is no point in giving a list of obscure titles of utopias and satires now known only to specialists, but mention must be made of Gabriel de Foigny, a Franciscan monk of scandalous life, who in 1676 published *La Terre Australe Connue* ("The Known Southern Land"), which set a record of some sort for wild imagination. The people of the Southern Land, it seemed, were hermaphrodites, and they did not have to till the ground because a species of long-nosed swine that rooted in straight lines had been domesticated and trained to do the plowing.[6]

Ninety-six years went by after Tasman's voyage before an ambitious young French sea captain of aristocratic Breton family named Jean-Baptiste-Charles de Lozier Bouvet talked the French East India Company into backing him for a voyage to southern waters, not specifically to search for Terra Australis but simply for general exploration. Bouvet sailed boldly southward into the world's worst weather region, the notorious Roaring Forties. And, on January 1, 1739, he made a land-sighting, a grim, glaciated double peak looming out of the sea.

The details are none too clear. Bouvet may have seen the island with a low-lying fog bank behind it. In any case, it appeared to him as a headland of an extensive land area lying southerly, and he returned to France and reported the discovery of a northern cape of the southern continent. Because of his sighting it on January 1, the Feast of the Circumcision in the Church calendar, he had named his find *Cap de la Circoncision*.

Geographers were skeptical. Pending further exploration, they named Bouvet's discovery in his honor, Bouvet Island. And, after two centuries of strange history for so insignificant an island, it still bears that name (Appendix VII).

One who believed Bouvet was Philippe Buache. In 1754 he brought out an arresting map, done in south polar projection. On it a Terra Australis of impressive size is shown split in two by an inland sea, the Mer Glaciale, at the approximate center of which is located the South Pole. The portion to the south of Africa and South America includes *Cap de la Circoncision* as its northern terminus; the portion below Australia, by far the larger, includes New Zealand on its northern coast. In the margin is an account of Bouvet's discovery, and a conjectural close-up map of the area of the Cap.

This map stirred up something. The famed naturalist-mathematician, the Comte de Buffon, went publicly on record as expressing his personal belief in the existence of this continent, and in its habitability. And the same was soon done by Alexander Dalrymple, chief hydrographer (or oceanographer, as we would now say) to the British East India Company, and later to the Royal Navy.

These opinions brought on their share of controversy. But the

Philippe Buache's map, illustrating his concept of the Southern Continent

CARTE
DES TERRES AUSTRALES,
Comprises entre le Tropique
du Capricorne et le Pôle Antarctique.
Où se voyent les Nouvelles decouvertes
faites en 1739. au Sud du Cap de
Bonne Esperance. Par les Ordres de
Mrs DE LA COMPAGNIE DES INDES.
Dressée sur les Mémoires et
sur la Carte Originale de
Mr de Lozier Bouvet
chargé de cette Expedition
Par Philippe Buache
de l'Academie Rle des
Sciences, Gendre de
feu Mr Delisle Pr
Géographe du ROY
De la même Acad
Augmentée
de diverses vues
Physiques &c.
1754
PLAN
et VUE des Terres
DU CAP DE LA
CIRCONCISION
Cap de la Circoncision
Capricorne
NOUVELLE HOLLANDE
MER DES INDES
AFRIQUE
sous le Privilege de l'Academie Rle des Sciences le 3 Septembre 1739.
nd showing (arrow) Cap de la Circoncision, as reported by Bouvet.

views of one of the most eminent living men of science, and of a ranking expert on oceans and what they contained, had to be taken seriously. The time had come to settle the Unknown Southland business once and for all.

The man chosen to do it was the magnificent James Cook, known to the world as Captain Cook, the explorer supreme, the man who made more of this world known to its inhabitants than did any other single man. In 1768 the Royal Society dispatched him to the South Pacific with a scientific party to observe a transit of Venus across the sun. British astronomers had selected Tahiti (first discovered by Queirós in 1605 on his second search for Terra Australis, rediscovered in 1766 by the Englishman Samuel Wallis) as the most advantageous point on earth for the observation. So Cook first made Tahiti. His account of the island and its people (and those of the German father-and-son scientific team of Johann Reinhold Forster and Johann Georg Forster, who sailed with him on a later voyage) was influential in establishing the sumptuous South Seas image of feathery palms, sleepy lagoons, and amorous maidens. Cook explored the islands around Tahiti and named them the Society Islands in honor of the Royal Society, his sponsors. Thence the expedition progressed to the land reported by Tasman and named New Zealand, which was discovered to be a chain of islands, with nothing to the southward but open water. On the return voyage he skirted and charted the eastern coast of Australia, and completed the roughing-in of this area on the map (it was not to be known precisely till 1822, when Philip Parker King completed his coastal surveys).[7]

The problem of the southern continent had come to fascinate Cook, and by 1772 he found backing for an expedition to make a really thorough search for it. His two vessels, the *Resolution* and the *Adventure*, were ideal for exploratory work. They were North-Country colliers, cargo vessels of shallow draught, roomy and capacious for carrying plenty of stores, able to operate in almost any waters, and easy to beach if their bottoms required cleaning. In this voyage Cook zigzagged back and forth across the South Pacific, discovering many islands, including New Caledonia and the group now known as the Cook Islands, but no continent. Three times he crossed

Captain James Cook.

the Antarctic Circle, the first European to do so (it may be that the Polynesian navigator Hui-te-Rangi-ora, of the Tonga Islands, reached the Antarctic in the eighth century, a thousand years earlier).[8]

Then Cook headed eastward, round the Horn, toward the South Atlantic area where Bouvet had reported finding the southern continent's northern extension. En route he discovered the grim sub-Antarctic island which he named South Georgia, and commented on its "savage and terrible" appearance, adding that "to judge of the bulk by the sample, [Terra Australis] would not be worth the discovery." His prolonged search for Bouvet's land turned up nothing. He missed the island in the fog, found no other traces of land, and concluded that Bouvet had probably been deceived by a giant iceberg. On his return to England, Cook reported that if any southern continent did exist, it had to be within the Antartic Circle.

So ended Terra Australis Incognita. What followed is another story, the discovery and exploration of the real Antarctica. Throughout the late eighteenth and early nineteenth centuries, whalers and

A north-of-England collier, of the kind used by Captain Cook.

sealers discovered various islands southward of South America—the South Orkneys, the South Shetlands, the Sandwich Group—and gradually closed in on the continent. It is impossible to say exactly who discovered the continent of Antarctica, since many of the voyagers' records are none too clear. In the year 1820 the British Navy captain Edward Bransfield and the American sealing skipper Nathaniel Palmer both made landings on the territory which has traditionally been mapped as a peninsula of Antarctica, and called on American maps "Palmer Land" and on British maps "Graham Land." There has been some controversy over which discovery preceded which, though the evidence indicates that Bransfield was first by a few months.[9] In any case it hardly matters, since surveys made during the International Geophysical Year of 1957–1958 proved that the "peninsula" is actually a group of islands bound together by the glacier, and not part of the mainland at all.

Perhaps the real credit for discovery should go to John Biscoe, an English sealing captain, who in 1831–1832 circumnavigated the continent, annexed Graham Land to the British crown, and sighted the mainland area that he named Enderby Land for his employers, the London firm of Enderby Brothers, who encouraged Antarctic exploration along with their commercial whaling and sealing ventures. But all this falls rather outside the story of the Unknown Southern Land of myth and fruitless quest.

Among the general public, the myth of the Southern Land, considering its two-thousand-year provenance, appears to have died remarkably easily. It seems to have left no such cultural hangovers as the myth of El Dorado. True, as late as 1845, when serious Antarctic exploration was under way, Edgar Allan Poe could use the traditional Terra Australis as setting for that finest of sea yarns, *The Narrative of Arthur Gordon Pym*. And the American scholar John Fiske relates that, during his mid-nineteenth-century boyhood, his nursemaid had him convinced that Tasmania was the land of ghosts and goblins.[10] This may have been a minor survival of the old legend of a southland full of wonders, or merely a misconstrual of the original name of Tasmania as "Van Demon's Land." Such is so often the course of a myth: beginning as legitimate speculation, it becomes a fabulous object of search, and ends as a nursery tale.

Postscript

At the time of writing this chapter, I had not yet read Charles Hapgood's *Maps of the Ancient Sea Kings*. In it he presents, rather convincingly, the flabbergasting theory that there existed, about ten thousand years ago and before the last Ice Age, an advanced seafaring culture that explored and mapped the entire world. He contends that some of the maps of this period survived until relatively modern times, and were known and copied by geographers, thus explaining the surprisingly modern accuracy of detail on some antique maps. In particular he maintains that the form of Terra Australis resulted from an accurate survey of the Antarctic coasts, made before the present glaciation, preserved through the ages on a few primeval maps, and copied on an exaggerated scale by Oronce Fine and other Renaissance cartographers. His primary source for the studies leading to this theory was the Piri Reis map, mentioned above in a footnote, page 40. I must admit to a streak of romanticism that makes me want to believe in Hapgood's hypothesis, but lack of evidence compels me to caution. The book is well worth the while of anyone interested in maps and geography.

In the interval between writing this chapter and retyping it, I found that I may have spoken too hastily in saying that Terra Australis Incognita left no popular cultural hangovers. Several people of my acquaintance, of metaphysical-occultist bent, have asked my "professional" opinion of the Piri Reis map. The question always seems to be whether the map is (a) a survival from lost Atlantis, or (b) the result of a survey made by flying saucer. I do not accept either explanation, but cannot dogmatically deny the theoretical possibility of either or both, and my reply to such people has been to refer them to Hapgood. Since I do not ordinarily follow their literature, I have no idea whether it was Hapgood's study or some independent discovery that brought the map to their attention.

CHAPTER 3.

The Very Strange Case of Friesland

South-west of *Iseland* lies another, and as cold an Isle, commonly called by the name of FREEZLAND, from the continual Frosts unto which it is subject. By the *Latines* it is called *Frislandia*, to distinguish it from the *Frisia* or *Friesland* in *Germany*.* It is situated under the North Frigid Zone; but not so much within the *Arctick* as *Iseland* is; the longest Day here in the height of Summer not exceeding 20 hours; and yet the Soil is so cold and barren, that it beareth neither Corn nor Fruit, the Inhabitants living most on Fish; which as it is their only Food, so is it also their chief Commodity wherewith to entertain or invite the Merchant. And hereof there is such abundance caught upon their Coasts, that they are never without the company of *Hanse-men*, *Scots*, *Hollanders*, *Danes*, and *English*; by which it hath been so frequented in these later times, that it hath been called by some the *Western England*. For quantity it is somewhat bigger than *Iseland*, but by reason of the bitter Air, and the Defects above mentioned, very thinly

---

* The North Sea coastal area of Germany and the Netherlands, inhabited by the Frisians.

inhabited. The chief Town of it is called *Freezland*, by the name of the Island; situate on the Eastern Shore of it. Besides which, there are others set down in the Maps; as 2. *Samescot*, 3. *Andefort*, 4. *Sorand*; but not much observable. Westward hereof, as *Zieglerus* (and out of him *Maginus*)* telleth us, is a less island, called *Icaria*, giving the name of *Mare Icarium* to the Sea adjoyning; so called (by his mistake or translation of the Fable) from Icarus the son of Daedalus, a King of Scotland, who did once (but no body knows when) Lord it over these Islands.

This paragraph appeared in the 1659 edition of Peter Heylyn's *Cosmography*. It seems to be a good, concise account of the physical and economic geography of a rather remote but fairly well-explored corner of the world, an island which is described in a previous paragraph, "belonging to the crown of *Norway*." Heylyn's spelling of "Freezland" is his own embellishment, invented to jibe with his explanation of the name; on maps of the period it is spelled Friesland, Frisland, or Frislandia. But except for this, the description seems quite circumstantial, credible, and not at all fabulous. The only difficulty is that there is no such island.

One question immediately rises to one's mind: Could it have sunk? And the answer to this is a very definite no. Not that the sinking of islands as such is impossible; many of them have been known to vanish in the heavily volcanic area of the Icelandic waters (Appendix II). But an island fitting these specifications—large, populated, supporting several towns, participating in world commerce, visited constantly by European vessels, and particularly well known in England—could not have simply disappeared when no one was looking. A catastrophe of this sort would have made history, dwarfing Pompeii and the Lisbon quake, and Friesland today would be a household word instead of a geographical obscurity.

But if the island was imaginary, it raises a very big question. The fabrication of a gold-glittering El Dorado or a beckoning southern

---

* "Maginus" is Giovanni Antonio Magini, a mathematician who brought out a new edition of Ptolemy (see Chapter 2) with modern maps in 1596. "Zieglerus" seems to be the Jakob Ziegler who, in 1536, published a confused map of the North Atlantic, which did not, however, show these islands. Heylyn apparently slipped up here.

DE I COMMENTARII DEL
.Viaggio in Perfia di M. Caterino Zeno il K.
& delle guerre fatte nell'Imperio Perfiano,
dal tempo di Vffuncaffano in quà.
LIBRI DVE.
ET DELLO SCOPRIMENTO
dell'Ifole Frislanda, Eslanda, Engroüelanda, Efto
tilanda, & Icaria, fatto fotto il Polo Artico, da
due fratelli zeni, M. Nicolò il K. e M. Antonio.
LIBRO VNO.
CON VN DISEGNO PARTICOLARE DI
tutte le dette parte di Tramontana da lor fcoperte.
CON GRATIA, ET PRIVILEGIO.

VERI   TAS.

Ant°   Gudalotto,

IN   VENETIA
Per Francefco Marcolini.   M D LVIII.

Title page of the original Venice edition of the Zeno Narrative. It was printed as one of two "blocks" in the same volume, the two unrelated except for both dealing with travels by members of the Zeno family. The Zeno Narrative is Book I, but for some reason the printer listed it second. (Courtesy of Rare Books Division, New York Public Library) continent (Chapter 2) is readily comprehensible. But what could possibly have been anyone's motivation in dreaming up a prosaic northern island of fishmongers?

The whole story began in Venice in 1558, with the publication of a small volume bearing a large title: *The Discovery of the Islands of Frislandia, Eslanda, Engroenlanda, Estotilanda, and Icaria: Made by the Two Brothers of the Zeno Family: viz: Messire Nicolò, the Chevalier, and Messire Antonio. With a Map of the Said Islands.*[1] The author (or part-author, or editor, whichever is the correct term) did not name himself, but he has been identified as Nicolò Zeno, of the same prominent Venetian family as the two brothers, and a member of the Venetian Republic's governing Council of Ten. And the story would be much easier to tell if it did not involve two men named Nicolò Zeno. For clarity we shall distinguish between Nicolò I, of the fourteenth century, the explorer, and Nicolò II, of the sixteenth century, who published the book.

With this book the world was given not only a whole archipelago of geographical myths, but also one of the most puzzling and problematical documents in all of travel literature.

The sixteenth and early seventeenth centuries accepted the Zeno Narrative, as it is generally known, at face value. After this period, geographers became increasingly dubious. Richard Henry Major, a distinguished English historian of geography, made an English translation of the narrative in 1873, marshaling all the evidence for its authenticity. His presentation is heavy with apriorism and circular reasoning, but it did establish some important points. In 1898 another Englishman, Frederick R. Lucas, made a new study of the Zeno Narrative, devoted chiefly to attacking Major's case. The American William H. Babcock in 1922 took a cautious middle position. Another American, Frederick J. Pohl (not to be confused with the science fiction writer Frederik Pohl), in 1951 made another study and, on the basis of recent findings, came out strongly in favor of the Zenos.[2]*

---

* I disagree entirely with Frederick J. Pohl's theory that Friesland was Fer Island, in the Orkneys, because the linguistic evidence is against it. That area was not then

Then, in 1954, an archaeological discovery was made that would seem to place the Zeno Narrative beyond all reasonable doubt as at least having a factual basis. But more of this in its proper place. The narrative needs to be examined in some detail, and fortunately it is short enough to make this possible here.

In an editorial note at the end of the book, Nicolò II admitted that as a small boy he had gone on a destructive kick and torn up some old family documents. Much later he learned of their contents, and tried to make amends by putting together and publishing the story as best he could from those remaining. The result is a scrappy, disconnected, frequently questionable, and thoroughly fascinating account.

It relates how Nicolò Zeno I sailed forth, in about the year 1390, to see a bit of the world, but en route to England was blown off course and wrecked on a strange northern shore. There he was in peril from pirates until rescued by the ruler of the land, with whom he was able to converse in Latin. In his account Nicolò II gave Frislanda as the name of the realm and an impossible jumble, "Zichmni," as the name of the prince. This lord "Zichmni" was favorably impressed with Nicolò's qualifications as a naval man (his brother Carlo had commanded the Venetian navy in a victory over the Genoese in 1382), and made him commander of the fleet for the subjugation of Frislanda, which apparently was in revolt against his rule.

Before we go further, it should be mentioned that *this* Frislanda, or Friesland, can be readily identified. It is the Faeroes Islands, called in medieval Norse *Faeroisland*, and regarded in medieval geography as a single land mass (actually, the islands are separated only by very narrow channels). The "later" Friesland of myth, so greatly displaced on the map, presents other problems which will be dealt with in due course, but there is nothing mysterious about Nicolò's landfall.

"Zichmni," too, can be identified. It was Captain Cook's sailing companion, Johann Reinhold Forster, who in 1784 first suggested that Zichmni might be Henry Sinclair, Earl of Orkney, on the

populated by English-speakers. An island named Fer could have given us a Ferland, or more likely a Feroe, but not a Friesland. Besides, that tiny isle could not possibly have been the scene of all the action described.

grounds that he was the only "ruling prince" in those northern waters at the time. However, the difficulty of getting "Zichmni" out of "Sinclair" has stopped most investigators. Some were led to hypothesize a pirate chief named Siegmund, or Sigmund, whom the Zenos might have glorified with a royal title to justify their joining his band.[3] But no evidence for the actual existence of this Sigmund has ever been turned up.

Palaeography provides the answer. Between 1400 and 1550, the introduction of the "fine Italian hand" revolutionized European handwriting, making medieval script difficult to read for anyone accustomed to the newer style. A medieval capital *S* looked like what a man of the Renaissance was accustomed to regarding as capital *Z*. Further, the name Sinclair was probably written without the *n*, and with a tilde above the *i* to indicate a nasal following the vowel (this abbreviation was in common use in medieval writing, and is still standard in Portuguese, as in the name João, pronounced roughly *Zhwoung*). Given this probable start of "Zĩclair," one can see how hasty or crude penmanship could result in a scrawl that one unaccustomed to medieval script could only make out as something like "Zichmni."[4]

So "Zichmni" was Henry Sinclair, Laird of Roslyn in Scotland, whom Haakon VI of Norway had in 1379 appointed Earl of Orkney, a position for some years vacant.* The vacancy of the earldom for these years apparently made it necessary for Sinclair to re-establish his authority over the Shetlands and Faeroes, which were included in the fief of Orkney. His original title of Laird of Roslyn explains the mysterious land of "Porland," which Nicolò I said that he also ruled; a mistake of *R* for *P*, and *s* for *r*, seems obvious (this business of assuming that one letter is really another may seem arbitrary to some readers, but it is a legitimate and very helpful procedure in many types of historical study).**

---

* The Orkneys and Shetlands did not pass to Scotland till 1468, as part of the dowry of Princess Margaret of Norway on her marriage to James III of Scotland.

** And in ordinary life as well. If in a newspaper one comes upon a reference to a "bottle-scarred veteran," one simply assumes that "bottle" is a mistake for "battle," and goes on from there.

To return to the narrative: Zichmni (henceforth we shall call him Sinclair) accomplished the subjugation of the Faeroes by land while Zeno handled naval operations. The account gives many geographical names, some easily identifiable and others not, but this need not detain us. What is important is that Nicolò I's description of the Faeroes fills in most of the salient details of Heylyn's description which begins this chapter: the capital named Friesland after the country, the economy based on fishing, the constant intercourse with European nations, including England. The business about the longest day in Friesland being no more than twenty hours is not from Zeno but merely the result of simple mathematics, which any geographer of Heylyn's time could have done, given the placement of Friesland on the map.

Nicolò Zeno I, though a man of the mild Mediterranean, found that adventuring in northern waters agreed with him, and he wrote a letter to his younger brother, Antonio, with an invitation to come out and join him. Antonio did so, arriving in 1392.

With two good Venetian navigators in his service, Sinclair undertook the subjugation of the Shetlands—which in the narrative are called Estlanda or "Eastland." (A glance at the map will show that the Shetlands lie considerably to the east of both the Orkneys and Faeroes.) The adventurers found the islands fortified against them, and conquered them only with difficulty. In the midst of the siege the king of Norway sent out a fleet to halt them, but it was destroyed by a storm.

This is a point which all detractors of the Zeno Narrative have seized upon. They object that the Norwegian crown could have had no reason for interfering with Sinclair's subjugation of the Shetlands, which were a legitimate part of his fief, and that Sinclair could not have made war on Norway, since that would have meant automatic revocation of his earldom. Further, no such naval action is recorded in Norwegian history, and in any case there was no king of Norway at the time, since the reigning sovereign was Queen Margaret.

Richard Henry Major suggested that the invasion was launched by one Malise Sperre, a rival claimant to the Earldom of Orkney, who had retired to Norway, and that Zeno knew only that the ships were coming from Norway, and drew the wrong conclusion. But this does not explain the statement, made a page or two previously, that Sinclair had won a victory over the king of Norway the year before Nicolò I joined him. One could make excuses for Nicolò II on the basis of the fragmentary material from which he worked, but this does not constitute an explanation, and it must be admitted that, were it not for the archaeological proof of what is to follow, the objection might be fatal to the authenticity of the whole document.

To return to the narrative. Having finished the conquest of the Shetlands, Sinclair returned to Friesland and left Nicolò I in command at the conquered capital, wherever it was (Lerwick, the present capital, did not come into existence till the seventeenth century). Nicolò I became bored with inaction and this renewed his ambition to see the world. He sailed northwestward and reached "Engroenland" (Greenland), a region then known only hazily to Europeans as the farthest Christian outpost (see Chapter 9). The Norse settlement in Greeland was then on its last legs, but Nicolò I reported finding there a monastery of the Franciscans, built close by a volcano and piping in water from neighboring hot springs for cookery and heating. Also in his account is a good description of the Eskimo kayak, and a reference to the discovery of a river which is now unidentifiable. But after his return to Friesland, from the unaccustomed cold climate, Nicolò I died, presumably of pneumonia, in 1396.

Here, for the first time, the historical implausibilities of the Zeno Narrative are redeemed by something tangible in the way of archaeological evidence. At three separate sites in Greenland, during the 1920s, finds were made of the sites of dwellings with plumbing installed to pipe in water from nearby hot springs.[5] These were attributed to the Norsemen, but the ground plans are quite different from those of all Norse sites, resembling instead the plans of tenth-century Irish dwellings.[6] Zeno had said that friars came to this monastery from Norway and Sweden, but primarily from the Shetlands, where the Irish had established religious foundations by the ninth century. Perhaps too much can be read into this, but at least we can definitely assume that the art of plumbing and utilizing hot springs was known and practiced in early Greenland.

As to the monastery itself, there is one vague reference that might support the Zeno Narrative.[7] Ivar Bardsen, a native Greenlander who wrote a description of the island some years before the time of Nicolò I, mentioned a monastery in southern Greenland, but of the Augustinians, not thè Franciscans. Bardsen was probably right and Zeno wrong as to the order of the monks. The site of the monastery has not been discovered so far, but it may have been close to Gardar, the bishop's seat, which is known to have been located in southern Greenland.

We have now reached the portion of the narrative that has brought it to the attention of numerous modern historians. Antonio Zeno, who inherited his brother Nicolò's position as naval commander, wrote to his elder brother in Venice a letter in which he related quite a story.

An old fisherman had turned up somewhere in the islands, and was brought before Sinclair because of an interesting tale he told. Twenty-six years earlier (around 1370), he said, he was one of the crew of a vessel blown about 1000 miles across the Atlantic to an island which he called Estotiland. The inhabitants of this island were evidently of European stock, and they were skilled in all the crafts; they maintained a city, had much gold, and their king possessed Latin books though the people had forgotten how to read them. They traded with Greenland, importing furs, sulphur, and pitch, and they raised grain and made beer, "which [the Italian Nicolò Zeno explains] is a kind of drink that northern people take as we do wine." A relatively civilized people inhabiting an unknown land.

The language of these people was unknown to the fishermen, who were, however, able to talk Latin with another castaway, and so establish communication. They became much admired for their knowledge of navigation with the compass, which was unknown in Estotiland, and the king kept them there five years, making coastal voyages. During this time they learned the language, but no examples of it were given in the fisherman's narrative as Zeno reports it. One of the fishermen explored the island, and he described it as smaller than Iceland, fertile, heavily forested, and with a mountain at its center from which four rivers flowed to water the country.

After five years, the fishermen were sent on a voyage south to a neighboring land called Drogeo, where they were captured by cannibals and most of them eaten. The narrator survived by teaching the savages how to fish with nets, and thus became a man of such importance among them that a neighboring tribe attacked in order to capture him. This was to happen to him again and again; he said that he spent thirteen years in Drogeo, and during this period changed hands twenty-five times by kidnaping. He reported that these people hunted with lances of wood, sharpened at the point, and that they suffered much from the cold because they were too stupid or ignorant to clothe themselves with the pelts of the animals they killed. In the course of his wanderings he had heard rumors of a land farther south, with a warmer climate, where the natives built cities and temples, used gold and silver, and made human sacrifices to their idols.

Finally, he managed to escape, and with the aid of friendly chiefs whom he had previously served, he returned to Drogeo, where he was picked up by a vessel off shore and brought back to Estotiland. There he became a trader on his own, prospered, and eventually was able to acquire his own vessel and return to Friesland. The narrative states that "the sailors, from having much experience in strange novelties, gave full credence to his statements." Sinclair at once projected an expedition to find this tempting land.

Here we are in the midst of incredibilities. Nicolò II undoubtedly believed the land of Estotiland to be on the eastern seaboard of North America, a region without gold and without any mountains from which four rivers flow. The native Indians of this area did not practice cannibalism, they had fished with nets from time immemorial, and they certainly knew how to clothe themselves when the need arose. And it is hard to swallow the idea of presumably uneducated fishermen speaking Latin. There may have been some sort of international seamen's lingo, like the lingua franca of the Mediterranean, which was slangily known as Latin, but the same word is used in reference to the king's Latin books, and this can only mean real Latin. The fact that the fishermen did not understand the Estotilanders' language does away with the theory advanced by some that Estotiland was a Norse settlement, because Norse was then the gen-

eral spoken language of the Orkneys and Shetlands, as it still is that
of the Faeroes, so the fishermen would certainly have recognized it.
The southern land where human sacrifice was practiced sounds teas-
ingly like Aztec Mexico, and Nicolò II, who lived after the time of
Cortes, may have dubbed this in. The civilized beer-drinking city-
dwellers of Estotiland cannot be identified; to explain them (in addition to the Norse colony theory that we have seen is untenable) some
historians have hypothesized an early colonization of America by
the Irish (see Appendix III).

Actually, the whole tangled mess is not important. A sailor's yarn,
told to impress a reigning earl, and recorded at third or fourth hand,
has no evidential value that we need consider. Too many defenders
of the Zeno Narrative have made the mistake of trying to substantiate
the document inch by inch, and have met their downfall at this point.
What is important is that this ancient mariner's tale sparked Sinclair's
westward voyage. Also of significance is the fact that the sailor's account of Drogeo described it as "a great country, and, as it were, a
new world" ("*il paese essere grandissimo, e quasi un nuovo mundo*"),
the first recorded use of the term "New World."

To return to the Zeno Narrative: Sinclair, with Antonio Zeno in
command of the fleet, set sail on a voyage to find this unknown land.
A terrific storm separated and sank many of the ships, but the one in
which Sinclair and Zeno were sailing survived the blow to reach a
land whose inhabitants turned out in force and in arms to keep the
strangers from landing. Sinclair managed to convince them that no
invasion was intended, and was told that their land was called Icaria
(see the Heylyn selection at the beginning of this chapter). Ten days'
sail followed—six due west and four against an unfavorable south-
west wind—and they made land, "and we did not know what country it was, and were afraid at first to approach it."

They soon found a good harbor and landed, and the famished
crew ate themselves full of birds' eggs. They named the harbor
"Trin," and "the month of June came in, and the air in the island was
mild and pleasant beyond description." An expedition was dispatched
inland, returning with a report of a smoking mountain, with springs
of pitch issuing from it, and of wild cave-dwelling savages inhabiting

NO LONGER ON THE MAP § 64

the surrounding countryside. On account of the country's richness and the mildness of its climate, Sinclair resolved to stay there and set up a colony. This touched off a near-mutiny, since most of the men wanted to return home before the winter made it impossible. Sinclair, who apparently was easy to get along with, agreed to their demands; he got volunteers to stay with him in the new land, and sent the rest of the men home under the command of Antonio Zeno ("against my will," says Antonio, who wanted to stay). There the narrative ends, except for a fragment stating that Sinclair remained in the newly discovered land and also explored both coasts of Greenland.

What happened subsequently can only be guessed. Sinclair must have returned to "Friesland" from his overseas colony, since he is known to have been killed in battle defending his earldom in 1400 or 1401. Antonio Zeno had wanted to return to Venice, but despite his entreaties, Sinclair would not let him go because he valued Antonio's services too highly. It is a matter of record, however, that he had died in Venice by 1405, so he must have returned after Sinclair's death. He may have written a complete account of his adventures, for Nicolò II refers vaguely to "the book" as one of the documents he tore up during his boyhood.

The learned Frederick J. Pohl believes that he can pinpoint in place and time the Sinclair landfall of America. On the eastern seaboard there are only three springs of pitch, and they, when set afire by lightning, could produce the "smoking mountain." One is in Venezuela and one in Trinidad, obviously much too far south; the third is near Stellarton, Nova Scotia, and could easily be reached by a voyage such as the one described.

The common practice of naming places for the day of their discovery led Pohl to play with the idea that "Trin," shortened because of the mutilated state of the original manuscripts, might actually have been "Trinity." He points out that the name was given to the harbor when "the month of June came in," and a check of the historical calendar showed that Trinity Sunday fell on June 2 in the year 1398. Since that date is quite in line with others that can be established for the narrative, Pohl suggested that this is the exact date of the naming, if not of the actual landfall.[8]

The Zeno Narrative, admittedly full of perplexities and improbabilities, is very dubious when judged in terms of internal evidence, and for centuries those who accepted it did so largely on faith. But about a decade ago, external evidence turned up that gave it a new credibility.

Near Westford, Massachusetts, is a large rock with a carving on it that from colonial times until 1954 was assumed to be an Indian sketch of a human figure. To amateur archaeologist Frank Glynn, it looked more like a sword, presumably of Norse origin. He sent a copy of it to Thomas Lethbridge, curator of the Museum of Archaeology and Ethnology at Cambridge, England. Lethbridge replied that the sword was of fourteenth-century style and wanted to know more.

Glynn cleared away the brush covering most of the rock, and carefully cleaned the surface. This revealed the incised figure, six feet tall, of a knight in full chain mail, his left hand resting on the hilt of the sword mentioned above, and his right arm bearing a shield with a coat of arms. Parts of the effigy had been weathered away, but English heraldic experts consulted by Lethbridge definitely identified the

Photograph of the Westford rock carving, with Frank Glynn.

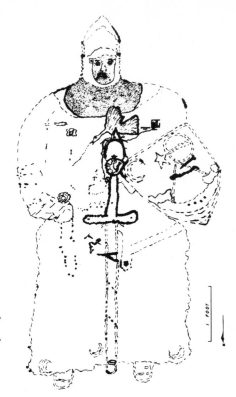

Glynn's hand-drawn copy of the
Westford rock carving.

arms on the shield as belonging to the Sinclairs of Scotland. And closer study of the figure revealed that the cutting had not been done with a modern chisel, but had been dinted into the rock with a medieval armorer's tool.[9]

In 1960 an improbable attempt was made to pass the carving off as of Indian origin.[10] But this hardly stands up. And no one so far seems to have suggested that it is a hoax perpetrated by some Scotsman of later date. It seems probable that someone, in the days of heraldry and chain mail, penetrated into what is now Massachusetts and left a memorial of his visit, with the Sinclair arms a prominent feature. And we have a historical account, sketchy but plausible, of the visit of a Sinclair to that general area. The Zeno Narrative, faulty as it is, would seem to stand verified in its general outlines.

The story of the Zeno Narrative has led us far away from Friesland. The geographical mystery still remains: how could the well-known Faeroes become transmuted into a nonexistent island southwest of Iceland, as it is shown in the map accompanying the Zeno Narrative and in most other maps of the period?

Part of the answer is found in the fact that in medieval England, and elsewhere in Europe, Iceland was best known for its fishing grounds. There is plenty of evidence that the English referred to Iceland as "Fish-land" and that the name spread.[11] Columbus's illegitimate son, Fernando, recorded his father's visit to Iceland in 1477 (he called it "Tile," meaning Ultima Thule), and he quoted from the great voyager's notes that "Tile mentioned by Ptolemy lies where he said it does, and this is called by the moderns *Frislanda*"—this was written eighty years before the Zeno Narrative appeared.[12] A Spanish map of around 1480 gives Iceland the name of "Fixland," and an anonymous map of about 1508 in the British Museum calls it "Fislanda." Then, fifty years later, "Frisland" appeared on the Zeno map, not as Iceland this time, but as a southerly companion to it.

This map was prepared by Nicolò II from an older original among the undestroyed family papers, and he said of it that "although it is rotten with age, I have succeeded with it tolerably well." The old map was obviously so illegible that it needed major reconstruction with the aid of other, more modern maps. The existing Zeno Narrative makes no mention of Iceland (other than as a misspelling of Ireland), but the original map undoubtedly showed it. Nicolò II would have wanted to call it by its modern name, but being confused by the two names (Iceland and Friesland) for the same island, he did what many other geographers of the period did. He simply assumed two islands to match the names.

He may have been quite unfamiliar with the remote Faeroes, and taken it for granted that the better-known Fishland-Fisland-Frisland was the scene of his ancestor's adventures. At least it is reasonably certain that he did not have a play on "Freeze-land" in mind, since the Italian word for "freeze" is *gelare*.

This map gives a number of place names in Friesland, most of

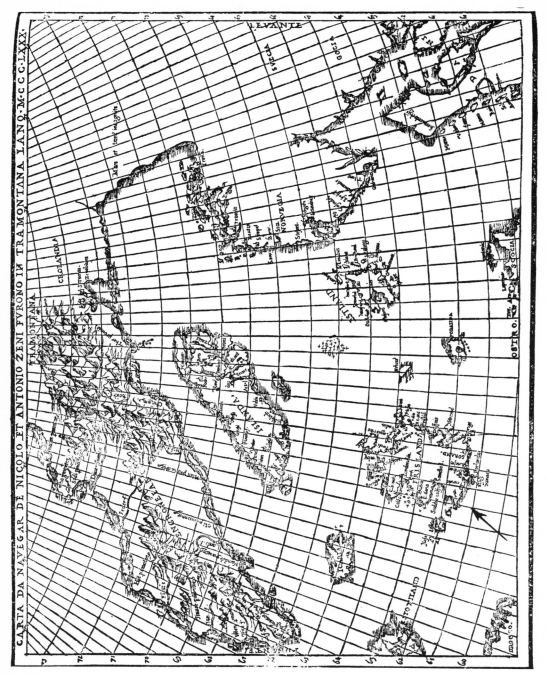

The Zeno map of the North Atlantic, showing Frisland.

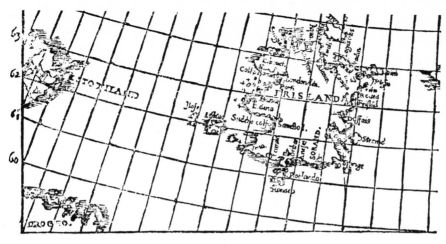

Friesland, or Frisland, as shown on the Zeno map.

them identifiable with place names in the Faeroes, and including those mentioned by Heylyn. Andefort (mentioned on the Zeno map as Andefard, but not in the text) is Andefjord in the island of Osteroe. From its association with a Gulf of Sudero, we can identify Samescot (on the map, Sanestol) with the Faeroese isle of Sandoe, to the north of Suderoe-fjord. Sorano or Sorand is given in the narrative as. the name of a territory subject to Sinclair, but it cannot be definitely identified, though various suggestions have been made.

One detail mentioned by Heylyn remains to be explained. Nowhere in Zeno is there any indication of Friesland's having been known as "West England." But on his Arctic voyage of 1577–1578, Martin Frobisher provided the explanation for this. He landed on a bleak unknown coast, probably in southern Greenland, which he thought to be an uninhabited portion of Friesland, and took possession of it for the Queen, naming it West England.* Heylyn's explanation of the name is as apocryphal as his attempt to account for the name of Friesland itself.

---

* This was on the return voyage; Dionise Settle, a crew member, recorded that on the voyage out in 1577, "the 4th of July we came within the making of Frisland," but he gave no details.[13]

So far as I can determine, this is the only instance of a mariner's claiming to have actually landed on Friesland. The only reference to it by another North Atlantic voyager that I have been able to find is that of James Hall, an English pilot in the Danish service, who mentioned in 1606 a strong southwesterly current, "the which I did suppose to set between Busse Island [of which more later] and Freseland over with America."[14]

The century-long cartographical career of Friesland, in whatever spelling, need not be recounted in detail.* The mythical island may be seen on any world map, polar map, or North Atlantic map of the

---

* One oddity which deserves to be mentioned is the Icelandic "Stefansson Map" of about 1570, probably based on an earlier original. It shows not only Friesland but also Vinland, which it says was visited by the "Angles."[15]

Sir Martin Frobisher.

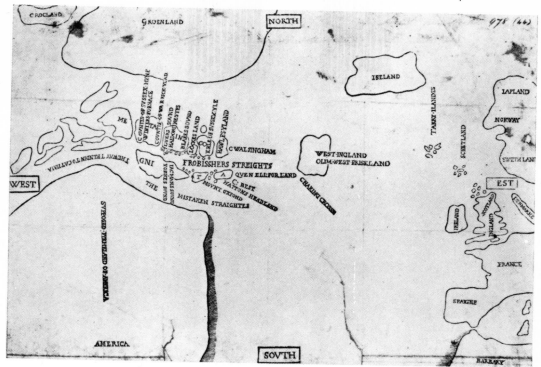

Map of Frobisher's explorations, showing Friesland as "West Ingland."

period from 1558 to the 1660s. It varies in size and shape, and it may be located directly to the south of Iceland or (usually) to the southwest. El Dorado was a myth that was whittled away, but Friesland was a myth that finally evaporated. By the late seventeenth century it had disappeared from all but the most cautiously conservative of charts. The 1701 edition of Peter Heylyn's *Cosmography*, published long after Heylyn himself had gone from this earth, gave the account of Friesland as in earlier editions, but a wry note was appended. "It is much disputed whether there be any such Island in the World, and by some positively denied."

But any map drawn around 1600 had to allow not only for the isle of Friesland, but also for an area somewhere on the Atlantic coast of North America that could be identified as Estotiland. Various suggestions have been advanced as to the origin of the name: "East-Out-Land"; "Estofiland," which uses the first three syllables of the motto *esto fidelis usque ad mortem* ("I am faithful unto death"); Estland, the Zeno Narrative's name for the Shetlands; and "Escociland" or "Escotiland" (Scotland), the latter particularly favored by those who believe in the sailor's story (see Appendix III).[16]

My own guess would be that the Nicolò I original read "Estofiland," and that the name the sailor actually used was something like "Stockfish Land." There is evidence[17] that fishermen of pre-Columbian times were familiar with, and made use of, the Grand Banks codfish (or stockfish) source, and that a western Atlantic region called Stockfish Land was vaguely known. The Andrea Bianco map of 1436 shows an *Isla de Stockafixa* at about the correct location for Newfoundland, and possibly identical with it. The fact that the alleged narrator was a fisherman would make this reading of "Estotiland" plausible.

Wherever or whatever Estotiland was, it vanished from the maps by the late seventeenth century. By then the entire eastern American seaboard had been explored and much of it colonized. No region called by its natives anything like Estotiland nor any trace of anything like the city and countryside described had turned up. All regions of the coast now had names given by Europeans, and "Estotiland" was no longer of any use as an identification.

Ortelius's world map of 1590 went the entire way, giving not only Friesland and Estotiland—the latter as a huge island, dwarfing Greenland, in the area actually occupied by Labrador and Quebec—but "Drogeo" as well, represented as a rather small island southeast of Estotiland, southwest of Friesland, and about equidistant from both. What the castaway had described as a great country and a new world had inexplicably dwindled into a pipsqueak isle. But Drogeo never caught on cartographically. Unlike the supposedly civilized

The Thorláksson map of Greenland, 1606.

Estotiland, Drogeo was a savage land with a savage name—the sort of place that its European discoverers would rename as they saw fit.

For some reason Ortelius failed to include Icaria. This land, which Sinclair's expedition visited when blown off course, was certainly either County Kerry in Ireland or the Outer Hebridean island of Saint Kilda. However, a new island of Icaria dutifully cropped up in the North Atlantic on many maps of the time. Its disappearance occurred before that of Friesland. Experienced navigators knew that the sea in those parts was not actually as cluttered up with islands as the maps indicated, so something had to go. The transfer of Greek mythical themes into those latitudes, as in the "King Daedalus of Scotland" story, was a barefaced attempt to explain the incongruous name of Icaria in some way, an attempt for which Nicolò II was undoubtedly responsible.

As for Engroenland, or Greenland, it has a long and intricate story of its own. But that must be deferred to Chapter 9.

And now for the irony. It appears quite possible that there may have been an actual island in about the attributed location of Friesland, and that it really did sink. During Frobisher's return from Greenland on his voyage of 1578, one of his vessels, the buss *Emmanuel*,* came into sight of a large island at about latitude 57° N, or so its captain later reported (the report was confirmed by one Thomas Wiars, a passenger on board). Apparently no landing was made; the crew observed it from seaward, and accounts differ as to whether it was wooded and fertile, or bleak and icebound. The island was named Buss, after the vessel.[18]

The next reported sighting of the island was made by the previously mentioned James Hall, on his 1606 voyage to Greenland. He said that he saw it but was unable to land because of ice.[19] The island went unreported then till 1668 when Captain Zachariah Gillam, en route to Hudson Bay, mentioned meeting it.[20] Three years later, in 1671, one Thomas Shepherd returned with a tale of having explored it, and with a very detailed map showing many geographical features such as Crown Point, Rupert's Harbor, Shaftsbury Harbor, Arlington Harbor, etc., plus a small offshore Shepherd's Island. But there is good reason to regard Shepherd as an out-and-out liar.[21]

There were no more reported sightings. Nicolas Visscher's world map, of about Shepherd's time, does not show it. A Dutch sailing chart of 1745 by one Van Keulen mentioned Buss as sunken, and suggested that it might have been the actual Friesland. Thereafter,

---

* A buss was a sturdy fishing vessel of Dutch design, capable of enduring rough weather.

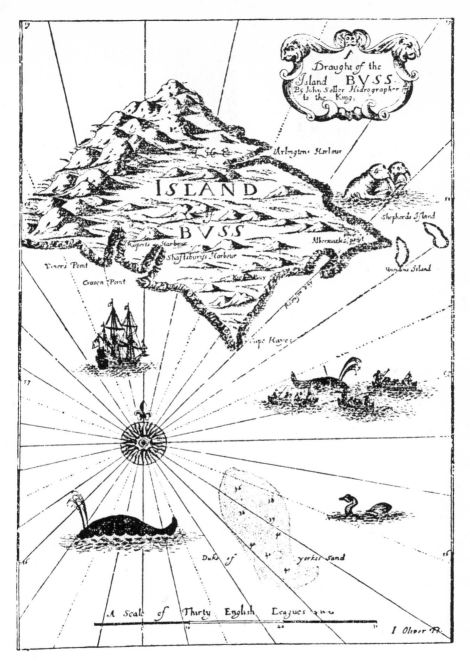

Detail map of Buss, 1673, based on Thomas Shepherd's account.

throughout the eighteenth century, the "Sunken Land of Buss" was generally accepted as a navigational hazard to the southeastward of Greenland, and marked on charts accordingly.[22]

Then occur a couple of trustworthy reports. Captain Richard Pickersgill, sailing from England to Hudson Bay in 1776, took soundings at the reported site of Buss, and found shallows. And in 1818 the Arctic explorer John Ross likewise took soundings at this spot, and got a depth of 180 fathoms, indicating a very considerable subsidence of the bottom over the previous forty years.[23]

This is sheer coincidence, having nothing to do with the Friesland myth. However, it seems highly possible that Nicolò Zeno II did place his imaginary island at or about the spot then occupied by a real one, and that this actual isle, as if to get into the spirit of things, then proceeded to sink.

CHAPTER 4.

Two Irish Questions:
Saint Brendan and Breasil

Ireland is the northwestern outpost of Europe, facing onto the wild Atlantic. For centuries Ireland has been renowned throughout the Western world as a land of rich legendry. It is not difficult to understand, therefore, that Ireland should have been the source of two of the greatest mythical Atlantic islands. Although the myths surrounding the island of Saint Brendan and the island of Breasil are in no way organically related to each other, it seems convenient and appropriate to treat them together, though consecutively, considering first the one of older origin.

We know disappointingly little about early Irish sea roving, but we do know that it occurred. The old Irish curragh, built of leather around a wooden frame, was an eminently seaworthy vessel, which could be constructed quite large (the word "curragh" is a cognate of "coracle," but must not be equated with the little round one-man boats associated with the early Britons and still used to some extent in Wales). We have the old Irish sea epics, the *Imrama*, as evidence of voyaging before Ireland came into history; and in recorded history we have the renowned Irish King Niall, "of the Nine Hostages,"* who late in the fourth century sent a fleet to the aid of the Picts against the Romans.

The Christianization of Ireland seems to have stimulated seafaring, at least among the religious element. Just as the anchorites of the early Church sought solitude in the Egyptian desert, the early Irish monks tended to sequester themselves on barren islets fronting on the ferocious western ocean, where perhaps the stark confrontation with the elements tended to foster spiritual experience. The great Saint Columba, who founded the monastery of Iona in the Hebrides in the year 563, is perhaps the most famous of them, but they were many.

This is the background against which the reputed voyaging of Saint Brendan must be considered. In its original form, the saint's name was Brenaind, but we shall use the customary modern spelling of Brendan. There is no question that he lived, and for nearly a hundred years (c. 484–577). He founded several monasteries during his long life, notably the one at Clonfert, and he is often called Brendan of Clonfert to distinguish him from another Irish saint, a contemporary, called Brendan of Birr (c. 490–573).

And there seems to be no question that he did some voyaging, the only uncertainty is how much. Our best source on Saint Brendan is the *Book of Lismore*, an Irish compilation of lives of saints, which was put together in the thirteenth century out of much older materials. In it we read that Saint Brendan desired to find a land of his own, far removed from other men, and that an angel appeared to him in a dream and assured him of the success of his quest. He and some companions sailed for five years, encountering various marvels, and finally reached the holy island, easily identifiable by the "trains of angels rising from it."[1]

If we allow for the embroideries common in medieval ecclesiastical literature, this sounds like a fairly plausible account of a voyage

---

* When an Irish king put down a revolt, he would take as hostage some kinsman of the rebel leader as surety for the latter's future good conduct. This attribution of nine hostages to King Niall indicates that he was a mighty ruler, who had suppressed nine attempts to overthrow him.

in search of a place of hermitage, the sort of voyage common among Irish monks. But about four centuries after the saint's death, in the tenth century, there appeared a Latin book of unknown source and authorship, the *Navigatio Sancti Brendani*, which was very popular throughout medieval Europe. It credited Saint Brendan with two voyages instead of just one.

At some point in early Irish history the old Greco-Roman belief in the Hesperides, or Fortunate Isles, must have become entangled with the old Celtic belief in the paradise of Avalon in the western sea, because in early Irish monastic circles there developed a vague concept of the Blessed Isles, or Isles of the Blessed, to the west. According to the dubious *Navigatio Sancti Brendani*, the good saint after finding his sacred isle returned to Ireland and later launched a second voyage in search of these Isles of the Blessed. He sailed for seven years, and eventually found them.

But we have two versions of the manuscript. In one, Brendan sailed southward in search of an island "just under Mount Atlas" (or off the coast of North Africa), where a holy man named Mernoc had formerly lived. Mernoc was rumored to have gone to the Garden of Eden, which in medieval belief was supposed still to exist somewhere

A landing on a sea monster, mistaken for an island. From Claus Magnus, Historia Septentrionalis.

Der Seedrache. Nach Klaus Groß.

on earth. Saint Brendan seems to have found the island without much trouble, though on his way thither he saw a hill all on fire (the volcanic peak of Tenerife?), and he visited a neighboring land (Africa?) from which he brought fruit and jewels.

The other version is better known and far more interesting. Saint Brendan, in search of the Blessed Isles, sailed westward from Ireland for fifteen days with a crew of sixty men, then was becalmed for a month and drifted to an isle where the crew found a palace with food which replaced their depleted stores, and where the Devil himself appeared but did them no harm. They then sailed for seven months (direction not given) to an island with gigantic sheep; they killed one, but before they could roast it, the island sank, becoming, most implausibly, a sea monster. The voyage went on, dragging out to many months between stops. They visited an island of birds (which were actually repentant fallen angels), an island with a monastery founded by an unknown "Saint Alben," an area where the sea turned into a swamp, an island where the fish were poisonous (a white bird warned them of the danger), and another sea monster resembling an island—which obligingly let them land on it, celebrate Pentecost, and stay seven weeks.

Eventually they reached the region where "the sea sleeps," and where "the cold is unendurable." Here a fire-breathing dragon pursued them, but in answer to their prayers another monster appeared to fight and kill it. They sighted an enormous glittering temple of crystal towering out of the sea (an iceberg?), and they visited more islands, some characterized by fire and smoke, others by a terrible stink. They saw a menacing demon appear before them and then dive into the sea. Then another island of fire and smoke, then one covered by clouds, then the entrance to hell, and the island where Judas Iscariot is held in torment. Finally the quest paid off; they reached an isle where a hoary-headed holy man told them how to reach the blessed island they sought.

They arrived at the island, and were met there by another holy man, totally unclothed but covered with feathers, who extolled in the most rapturous terms the island's balmy weather and fertility. In a cave Saint Brendan found a dead giant, whom the saint by his own holiness was able to bring back to life. The giant gave his name as Maclovius, accepted baptism, said that his people had known the doctrines of Christianity, and as a favor asked to be allowed to return to his eternal rest, which was granted. When the Saint Brendan story became generally known, "Saint Maclovius" passed into the popular hagiology, though he was never officially recognized by the Church.[2]

It makes a beautiful tale, but unfortunately that is all. It is very much open to doubt that Saint Brendan made any voyage that would furnish a real-life basis for this story—let alone indicate that he discovered America, as some have maintained (Appendix III). The whole thing would appear to be a Christianized reworking of material indigenous to the Erse folklore and drawn largely from the *Imrama*—particularly from the legendary voyage of Maildun, who also encountered demons and islands of fire. Why Saint Brendan should have been picked out of all the holy Irish voyagers to have this story foisted upon him is a question that perhaps an expert Gaelicist could answer. But it probably has no real relevance to the legendary island, our actual point of concern.

It is worth mentioning that the learned Geoffrey Ashe, after an intensive study of the Saint Brendan problem, advanced a very imaginative and cogent case for his belief that, whether the actual voyaging of Saint Brendan ever took place or not, the *Navigatio Sancti Brendani* shows a sound knowledge of North Atlantic geography. He believes that he can identify at least the more salient of the places mentioned in the *Navigatio*, and retrace the supposed course of the perhaps fictitious voyage. The book is well worth reading, though it deals only marginally with the legend as legend.[3]

It is not clear whether the people of early medieval times took the voyage of Saint Brendan as the literal truth or as pious allegory. But by the High Gothic period, when the tale had made its mark on the map, there was little tendency among the learned to take seriously old semi-pagan legends of blessed isles in the distant ocean. By the thirteenth century the assumption was that Saint Brendan had made a quite ordinary voyage, on which he had discovered an island or islands, presumably to be found among those which were (at least supposedly) known.

A huge world map, completed circa 1275, which adorns a wall in the cathedral at Hereford, England, is the first known map to feature Saint Brendan's discovery. At about the proper site of the Canary Islands are placed the "Six Fortunate Islands, which are the Islands of Saint Brendan" (*Fortunate Insulae sex sunt Insulae Sct Brandani*), of which only five seem to be shown. The Canaries had been known in classical times (King Juba II of Mauretania had sent an expedition there during the first century B.C.),[4] and for some reason the rugged and none-to-fertile islands had been identified with the mythical Fortunate Islands. This could explain the Hereford mapmaker's

Section of Pizigani map of 1367, showing Saint Brendan in lower left-hand corner.

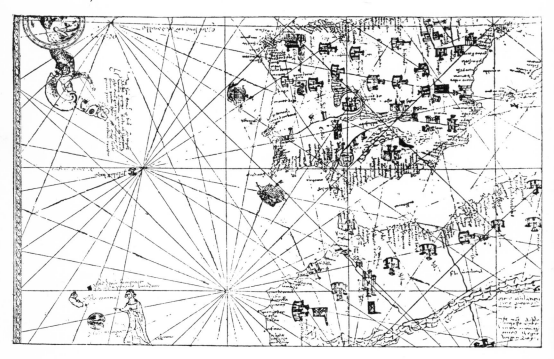

confusion of the Canaries with the Blessed Isles found by the Irish saint.

But the whole tone of the *Navigatio Sancti Brendani* suggests a voyage into the unknown and a brand-new discovery, not a landfall already fairly familiar—as the Canaries had become by the late thirteenth century. Accordingly, the island of Saint Brendan in its next known cartographic appearance—a map of 1339 made by the Majorcan Angelino Dulcert, or Dalorto—is identified with a more recent discovery, the Madeiras.

Officially, the Madeiras were discovered and claimed for Portugal by the great navigator João Gonsalves Zarco in 1418. But the medieval maps give us good reason to believe that the islands were known earlier, though perhaps only in seafaring circles. They may have been known to the Phoenicians and Romans; and the Portuguese themselves (as in Galvano's *Discoveries of the World*) attributed the original discovery to an Englishman named Machen, or Macham, about 1345.[5]

Angelino Dulcert was a member of the flourishing Majorcan school of cartography that produced the handsomest and most accurate maps of medieval times. On his aforesaid map of 1339, the Madeiras are indicated in approximately the right position as *Insulle Sa Brandani siue puellan*, which in properly spelled Latin would read "Islands of Saint Brendan, or the Girl." Who the Girl was, and how she came into it, is now hard to guess.* Almost thirty years later, in 1367, the Pizigani brothers of Venice produced a map on which the isles of Saint Brendan are apparently equated again with the Madeiras, and made easily identifiable by the monkish figure drawn beside them. The inscription on this map is barely legible, but one suggested reading is *Ysole dictur sommare sey ysole pone le brandany*, translatable as "The So-Called Sleepy Islands, or Islands of Saint Brendan." This attribution, if authentic, is as inexplicable as the one involving "the Girl."**

---

* Geoffrey Ashe has suggested a translation as "Isle of Maidens," and a linkage with Irish folklore, but he failed to reconcile this with the fact that *puellan* (correct Latin, *puellam*) is a singular, not a plural form.[6]

** To show what a student of old maps is up against linguistically, I should mention

But in the meantime, indications of knowledge of the Madeiras, with no reference to Saint Brendan, had multiplied. There was the so-called Medici map of the Atlantic in 1351, showing islands at that position called Lecname and Porto Santo. Also in the 1350s there appeared a very curious book by an unknown author who identified himself only as a Spanish Franciscan born in 1305. It purported to be an account of the entire earth, based on the author's travels to every part of it. Though undoubtedly a hoax, it reflected the geographical knowledge of its time, and it mentioned "Lecname" and "Puerto Santo" as names of Atlantic islands.[7] When the Portuguese did rediscover the Madeiras they gave the name of Porto Santo to one of the islands, and the name "Madeiras" is simply a Portuguese translation of the Italian "Legname," or "Forest Islands."

After the discovery of the Azores in 1427 by the Spaniard Diego de Seville, who sailed for the Portuguese, these islands too came to be included in Saint Brendan's diocese. Various maps of the fifteenth century show it thus, and a full list would only tire the reader.

The point is that up until now the island(s) of Saint Brendan were not so much a myth as a question of location. There were known islands in the Atlantic, the Irish saint was believed to have discovered something, and the problem was simply to correlate the two. The great Venetian cartographer Andrea Bianco followed tradition on his map of 1436 by associating the Madeiras with Saint Brendan's discovery. But Bianco, on his better-known map of 1448, reduced the Madeiras and Azores to an inaccurate north-and-south string of islands, located to the east of another group of islands; these latter were apparently the real Azores, reproduced from a Portuguese source and added to traditional Italian concepts of the Atlantic islands. However, Bianco, having to call them something, foisted onto the largest island of the group the name of *yª fortunat de sa. beati blandan.**

---

that a literal translation of this very corrupt late-Latin caption would be "Islands Called Pertaining-to-Sleep, or Islands Behind Holy the Brendan."

* It could signify English *island*, German *Insel*, French *île*, Italian *isola*, Spanish *isla*, Portuguese *ilha*, Latin *insula*, or Gaelic *innis*.

It is at this point that the Isle of Saint Brendan begins to become mythical, in our present sense. It was no longer simply a tag attached to the known Madeiras or Azores, but a name cut loose to wander freely on the map.

In its mythical form, the name seems to have appeared first on the famous 1492 globe of Martin Behaim, the German cartographer who worked for the Portuguese and who apparently influenced Columbus. On the Behaim globe, Saint Brendan's Island appears to the west of the actual Cape Verde group, and it is represented as being of considerable size.

The career of Saint Brendan's Island as a myth lasted for a century or so. On an English map of 1544, attributed to Sebastian Cabot, it was placed in mid-Atlantic at about the latitude of northern Newfoundland. The great influential maps of Mercator in 1567 and of Ortelius in 1571 duplicated this placement of "S. Brandain." Other cartographers copied the English map well on into the seventeenth century, and it still loitered on Michael Mercator's map of about 1620. But by the mid-century it had disappeared.

"Saint Brendan's" was still not entirely finished. It drifted back to its original point of appearance, the Canaries. Among the Canarians of the late seventeenth century it was believed that there was an eighth island in their seven-island group, and they called it by the name of San Borondon.[8] Even today the people of the Canary Islands tend to live strictly parochial lives, so that a Canarian seldom leaves his native island, and thus their faith in the existence of one more isle could have a certain viability. There were reported sightings of the island, which was supposed to be 87 leagues long by 28 wide, situated about 40 leagues from the Island of Palma. Various expeditions of Canarian fishermen, the last in 1721, searched for it in vain. Nevertheless, "San Borondon" was officially claimed as a property of the Spanish crown, and there is a rumor of someone's sighting it as late as 1759.[9]

Today most historians believe that, if there is any truth to the story of Saint Brendan's second voyage and discovery, he probably touched at the Madeiras or Azores. But his island is no longer with us, and has not been for two centuries.

Before we take up the story of Breasil, there is one point which should perhaps be clarified. Breasil, however spelled—Breasail, Brassil, Brasylle, Berzil, even Brazil—has nothing to do with the Brazil that we now know, despite the similarity of name. In the tangled etymology of the word there is a remote connection, but that is all.

In other variants of the name Breasil has actually become more famed in folklore than in historical geography, and we shall consider this aspect of the story shortly. But Breasil was more than a legend. In Europe of the fourteenth and fifteenth centuries, it was believed to be a good solid island, some distance from Europe, and worth sailing for. The tale of Saint Brendan had to be studied chiefly from map and manuscript, but the tale of Breasil involves a few very concrete voyagings.

The most plausible guess as to the origin of the name Breasil, or Breasail, seems to be that the word combines two Irish Gaelic words, *breas* and *ail*. Both had highly laudatory meanings, so that *breas-ail* could be translated as something like "superbly fine," "grand and wonderful," or "the most of the greatest." The first Breasail recorded was a pagan deity of pre-Christian Ireland, and Breasail is also mentioned in ancient annals as a masculine personal name. Saint Breca, for example, an anchorite of the Aran Islands of around 480, was originally named Breasail.

Exactly how and when "Breasail" came into currency as the name of an island we do not know. (Some have theorized that early Irish voyagers reached America and gave this name to the newly discovered land—see Appendix III.) Nor are we certain when the mythical Irish island became more generally known in Europe, though when it did, it encountered another similar name that may have influenced the whole concept.

The flourishing textile industry of the Mediterranean had created a constant demand for dyestuffs, and there are a variety of records (the earliest in 1193) of some sort of "grain" which yielded dye and was in great demand in Europe. Marco Polo mentioned *brazil* as a crop grown in Sumatra, and his secretary, Rustician of Pisa, added the note that Polo brought some of this grain home with him, but that it would not grow in Italy. Just what sort of grain seed this might have been is not clear, but we do have some idea as to the origin of its name. We know that *brazil* was a term in the Mediterranean lingua franca meaning coal (Spanish *brasero*; Portuguese *braza*; Italian *braciere*; French *braise*, now used only in the sense of a burning coal), and we know that dyes had been made from coal since ancient times. It seems probable that some compromise form of the various Romance words for coal came into currency as a term for whatever materials were used for the purpose of dyeing. And this is where the name of the present Brazil comes in: that South American region was named for its extensive forests of dyewood trees.[10]

It seems that the Irish term that could be translated as "Most-Best Island" became confused with the Mediterranean term that could be translated as "Dye Island." This confusion may have been influenced by the Arabic geographer Idrisi. His account of the island Sahelia will be considered at further length in Chapter 6 in connection with the legend of the island of seven cities; suffice it to say here that, according to Idrisi, ships came from all over the world to trade for dyes and gems. This may have established the idea of a dye-producing island in the Atlantic, which became confused with the concurrent Irish belief in an island in the same area bearing a name that seemed to confirm the idea.

Unfortunately, theories of early Irish belief in an Island of Breasil are based on conjecture and extrapolation. The name is of undoubted Irish provenance, but Irish references to the island as such seem not to occur until a later period. Its first actual appearance is on the Angelino Dulcert map of 1325; it appears as a fairly large circle in the latitude of southern Ireland, identified as *Insula montonis sive abresil*, which could be translated as "Island of Rams, or Breasil." It is also possible that *montonis* is actually intended as a reference to mountains, and should read *montanis*. Several later maps give Montanis, Montorius, or Monte Orius as descriptive or alternative names for Breasil, indicating that Breasil, outside of Ireland, was thought of as a mountainous island which yielded dye.*

---

* This description brings the Canaries to mind, since they are mountainous enough, and until recent years one of their chief products was cochineal dye. But this identi-

Following its probable first mapping by Dulcert, Breasil became fixed as a circular island in the Atlantic, at about the latitude of southern Ireland. The maps already cited in connection with Saint Brendan all show it. The barely legible Pizigani map of 1367, which credited Saint Brendan with discovering the "So-Called Sleepy Islands," gives an even stranger appellation to Breasil, if the suggested reading is correct: *Isola de nocorus sur de brazar*. It is difficult to render this sensibly into English, but it would seem to make Breasil the Harmful Island as well as the Island of Dye. As we shall see in Chapter 6, the inhabitants of the Isle of Sahelia were supposed to have killed each other off in civil wars, and possibly this term was influenced by that idea.

An anonymous Catalan map, drawn in 1375, showed something different. It kept Breasil in its accustomed place but turned it into a sort of atoll, enclosing a lagoon in which there are nine tiny islets. Another Catalan map of about a century later shows two Breasils. One is in its usual place in relation to southern Ireland, though farther west than on earlier maps. The other is at the far side of the Atlantic, represented by a circular atoll that fits neatly into a concave bay at the southern end of an Isla Verde, which can only be a misplaced Greenland (see Chapter 9).

The learned William H. Babcock, authority on mythical Atlantic islands, has suggested that this atoll-form of Breasil might be a stylized representation of the Gulf of Saint Lawrence, which is semi-enclosed from the sea and studded with islands, lying in an area of the Atlantic where prevailing winds and currents could have brought a European voyager of pre-Columbian times. If this is true, the 1375 Catalan map would be the earliest known rendering of a portion of the American coast.

Outside of maps, the earliest reference to Breasil is found in the curious book of the anonymous Spanish Franciscan, cited earlier, which names Brazil as one of the Atlantic islands.[11] The first recorded voyage in search of the island appears to have been made in

fication will not work. The Canarian cochineal industry was not established until the sixteenth century after the Spanish conquest.

1452. In that year, Diogo de Teive, a Portuguese sea captain operating out of Madeira, was dispatched by Prince Henry the Navigator to cast about the North Atlantic and see what was to be found. He sailed west-southwest as far as the Sargasso Sea, then turned north, and discovered the two westernmost of the Azores, until then unknown to the Portuguese. Continuing northward, he searched for Breasil, and got as far as the latitude of southern Ireland, where, he later said, he felt he was close to undiscovered land. But, when a reasonable search turned up nothing, he returned home. One of his crew members was a Spaniard, Pedro Vásquez de la Frontera. Forty years later, this old sailor, retired and living in Palos in Spain, met an Italian adventurer named Cristoforo Colombo, who was projecting an Atlantic voyage. The old salt told the would-be voyager about the Sargasso Sea and assured him that it was nothing to fear, and he also did a great deal toward recruiting Columbus's crew.[12]

About 1482 William of Worcester, by origin a Bristol man, completed his *Itinerarium*, a valuable description of southern and western England. In it he gave the version of his brother-in-law John Jay, a Bristol merchant, who in July 1480 had sent out John Lloyd, "most expert shipmaster in all England," in search of "the island of Brasylle in the western part of Ireland, to traverse the seas." Lloyd voyaged unsuccessfully on his quest, was hampered by storms, and after nine weeks had to return as the supplies ran low.[13]

Pedro de Ayala, the Spanish ambassador to England, in 1498 made the not-too-clear statement that "for the last seven years the people of Bristol have equipped two, three and four caravels in search of the island of Breasil and the seven cities." (The seven cities will be dealt with at more length in Chapter 6.) Does this mean that voyages had been undertaken over the past seven years, or that seven years had been taken up in preparing one fleet? Either way, it indicates a serious desire among the Bristol merchants to discover Breasil.[14]

Although the legend of Breasil was most probably of Irish origin, we seek in vain for any records of Irish voyages in search of the island. It is true that from the twelfth century on, the Irish were a conquered and oppressed people, not in a position to launch many ships. But somehow the Anglo-Irish, the English occupying the country, who showed a notorious tendency to become "more Irish than the Irish," never became interested. As far as Ireland was concerned, the Island of Breasil passed almost completely into occult legendry.

Disappearing islands, or islands which can be seen only by the elect, are a familiar feature of Celtic myth. They range from the earthly western paradise of Avalon, familiar from Arthurian story and song, down to many more workaday examples. For example, there are the nine islands that rise out of the sea every seven years; they can be plainly seen from the coast of Galway, but will vanish if anyone attempts to sail out to them. Some witnesses have claimed to have seen people on the islands going about commonplace daily tasks. Two distinguished men who claimed to have personally seen these islands were Thomas Otway, the famous Restoration dramatist, and Thomas J. Westropp, a noted Irish folklorist of the nineteenth century, who devoted some study to the Breasil legend. (Apparently neither of these Thomases was much given to doubting.)[15]

And there is the Isle of Eynhallow, in the Orkneys. Allegedly it was once under enchantment, and would rise from the sea at times yet sink before anyone could reach it. The story had been that if a man could sail out to the island, without looking away from it and holding steel in his hand, he would break the enchantment. During the seventeenth century, someone succeeded in doing so, and the island has stayed put ever since.[16]

The existing records are too sparse to indicate exactly when Breasil became mythical to the Irish. It may have been early enough to have made Breasil the original Lost Island mentioned by the chronicler Honorius of Autun in the twelfth century. It existed somewhere in the Atlantic, and was the most fertile and beautiful land on earth, but no one who discovered it could ever find it again.

In its mythical form, Breasil became known in a form variously rendered as Hi-Brasil or O'Breasil (or some variant spelling of either). Both prefixes are forms of the Gaelic word meaning "ancestor," and serve to enhance the legendary element. The story took bizarre forms. In the province of Munster, for example, it was believed that one of the mountains of the area had been known as Callan, though no one knew which mountain this was. On it was a tomb, never discovered, of an early Irish king named Conan, and in the tomb was a key that, if anyone should find it, could be used to cause Hi-Breasil to rise out of the sea. It appears that by now Breasil had come to be identified with one of the nine islands previously mentioned.

And during the 1680s there was recorded living in Galway one Morrogh O'Ley, who had spent six or eight years in Hi-Breasil, and on his return was able to practice medicine successfully.[17] The folklore pattern here is well known. Joseph Campbell in *The Hero with a Thousand Faces* examined it in detail; the hero ventures into the supernatural world and returns with some power to do good for his people. In the popular legendry of the British Isles, this motif took the familiar form of the man who spends some time among the fairies and returns with healing powers. Breasil is here equated with Fairyland.

But during the seventeenth century, something stirred an interest among the Anglo-Irish in Breasil as a concrete possibility. In about 1625 one of the Leslies of County Monaghan secured a royal grant for Breasil, whenever it was discovered.[18] And Hardiman's *Irish Minstrelsy* of about 1636 mentions a Captain Rich, sailing out of Dublin, who had recently discovered Breasil but could not land because of fog; his bearings would place Breasil in the Bay of Biscay.[19]

Apparently the only man ever to claim an actual landing on Breasil was John Nisbet, an Irish sea captain. In 1674 he landed at Killibega Harbor and told his tale. Breasil was a great black rock, inhabited by great black rabbits, and by a wicked wizard who dwelt in a strong castle. Nisbet had managed to defeat the wizard and to resist his magic by setting a huge fire—for fire, as anyone knows, is the power of light against the power of darkness, hence the practice of burning witches. He brought with him several Scottish "castaways" whom he had apparently coached in their stories so that they would back him up. There is no indication that anyone took his yarn seriously.[20]

From the early sixteenth century on, Breasil consistently appeared on the map as being in American waters, with the exception of the Ortelius map of 1571, which restored the island to its traditional position off southern Ireland. The eighteenth century kept it close to mid-Atlantic.

And Breasil died hard. It lingered on the map long into the nineteenth century, in fact until less than a hundred years ago. But by this time it had dwindled from a considerable island to the small supposed Brazil Rock, the portion of which became fixed by John Purdy's important 1825 map of the North Atlantic. In 1836 the great German man-about-science, Alexander von Humboldt, could comment that, of all the fictitious North Atlantic islands, only Brazil Rock and Mayda still remained (for Mayda, see Chapter 10). Finally in 1873, when navigations in this much-traveled span of ocean failed to bring in any concrete reports of the supposed Brazil Rock, the British Admiralty saw fit to remove it from their charts.

CHAPTER 5.

Various Islands,
Some of Them Devilish

Anyone familiar with navigational charts has seen shoals and reefs, and sometimes islands, marked with the abbreviated disclaimer of "P. D." (Position Doubtful), or "E. D." (Existence Doubtful). The conservatism of cartographers is commendable here; they would rather commit the scientific error of perpetuating a nonexistent island than the practical error of allowing a shipwreck to occur on an island that might be there after all. So, some nonexistent islands may quite possibly be still on the map, and some future study of what is no longer on the map may have to include them.

The islands involved range from fabulous to dubious; one or two of them may in fact exist, but the lack of sustaining evidence has caused them to be dropped from the map. There is no actual connection between them, but since none of them has a story of its own worth expanding to chapter length, it seemed most convenient to treat them one by one, alphabetically, in a single chapter, followed by special consideration of a couple of especially intriguing matters.

Antillia

This name is still preserved in the term Antilles, applied to the West Indies, and more particularly to the long scimitar-curve of small isles sweeping south-by-east from Puerto Rico down toward the Venezuelan coast. But the name and concept of the Island of Antillia predates the discovery of the West Indies, or at least, the Columbian discovery.[1]

The name itself is no help; in Latin it merely means "Opposite Island."* Its possible first appearance, as "Atilae," was on the Pizigani brothers' map of 1367, in the approximate position of the Azores, at that time not yet discovered, or recorded to have been discovered. It shows up again, more definitely, as "Attiaela," on an anonymous Catalan map of about 1425. On Battista Beccario's important map of 1435, it first appears in what was to become its standard form, a rough rectangle in the western Atlantic, far to the westward of Spain and in its approximate latitude, with its name spelled Antilia or Antillia, and accompanied by three smaller isles, Reylla, Salvagio, and I in Mar. It should be noted that "I in Mar" merely means "Island in the Sea," and that this Salvagio is a freakish occurrence, so far south, of an island usually placed in Newfoundland waters. We shall consider Salvagio later in this chapter.

Some maps identified Antillia as the Island of the Seven Cities (Chapter 6), and after the discovery of America some maps transferred Antillia to the mainland. A map of about 1508 which locates the Seven Cities along the eastern coast of North America also gives "Antiglia" as the name of an inland region of South America, roughly in modern Venezuela. The new discoveries of that period, crossed with traditional geographic concepts, gave rise to some wild and wonderful new notions. One finds this out from reading old maps, and one must bear it in mind while reading them.

In any case, by the time of Columbus, European geographers apparently took for granted the existence of a large island out in the

---

* Though Alexander von Humboldt, for no apparent reason, suggested an alternative derivation, from the Arabic *al-tin*, "the dragon."

west Atlantic, so much so in fact that they tossed off casual references to its supposed discovery.

Martin Behaim on his globe of 1492 showed Antillia with a notation that in 1414 a Spanish ship "got closest to it without danger." This would seem to imply that the island was known, and regarded as a sailing hazard, even earlier than that. There are also references to a Portuguese voyage of the 1440s as having reached Antillia, but this is most likely the same one which was supposed to have visited the Seven Cities (see Chapter 6). And Columbus himself, while in Lisbon about the year 1480, wrote a letter to King Alfonso V in which he mentioned "the island of Antillia, which is known to you."

As we have seen in Chapter 2, Columbus was not the propounder of a wild new theory that the world is round, and his opponents did not base their argument on belief in a flat earth. The question at issue was the circumference of the earth, and here Columbus was dead wrong and his opponents much closer to right. On not much besides wishful thinking and hand-picked evidence from geographers whose views fitted his preconceptions, Columbus shrank the distance round the world to one that would make a westward voyage to the Orient feasible.[2] Orthodox geographers who had a better estimate of the true circumference, knew that no vessel could possibly carry the necessary supplies for so long a voyage. But even to this, Columbus had an answer.

There was in Florence at that time one Paolo Toscanelli, a physician by vocation and a rather wrongheaded enthusiast of geography by avocation. He had some unorthodox ideas of his own, and he argued for them, but he was learned enough to have a considerable degree of respect from more cautious geographers. And Columbus had a letter from Toscanelli, dated 1474, recommending Antillia as a good stopping-point to break his voyage and take on stores.

So Columbus sailed, evidently expecting that if worse came to worst he could always make for Antillia. Perhaps he made it, for some historians have identified Antillia as Cuba. Columbus was convinced that he had made the eastern coasts of Asia, or at least some islands of that area, and he died convinced of it. But his voyagings,

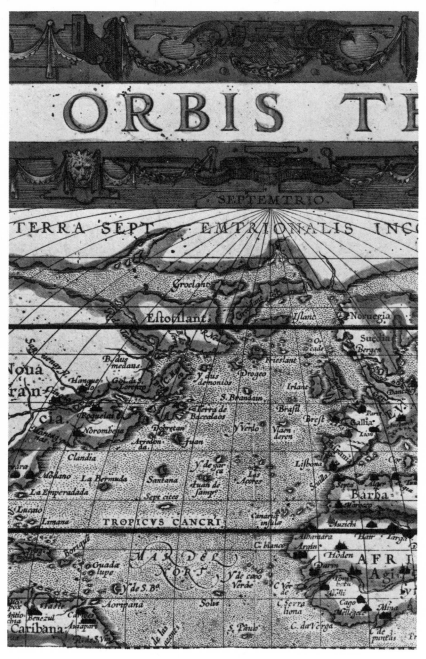

Section of the Ortelius map of 1571, showing Friesland, Estoti-land, Drogeo, "S. Brandain," "Y. Dus Demonios," "Brasil," "Y. Verdo," Vlaenderen, Santana, and "Sept Cites."

while they placed the present Antilles on the map, made an end of Antillia.

Peter Martyr, the historian of Columbus's voyages, wrote in 1511 that the great discoverer believed himself to have found the land of Ophir, whither King Solomon's ships had sailed for gold,* "but, the descriptions of the cosmographers well considered, it seemeth that both these and the other islands adjoining are the islands of Antillia."

Antillia did straggle along, on a few maps, for a couple of decades into the sixteenth century. But its reason for existence was gone. There remained only the question of which of the increasingly well-known West Indies it should be identified with. Today, there remains the possibility that Antillia was not fabulous, but was established by some ill-recorded and forgotten voyage that did reach Cuba, or possibly Florida. But at present this remains unproved, and Antillia is no longer on the map.

Aurora Islands

There were three of them, and they lay southeastward of the Falklands, about halfway between there and South Georgia, and they took their name from the Spanish ship *Aurora* that first reported them in 1762, and nobody has had a sight of them since 1856. They raise some interesting questions.[3]

For one thing, they seem to have been the only questionable islands on record sighted twice from the same ship, for the *Aurora*'s officers in 1774 reported having seen them again. In the interval another Spanish vessel, the *San Miguel*, had fixed their location at latitude 52° 37' S, longitude 47° 49' W. During the last two decades of the eighteenth century, several more sightings were reported.

Then in 1794 the Spanish corvette *Atrevida*, under command of a

---

* This "Ophir" was the island of Haiti, or Hispaniola, where Columbus found abandoned gold mines. His son Bartolomé confirms Columbus's identification of the island as the one to which King Solomon sent his ships. This conjecture, made by Columbus himself, is of interest as the first post-Columbian theory of a pre-Columbia discovery of America.

captain whose name is recorded as J. de Bustamente, set out to make a real survey of the Auroras, and found them. Bustamente's report described the central and largest island as a tent-shaped peak, the southern side white with snow and the other side dark; the island to the north of this was a smaller peak, also snow-covered; and the southernmost island was a large saddle-shaped rock, which at first they took for an iceberg. They confirmed the latitude and longitude of the Auroras, and this placed them definitely on the map.

But thereafter nobody seems to have paid much atention to these three useless excrescences in the midst of icy waters, except to avoid them as a danger. The next voyager to look for them was Captain James Weddell, the renowned Antarctic explorer. In 1820 he searched the reported area, and found nothing. The American sealer Benjamin Morrell made a similar unsuccessful attempt in 1822.

From then on, all searches were fruitless, but the Auroras stayed on many maps at least until the 1870s. Readers of Poe will remember that part of the purpose of the voyage in *The Narrative of Arthur Gordon Pym* was to make a search for these islands. Among Cape Horn sailors they became an article of faith, and a further legend grew up of a Spanish treasure galleon cast away on one of the Auroras, with wealth available for the salvaging. The origin of this belief may have been in the Spanish vessel *San Telmo*, lost with all hands in the South Shetlands in 1819—but probably with no treasure aboard.

How then to explain the Aurora Islands? Icebergs? Were a succession of experienced mariners taken in, time after time, by a coincidental conjunction of three icebergs in the same place, during the late eighteenth century and then never again? As an explanation, this lacks something of probability.

The Shag Rocks have also been brought up as a possible explanation. There do exist, at about latitude 53° S, longitude 43° W, a group of three rocks, all visible above water within an over-all distance of about 1 mile. The suggestion has been made that an erroneous fix on the Shag Rocks might have accounted for the reports of the Auroras. But this hardly squares with the Bustamente account. The Shag Rocks are too small and unimpressive to fit his description, and they

A Spanish galleon, such as the San Telmo, *in distress.*

are much too far east—6 degrees of longitude, or over 100 miles—to make it plausible that a navigator qualified to do marine surveying would have made such a mistake.

The romantically minded reader may wonder if perhaps they sank. The possibility cannot be categorically denied, but unfortunately we have no records of any islands ever being known to sink in sub-Antarctic waters.

There is actually no wholly satisfactory explanation for the Aurora Islands, and they remain one of the great unsolved mysteries of the sea.

Mention should be made of one last, and very questionable, reappearance of the Auroras. In 1856 the captain of the *Helen Baird* recounted in his log a sighting of the Auroras, which he placed at latitude 52° 42′ S, longitude 48° 22′ W, or reasonably close to the first attributed location. He made them five islands, not three, and described them as snow-covered and extending over a range of 20 to 25 miles. But his report was generally disbelieved, and since that time the Auroras have never been seen again.

Daculi

Daculi, an island not mentioned in histories of exploration, must be studied because of its appearance on early maps.[4]

Daculi first showed up on the Dulcert-Dalorto map of 1325, north of Breasil and to the northwest of Ireland. To the east of Daculi is another island, called Bra, which cannot be described as mythical because it seems to be a misplacement of the Hebridean island of Barra. But it came into a strange relationship with Daculi on maps of the period.

Daculi appeared on most of the famous early maps previously mentioned: the Dulcert of 1339, the Medici of 1351, the Pizigani of 1367, the Beccario of 1435, the Pareto of 1455. The spelling varied, but the island's position remained roughly the same. And it was always accompanied, to the east, by Bra. The Pizigani map—the same that had strange things to say about Saint Brendan and Breasil—

attached to Bra a notation in doubtful and now-illegible Latin, the meaning of which is questionable but has been construed to indicate that the mortality rate was high on the island.

One suggested derivation for the name Daculi is from the Italian word *culla*, "cradle." Next to Daculi the Pareto map gives a caption in Latin which has been taken by some to substantiate this theory. Its point is that pregnant women of Bra who have difficulty in delivery will give birth easily if taken over to Daculi. This would seem to make a name meaning "cradle" somewhat appropriate. But is this actually related to the name's derivation, or is it a story made up to explain it? No one now can say.

On the map, Daculi did not survive the fifteenth century. Remote as northern Irish waters were to Italian cartographers, they were visited regularly by Italian traders, so that an imaginary island located in this area could not last long.

Davis Land

Lionel Wafer was one of the most colorful characters of the Spanish Main. A native speaker of Gaelic as well as English, he was apparently a born linguist, who spent some time as a captive of the Indians of Panama, learned their language, took to their ways, and got along well with them. Most histories of the period mention him as a pirate, but it appears that he served as surgeon aboard pirate ships, and never actually helped to take any prizes.

In 1687 Wafer was aboard the *Bachelor's Delight*, commanded by a Dutch pirate whose name is recorded as John Davis.* Following a raid on Panama from the Pacific side, this vessel swung southward to round the Horn.[5] What occurred on this voyage was recounted by Wafer in his *Description of the Isthmus of Darien*, published in London a year later. The ship was shaken and rocked by some sort of undersea disturbance, which was later found to coincide with the

---

* Not to be confused with the great Elizabethan explorer of that name. However, I must admit that in my preliminary notes for this chapter, I did confuse them. We "experts" can make mistakes at times, too.

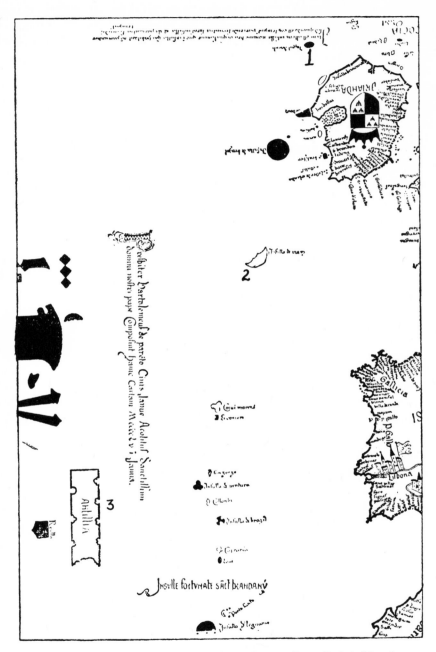

Section of the Pareto map of 1455 showing (1) Daculi, (2) Mayda, and (3) Antillia.

Callao earthquake of 1687. And shortly after (Wafer's dating is imprecise), at about latitude 20° 27′ S, a sighting was made of an extensive tract of land in the sea, "which we took to be islands." Wafer estimated its length at 40 to 45 miles. The most cogent and convincing detail of his account is the mention of large flocks of birds seen rising from this land. If reliable, this would seem to do away with any explanations in terms of optical illusions or cloud formations seen on the horizon. Wafer (or perhaps Davis himself) named the discovery Davis Land.[6]

Captain William Dampier, another part-time pirate who did important exploratory work in the Pacific in 1688, took Wafer's report seriously, and made an unsuccessful search for Davis Land. In 1721 the Dutch skipper Jakob Roggeween also tried, and did discover Easter Island. Apparently the last search was made by a Spaniard named González in 1771, after which date Davis Land dropped off the map.

What was Davis Land? Perhaps the best guess might be that it was Easter Island. It fits Wafer's description well enough, and could easily have been mislocated, owing to the uncertainty of determining longitude in the days before the chronometer. The latitude given is a good 400 miles too far north, but Wafer himself was not a navigator, and his book is not distinguished by meticulous accuracy. Captain Davis, too, may have made a bad observation.

Davis Land has been much favored by partisans of lost continents, who see it as one of the last high grounds above water of sunken Lemuria, or Mu.[7] It is possible that Davis Land was thrown up by the earthquake mentioned, and that it later sank. But in more modern times, enough islands have been known to sink in the South Pacific from volcanic activity that there is no need to bring in any lost-continent theories to complicate the matter.

Dougherty Island

In some respects, Dougherty appears as one of the strangest of dubious isles. The evidence for its existence is very compelling, yet it is not there. In fact, the special interest of this island is such that it seems advisable to give some clear idea of its reported location to the reader unfamiliar with the finding of latitudes and longitudes.

Take a good up-to-date map of the Antarctic, drawn on the South Polar projection. Draw a line connecting the northernmost point of Tierra del Fuego with the northwesternmost point of South Graham Island. Use this as a base on which to erect an equilateral triangle, with the apex pointing west. This apex will give the approximate location of Dougherty Island, if it exists.

It was roughly here that Captain Swain, a Nantucket whaler, reported sighting an island in the year 1800. He described it as high, snow-covered, and with many seals and sea birds. In all modesty he named it Swain's Island, and gave its position as latitude 59° S, longitude 90°–100° W. The chronometer had been invented some thirty years before, and longitudes could be computed much more accurately than this, but whalers seldom carried the most modern equipment, and their longitudinal fixes were usually sheer dead reckoning (which in nautical terminology means experienced guesswork).

In the years following, two other New England whalers are supposed to have sighted this same island, but the details are not clear, and it seems to have excited little interest. In 1830 the two American vessels, the *Anawan* and *Penguin*, set out under command of Nathaniel Palmer (the same whom American maps long credited with discovering the Antarctic continent) to get a fix on Swain's Island. The details are vague, but it seems that they made a rather loose search, and came up with nothing.

Then in 1841 Captain Dougherty, an English whaling skipper in command of the *James Stewart*, reported the discovery of an island. It was 5 or 6 miles long, with a high bluff to the northeast end and lower land beyond, and covered with snow. Dougherty fixed its position at latitude 59° 20′ S, longitude 120° 20′ W.

The discrepancy here has to be borne in mind. Both islands were supposedly in latitude 59° S, but 20 to 30 degrees of longitude lies between Swain's and Dougherty's alleged discoveries. It is true that as one approaches the Poles, degrees of longitude become smaller and smaller; it is also true that Captain Dougherty admitted he was not sure of his observations because of several preceding days of poor visibility. Nevertheless, such a gaping error as this leads one to wonder whether Swain's and Dougherty's reports had any reference to the same island.

It seems to have been only in the twentieth century that the two were correlated. At the time, Dougherty's discovery was accepted as new, and quite his own. And in the years that followed, a number of navigators confirmed the report of an island at about latitude 59° S, longitude 120° W. Captain Keates of the *Louise*, out of Bristol, described the island in detail in 1860, even to mentioning an iceberg grounded on the northwest shore. Keates fixed the island at latitude 59° 21′ S, longitude 119° 7′ W; his chronometer was later checked and found to be in error by less than a quarter of a mile.

Dougherty Island was now very much on the map, including British Admiralty charts. The last reported sighting was in 1886. Captain William Stannard of the *Cingalese* told of having seen it five years later, said that there were many seals in the vicinity, and gave its location at latitude 59° 20′ S, longitude 120° 18′ W.

From 1889 on, numerous searches were made for the island, and all without success. Captain Greenstreet, in command of the British steamer *Ruapehu*, tried five times between 1894 and 1910. Robert Falcon Scott, the renowned Antarctic explorer, combed the area in 1904, and at the reputed position of Dougherty Island got soundings of 2558 fathoms, or about 3 miles. Sir Ernest Shackleton, another famed Antarctic explorer, passed over the charted side of Dougherty Island in 1909 and found nothing. It must be pointed out, however, that this occurred in the midst of the Antarctic winter, when conditions of navigation and visibility are incomparably bad, so that this in itself may prove nothing. In 1915 the survey vessel *Carnegie* passed within 3 miles of the alleged position of the island, and the report stated afterward that conditions of visibility were such that the island, if existent, could have been seen from the crow's nest to a distance of 35 miles on any side.

Thus ended the search for Dougherty Island. The question remains: What happened to it? Did it suddenly sink to unthinkable depths? Or were Dougherty and a number of other navigators deceived, coincidentally, in about the same position, by sight of some of the vast Antarctic icebergs which at times are miles in extent? It seems to require a mighty act of faith to believe this; still, there is the significant point that none of those who reported sighting Dougherty Island ever seems to have claimed to have landed on it.

Dougherty Island remains one of the most teasing mysteries of the sea. But the mystery does not stop there. It will be remembered that Captain Swain had reported the discovery of an island in 1800, forty-one years before Dougherty's report. Modern students have generally equated the two, chiefly because both are sub-Antarctic islands in 59° of latitude, playing down the tremendous discrepancy between the longitude of Swain's Island (fixed by Swain at somewhere between 90° and 100° west longitude) and Dougherty Island (fixed by all who claim to have seen it at about 120° west longitude). The reported position of Dougherty Island has been so thoroughly combed as to justify the statement that it is not there, however the fact may be explained. The reported position of Swain's discovery has not so far been thus thoroughly investigated, and there just might be, at the apex of the triangle previously mentioned, an actual small and unimportant Antarctic island which started all the fuss. One of the early captains to report it during the 1820s was Richard Macy of Nantucket, who gave its position at latitude 59° S, longitude 91° W, and that is just about where this triangulation brings us. In this area there may be an island that (combining its location in 59° S with iceberg sightings or visual disturbances noted in that latitude) could have given rise to the yarn of Dougherty Island, and seamen expected to find it at that given place, and interpreted whatever they saw in accordance. Then again, an iceberg or one of the visual disturbances for which the Antarctic is notorious, may have caused Captain Swain to see an island that was not there.

As to its career on the map, I have not been able to determine when it was last mapped, but Dougherty Island shows up clear on a Rand McNally map of about 1938 in my possession. As far as I can tell, maps of the 1950s seem to have dropped it.[8]

Isla Grande

The Spanish skipper Antonio de la Roche was a mighty voyager in sub-Antarctic waters, and he apparently discovered the island of South Georgia a century before Captain Cook. On the same voyage, in 1675, he came upon "a very large and pleasant island, with a good harbor to the eastward." He gave its latitude as 45° S, with no longitude, and named it Isla Grande. Since he was cruising in Atlantic waters at the time, this would place the island somewhere east of southern Argentina. One theory has been advanced that de la Roche was deceived by a couple of headlands on the Argentine coast, in 45° S, and that by failing to sail round his "island" he failed to discover that it was in reality part of the mainland.[9]

Isla Grande has the distinction of being one of the few fabulous islands to be an object of search by a really top-caliber explorer. Jean François de Galaup, Comte de Lapérouse, was dispatched by the French government in 1785 to survey Asian waters, and one part of his instructions was to search en route for the island of "La Grande." He spent some time in the search, but with no success, then went on to complete his assignment, and did important work in Asian and Australian surveying until his expedition came to grief in the New Hebrides.

Later navigators thoroughly searched the entire zone, the last being the American sealer Benjamin Morrell, in 1826. From no specified source he gave the supposed location of his quarry at latitude 43° 10' S, longitude 31° 15' W. He expressed disbelief in the island's existence, but tried anyway, half-heartedly, and found nothing. This seems to have ended it, and Isla Grande was forgotten.[10]

La Catholique

This appeared on the Desceliers map of 1546, in the latitude of southern Florida, and along with it were shown three other islands of unidentifiable origin. Later Portuguese maps were to copy La Catholique, in roughly the original position, as "La Católico." The other three islands shown by Desceliers were Saint Anne, in the mid-

Atlantic east of New England, and two isles named for an unknown "Saint X" (Saint Francis Xavier was not canonized until 1622). One of these was to the south of the Azores, the other to the east of Long Island. Nobody else seems to have copied them, unless Saint Anne was the original of Mercator's "Santana," to be considered later in this chapter.

There is nothing in the annals of voyage and discovery to explain any of these islands or their names. The best guess may be that since tradition had placed demonic islands in North Atlantic waters, the good Desceliers (of whom we know nothing personally) would have felt impelled to exorcise the area by including a few with sanctified names.[11]

Saint Matthew's Island

Exactly who reported discovery of Saint Matthew's Island seems not to be a matter of record, but the year was 1516 and the expedi-

Section of Desceliers' map of 1546, showing (arrow in lower left-hand corner) La Catholique. The names are mostly upside down because on the original south is at the top.

tion Portuguese. It was supposed to be in the Gulf of Guinea, and although it stayed on the maps until well into the nineteenth century, its story can be briefly told.*

There is an actual island of Annobón, now a Spanish possession, in the Gulf of Guinea, in the same latitude reported for Saint Matthew's, and at about 5 degrees east. Saint Matthew's was supposed to lie at 5 degrees west. Apparently it was a simple error of misreading (or miswriting) of the longitudinal reading as west instead of east, which led to a long-lasting belief in an nonexistent island in that position.[12]

Saxemberg Island

The discoverer of this island was a Dutch captain named Lindeman, and the year 1670. According to his log, he was at latitude 30° 40′ S, longitude 19° 30′ W. (It must be borne in mind that finding longitude was strictly by-guess-and-by-God in those days before the chronometer.) Accompanying his report was a sketch of the island, which shows it as low-lying but with a sudden high peak in the center, looking a great deal like a witch's hat. It was Lindeman who named the island Saxemberg (some times erroneously spelled Saxemburgh).

That no further searches for it seem to have been made appears to indicate a certain skepticism among geographers of the time. It was next heard of in 1804, when Captain Galloway, of the American vessel *Fanny*, reported not only sighting it but having it in view for four hours. He confirmed the description, complete to the peak in the middle, and also confirmed Lindeman's latitude, but made the longitude about 2 degrees farther east. Considering that Galloway had the advantage of the chronometer, which Lindeman had not, this would seem more of a confirmation than the contrary. Lindeman's

---

* There are actually two Saint Matthew Islands: in the Bering Sea, and off the coast of Burma.

old, doubtful account was dusted off, and Saxemberg Island was restored to the map.

This restoration seemed amply justified in 1816, when the skipper of the *True Briton*, Captain Head, gave a report that entirely agreed with Galloway's, except for his statement that he had the island in view for six hours. Actually, this was not a very good corroboration, since Head was undoubtedly familiar with Galloway's account, and thus very likely saw what he expected to see. That Galloway knew of Lindeman's old, forgotten, and never really believed account is more than we can assume. It appears definite that both Lindeman and Galloway independently did see something, and at about the same spot.

But no one else has seen it since. Several systematic searches which were made later turned up nothing. If any further proof of the non-existence of Saxemberg were needed, it would be that the reported location of the island is within 500 miles of the island of Tristan da Cunha, in the South Atlantic. And the hardy seagoing people of that island, thoroughly familiar with the seas for some hundreds of miles about, apparently know nothing of Saxemberg, or of anything fitting its description.

How did it all originate? Were Lindeman and Galloway both coincidentally deceived by the same sort of cloud formation on the horizon? This has been suggested as an explanation, but it seems rather far-fetched. There is no need to assume that it sank, though that is remotely possible. The most we can say is that two seamen, experienced enough to be captains, saw in the same place something which they took to be an island. But neither of them landed on it to make sure that it was actually firm ground, and it is not there now.[13]

This completes the alphabetical roundup of islands. It is far from being an exhaustive list. A number of others could have been included, such as Incorporado and Podesta (geographically unimportant and without interesting stories) or Saint John of Lisbon (for which I have been unable to find a satisfactory source).[14] So let us now pass on to consider the very interesting topic of:

Devil's Islands

Among readers of geographical material there is a distinct class of people, including myself, who could be referred to as "island buffs." There is something about an island. Perhaps it is, as Rachel Carson suggests, that man as a land-dweller experiences the sea as alien territory, and has an instinctive attraction to a suddenly-appearing bit of his own habitat in all that hostile vastness.[15]

But however one explains it, the fact remains that islands possess a particular fascination of their own. The fact is familiar to any small boy who got a special enjoyment out of rowing out to that tiny island in the river or lake and playing pirate there, when he could equally well have played pirate along the main shore. No one ever daydreams of being shipwrecked on a tropical mainland coast, even though the climate and the girls there could be equally as inviting as on any island. An incident that would be regarded as minor and quickly forgotten if it occurred anywhere on a continental landmass, may be enough to make an island forever famous. Consider, for example, how few people have even heard of the Steinheimer treasure, reputed to have been buried somewhere in northern Texas, as against how many have gone on fruitless quests to find the alleged treasure buried on Cocos Island.[16]

There does seem to be some never-spelled-out popular mystique of islands, and it appears to go far back in history. Classical geographers provided tale after tale of discoveries of strange and interesting islands. The interest may have been intensified by the common practice in medieval geography of using the word "island" (*iland*, *yslant*, *insula*, or however spelled) not in the modern sense, but as referring vaguely to some far and remote land considered to be of interest, the visiting of which involved a long sea voyage.* The truthful Marco

---

* Antonio Galvano, writing about 1555, mentioned the Pharaoh Sesostris III's unrealized project of the nineteenth century B.C. to dig a canal linking the Nile with the Red Sea, and commented that this if completed would have made Africa "an Island all compassed with waters." This is the earliest rigidly defined use of the word "island" in the modern sense that I have been able to locate.[17]

The Vale of Devils, on one of Sir John Mandeville's fabulous "islands." Fifteenth-century English engraving.

Polo thus referred to as "islands" all lands of which he had heard something remarkable but which he had not personally visited. Half a century later the mendacious author of the famous *Voiage and Travaile*, attributed to Sir John Mandeville, filled the Orient with "islands" of wonder, which he did claim to have visited—and most of which would have been parts of the mainland if they had existed in fact.

When we take into account this apparently widespread human fascination with actual physical islands, and add to it the medieval convention that the site of anything marvelous was always an "Island," it will be easy to see how in late-medieval geography there should come to be a belief in certain islands as scenes of fearsome supernatural phenomena.

The idea of a distant island as haunted, or enchanted, or as the earthly site of some unearthly marvel, is certainly not confined to medieval Europe. It is common to all early maritime cultures. There is the famed blessed isle of Avalon, and the various demon-haunted islands which the old Irish sea-sagas of the *Imrama* treat (notably in the legendary voyage of Maildun). I mentioned some of these in Chapter 4, along with the marvelous isles which Saint Brendan was said to have visited in the course of his wanderings. And we shall consider in Chapter 9 the western island on which Cronus, or Saturn —the dethroned father of Zeus—was supposed in classical times to have been imprisoned. There are many more islands that could be mentioned, as for example the isle of P'eng-Lai which, in ancient Chinese belief, was supposed to lie somewhere out in the Pacific and to hold the elixir of bodily immortality—except that every expedition in search of it found it upside down.[18] But these are not our present concern, since they did not appear on maps.

One that did appear on the map, at least on the twelfth-century map of the Arab geographer Idrisi, is the island of El Wakwak. On this remarkable isle, which was inhabited by women only, there grew a sort of tree whose fruit was shaped like the heads of women and hung from the trees by its hair. The heads continually cried out the meaningless call, "Wak-Wak!" and if cut off the trees, they died. No one has ever been able to discover a satisfactory explanation for this bizarre myth, though Sir Richard Burton in his annotations to the *Arabian Nights*, in which Wakwak is mentioned, pointed to the possibly connected fact that in the Cantonese dialect Japan is sometimes called *Wo-Kwok*.[19]

In medieval European Christian belief there was a heaven above and a hell below—a hell very concretely located at the core of the planet. This raised the possibility of hell's having its inlets or outlets on the surface of the earth, and late-medieval geographers found several. The openings were most plausible in areas of volcanic action, and the isle of Stromboli in the Mediterranean and Mount Hekla in Iceland became the most celebrated. An anonymous Spanish Franciscan cartographer located an *Isla del Infierno* in the Atlantic; since it appears to be one of the Canaries, he probably had the volcanic peak of Tenerife in mind.[20] And in the distant unknown reaches— those remote "islands where anything could happen"—how many more might there not be?

In reading about medieval European civilization—or at least of certain periods of it—one gets the impression that men of the time felt themselves to be holding an embattled ground against a dire enemy. There was the rather small area of the world called Christendom, where the will of God was known and followed, and there were vast unknown reaches beyond, which were the domain of the Foe. Seen thus, medieval Catholic missionary efforts appear not so much as attempts to save individual souls as military forays into Satan's territory; and the ferocities of the Inquisition and the Albigensian Crusade seem to be aimed less at the halting of doctrinal error than at taking measures against a perilous enemy movement carried out through subversion. It is true that many quotations from medieval authors could be marshaled to refute this interpretation, but there is enough evidence to give a modern student the definite feeling that, at least on the popular level, something of this sort was believed. Thus, one need not assume any abysmal depths of credulity

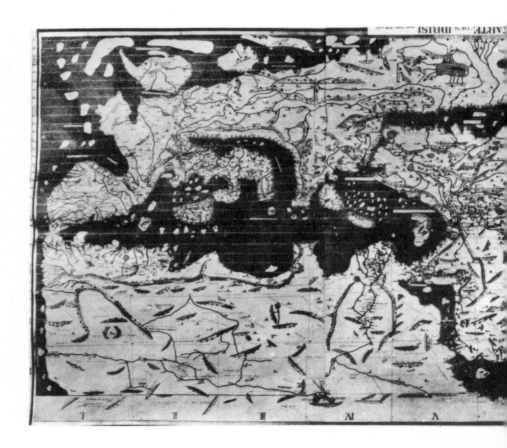

or superstition to understand how the culture of the time could have believed in Atlantic islands as the haunts of devils.

Exactly when this belief arose, and how long it existed in the common mind and in sailors' folklore, it is impossible now to say. That it did so is certain, for mythical islands are not mapped without a reason. The first known appearance of a demonic island on the map seems to have been with the Andrea Bianco map of 1436. The map is badly chopped off at the edges, but it does give in the far Atlantic an island of Antillia, mentioned earlier, and, at about the longitude of New Jersey but to the north at about the proper position for Nova Scotia, the southern tip of an isle with the arresting name of Satanaxio.

Though rather illegible on this map, the full name appears to be La Mão Satanaxio, or La Man Satanaxio. For the latter possibility, the translation "Hand of Satan" has been suggested, though this

Indrisi's world map of the eleventh century.

leaves unexplained the grotesque suffix tacked onto Satan's name. Nils Nordenskjöld, the eminent Finnish Swede, who did extensive exploration in the Arctic and later made himself a pioneer authority on old maps, suggested as a possible original Santanagio, the Basque form of the name Saint Anastasius, and advanced this as possible evidence for Basque knowledge of American waters before Columbus.[21] Perhaps this is true, and a misunderstanding of the outlandish Basque tongue led the Italian cartographer to believe in a western Atlantic island somehow associated with the devil.

In any case, the Bianco map placed a devil's island in what were later to be known as American waters, and later cartographers copied Bianco. But in the interval the name Satanaxio (which Bianco seems to have been the only one to use) underwent a few changes. On some maps, in the location of Satanaxio, there appeared an island called Salvagio. As to its Latin original, this name is ambiguous; it could refer either to "savagery" or "salvation," and it can be interpreted either way, depending on whether one prefers a diabolical or a saintly source as the original of Satanaxio. The island of Salvagio remained on the map as late as the mid-sixteenth century, but by then two other variations on Satanaxio had begun to replace it.

There was the island of Santana, which appears as an intriguing cross between "Saint" and "Satan," though it may also have originated from Santa Ana (see above under La Catholique for an island named Saint Anne). Whatever its source, Mercator showed the island, and after him Ortelius, in the mid-Atlantic, east and a little north of Bermuda. It seems to have had a rather brief run on the map. The English colonization of Bermuda during the early 1600s, and the resultant sea traffic in the area, apparently did away with belief in Santana.

The "Isles of Demons" in the Newfoundland-Labrador area had a rather longer career. They first appeared, called the *Insulae Demonium*, on the Johann Ruysch map of 1507, as two islands just to the north of Labrador, at the entrance to what is now called Hudson Strait, and they are shown with imps cavorting all over the place. Their next appearance seems to be on an English map of 1544,

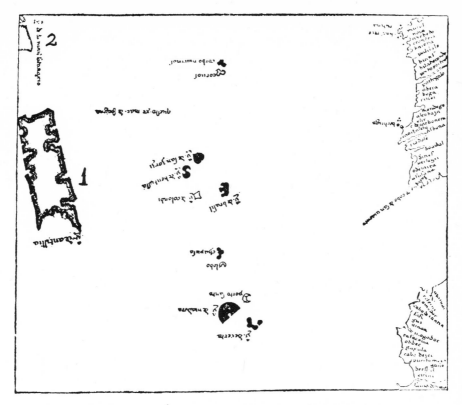

Section of the Bianco map of 1436, showing (1) Antillia, and (2)
La Man Satanaxio.

attributed to Sebastian Cabot, which makes the haunt of devils a
single island off the coast of Labrador. Another map, published in
1550 to accompany the Italian scholar Giambattista Ramusio's
classic collection of travels, *Della Navigazioni e Viaggi*, retains it
as a single island, but moves it south, to the northern coast of
Newfoundland.

The two map-making greats of the sixteenth century, Mercator
and Ortelius, both showed the devil's land. Both broke it up into two
islands once more, Mercator in 1569 keeping them still just north of
Newfoundland, and Ortelius in 1571 moving his *y das demonios*
north to the earlier position off Labrador. The Devil's Islands

barely survived into the following century. English and Danish voyagings into the area in question had turned up nothing to substantiate them, and these Protestant voyagers were highly skeptical in any case of such Popish superstitions. Nevertheless, as late as about 1620, Willem Blaeu and Michael Mercator were still copying them off older maps, and locating them somewhere off Labrador. By 1645, however, when Blaeu brought out his great map of the polar regions, he had discarded them.

Actually there are no islands off Labrador, except for a few tiny coastal ones. But at the entrance to the strait separating Newfoundland from Labrador, the other location as given by Mercator and the aforesaid 1550 map, there are two islands: Belle Isle and the neighboring, much smaller Quirpon. And it does seem that sixteenth-century French fishermen regarded them as isles of demons. Was this simply a notion based on what the map showed, or was the map influenced by what the fishermen reported?

Mention has been made earlier in this chapter of some of the traditional sources and beliefs that probably contributed to the belief in (or at least, the acceptance of belief in) uncanny islands somewhere in the North Atlantic. The problem now is why a special area of demonic activity came to be traditionally placed in the vicinity of Newfoundland and Labrador.

The ferocious climate and frequently diabolical ice conditions might in themselves be enough to explain it. Some sailor's comment, characterizing it as something like "the devil's own sea," could have been taken up by a literal-minded cartographer. The Devil's Islands first appeared in clear and recognizable form on the Ruysch map of 1507. Not long before, in 1501, the remnant of Gaspar Corterreal's expedition had returned to Europe after discovering the land they called Labrador (Chapter 9). Something said by one of Corterreal's men could have influenced Ruysch, who placed the islands on the map. The earlier "Satanaxio" on Bianco's map may have been a butchery of a Basque name of a quite different meaning, and its place on the map a pure accident. The Bianco map's strange wording, which seems to allow of a translation as "Hand of Satan," remains a problem, but the actual writing on the map is now too illegible to justify anything but conjecture.

Norse sources also may have contributed to the concept of Devil's Islands in the North Atlantic. The medieval Norsemen believed in a flat earth, with the Atlantic as a landlocked sea except for the Skuggifjord, a gap through which the Atlantic flowed out into the great Ocean surrounding the world. This flowing out, and back again, accounted for the tides. In general Norse belief, the Skuggifjord was vaguely located, but the Greenland Norse believed themselves to be living in the vicinity of it. In fact, there is reason to believe that they were acquainted with Hudson Strait, with its tremendous towering tides, and believed it to be the Skuggifjord.[22] It is quite possible, considering the internationality of sailors, that some memory of the belief in the off-Labrador zone as a region of especial peril and terror may have percolated down the centuries through seagoing channels, and survived in altered form to the sixteenth century to influence geographers' concepts. In the process it could well have been reshaped by the dominant theology.

An additional point is that the Norsemen referred to the natives of North America with whom they came in contact as *Skraelings*, a word which has been translated in various ways, most often as "Screamers." At a later date it seems that the Norse applied the word loosely to Eskimos. But Eskimos are not noted for screaming, while Indian war whoops are well known, and it appears that these "Screamers" were the now-extinct Beothuk Indians, who, during the sixteenth and seventeenth centuries and earlier, occupied the Newfoundland-Labrador territory. At the time of the Norse explorations in North America, circa 1000, their range of habitat is uncertain, so that the fact that the Norse apparently made contact with them is no aid in pinpointing what they discovered.[23]

This seems to tie in with the fact that the French fishermen considered the present Belle Isle as demon-haunted because of terrible screams heard from its shores. They may well have heard the Beothuks performing some sort of ritual there. How frequently this happened hardly matters. Once could have been sufficient to get the story into circulation, and to influence sailors' superstitions and mapmakers' concepts. The records are too meager for anyone to do more than speculate. But it appears likely that the name Belle Isle, "Beautiful Island," was an attempt at exorcism, at driving the evil away by giving the place a good name.

And as an ending to this chapter on various islands, it seems fitting to wind up with the

Painter's Wife's Island

Exactly what map the Painter's Wife's Island appeared on is now unknown, but it is a merry tale, and cannot be told better than in the words of Peter Heylyn's *Cosmography* of 1659:

THE PAINTERS WIVES ISLAND is an Island of this Tract [of unknown or doubtful territory], mentioned by *Sir Walter Raleigh*, in his *History of the World*. Of which he was informed by *Don Pedro de Sarmiento*, a *Spanish* Gentleman, employed by his King in planting some Colonies in the Streights of Magellan . . . who being taken Prisoner by Sir Walter in his going home, was asked of him about some Islands which the Maps presented in these Streights, and might have been of great use to him in his Undertaking. To which he merrily replied, that it was to be called the *Painter's Wive's Island*, saying, that whilst the Painter drew that Map, his Wife sitting by, *desired him to put in one Countrey for her, that she in her imagination might have an Island of her own*. His meaning was, that there was no such Island as the Map pretended. And I fear the Painter's Wife hath many Islands and some Countreys too upon the Continent in our common Maps, which are not really to be found on the strictest search.

It might be added that the same is still not entirely untrue today, though certainly not to the same extent as in Heylyn's time.

From Seven Cities to None

This chapter involves three separate geographical myths: the myth of the Seven Cities, the myth of Cíbola, and the myth of Quivira. The three are not organically related, exactly, but to some extent each grew from the one before, and linked as they became, they spanned a full millennium.

Most readers probably know that a vague rumor of the Seven Cities of Cíbola impelled Coronado to explore the American Southwest and think of Quivira as an alternate name for the same region. But in fact this is not quite the way it happened; the real story is more complicated and far more interesting.

It began in eighth-century Spain. In the year 711 the North African Moors under their general Tariq* descended upon the Visigoth, or "West-Goth," kingdom which had once dominated the western area of the late Roman Empire, but which since its defeat by Clovis the Frank in 507 had been reduced to a feeble remnant of its former glory. King Roderick (Rodrigo in Spanish) rode to battle at the head of his troops, but he was killed and his forces were defeated in the battle of Guadalete. The next decade and a half were

---

* Now remembered chiefly for giving his name to *Jebal al-Tariq,* or "Mount Tariq," which later centuries corrupted into Gibraltar.

a horror, the Moorish forces overrunning all of present Spain and Portugal up to the Pyrenees with fire and steel.* Christian refugees escaped in every available direction, and there is reason to believe that some fled by sea and tried to reach the vaguely known Canary Islands and possibly the Madeiras.

There arose a legend, which persisted throughout the Middle Ages, of seven Portuguese bishops who managed to escape by ship, with a considerable number of the people of their dioceses, and to reach an island somewhere out in the Atlantic where they established seven cities. Part of the legend, of course, was that the people of the Seven Cities would one day return in force to help their Spanish compatriots defeat the Moors.[1]

Was this a rumor contemporary with the events, or a story which grew up in later ages? There is no longer any way to be sure. In any event, the legend of the Isle of Seven Cities was kept up in Spain, and apparently became known elsewhere. In the twelfth century the Arab geographer Idrisi spoke of an Atlantic island of Sahelia (previously mentioned in Chapter 4), which had once contained seven cities until the inhabitants killed each other off in civil wars.[2] By the late fourteenth century, suppositious locations of the Seven Cities were beginning to show up via Spanish and Italian maps on one or another of the imaginary islands of the North Atlantic. Sometimes the Seven Cities were shown on Breasil but more usually on Antillia, as we have already seen in Chapters 4 and 5. A French map of 1546 appears to be the first to place a specific island of *Sete Cidades* in the Atlantic, where it was to remain for half a century or so.

Before this time, however, an anonymous and undated map, now in the British Museum and believed to be of about 1508, had located the Seven Cities along the eastern seaboard of North America (Chapter 5)—though on this map the area is distorted so as to make it the southern rather than the eastern coast. This early placement of the mythical cities on the American mainland occurred in an

---

* In fairness to the Moors, we must remember that within a century they had made Spain the most civilized realm in Europe.

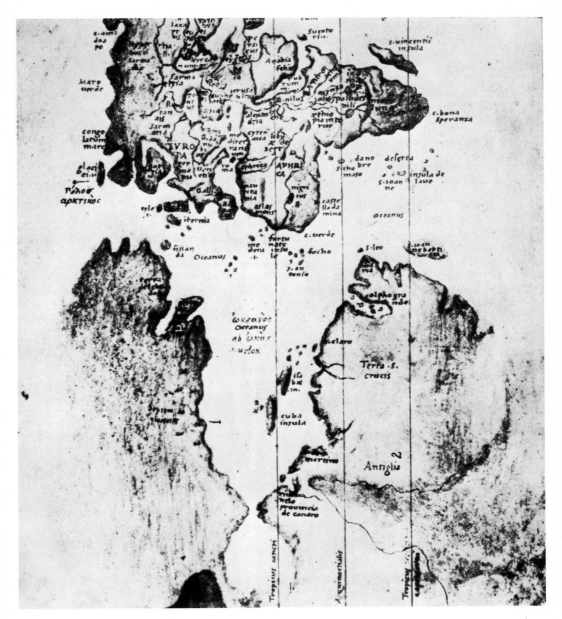

Part of a map of about 1508 showing (1) the Seven Cities on the North American coast, and (2) the name Antiglia in the South American continent.

obscure source, which probably had no influence upon what followed, but it may have reflected a widespread belief of the time.

As for exploration, there were rumors during the 1430s and 1440s of a couple of Portuguese expeditions (or perhaps the same one) which were blown off course in the Atlantic to end up at the Isle of Seven Cities, where the people still spoke Portuguese and asked if the Moors were yet in control of their ancestral land (Chapter 5). In each case, the report had it that that some sand from the beaches of the isle was brought home and proved to be rich in gold.[3]

There is the more authentic record of a Fleming whose name is given as "Ferdinand Dulmo," who in 1486 requested the permission of King João II of Portugal to take possession of the Seven Cities, but there is no record that anything was done about it.[4] Also, there is the 1498 report of Pedro de Ayala, Spanish ambassador to England, that the people of Bristol had, during the past seven years, sent out one or more expeditions in search of Breasil (Chapter 4) "and the seven cities."[5] But it is doubtful that the hardheaded merchants of Bristol sent any expeditions chasing after Iberian legends, and the Spanish ambassador's inclusion of the "seven cities" among their objectives probably reflects his own preassumptions as to where the cities were to be found.

The first substantial connection of the Seven Cities story with the North American continent can be said to have begun in 1528. In that year Panfilo de Narváez launched his ill-advised and badly planned attempt to set up a colony on the Gulf of Mexico. The expedition came to grief on the coast of Texas, and some of its members were forced to resort to cannibalism. One who survived, known to fame as Alvar Núñez Cabeza de Vaca,* was captured by the half-starved Indians of the arid Texas plain. The story of his ghastly eight years' wandering is a tremendous epic in raw courage, too long

---

* As any first-year student of Spanish knows, Cabeza de Vaca means Cow's Head. In 1212 an ancestor of his, a shepherd named Martin Alhaja, was acting as guide to the army of King Sancho VII of Navarre and placed a cow's skull to mark the entrance to the mountain pass, so that the army was able to cross and defeat the Moors at the battle of Las Navas de Tolosa. Consequently the shepherd was ennobled and his descendants granted use of the honorary name Cabeza de Vaca.

to be given here. He earned prestige among the Indians by building up a reputation as a healer; indeed, he claimed once, with the help of God, to have restored a dead man to life. Whenever possible, he utilized his standing with the Indians to rescue their Spanish captives, and finally in 1536 he appeared on the northern border of Spanish-held Mexico with three men whom he had managed to liberate. Among them was a Negro named Esteban, a fellow castaway member of the Narváez expedition.

Border guards picked up these stragglers and brought them to Mexico City. Cabeza de Vaca's account of the country he had crossed had its points of interest, such as his "hunchback cattle," the first Spanish mention of the buffalo, but by and large it was not such as would be likely to induce anyone to visit that territory. The Spanish authorities were not satisfied with that, and they kept pumping him for information. Eventually they drew out what would seem to be his unclear recollections of what he had heard from the Indians, about tribes to the north and east, whose living standards were sumptuous by comparison with their own. And the late conquerors of Mexico read into this what they wanted to believe.

It appears that de Vaca's story, if only indirectly, had something to do with launching Hernando de Soto's explorations of our present South, where he hoped to find "another treasure like that of Atahualpa, Lord of Peru," but found only hardship, hostility, and death. De Soto was not hunting specifically for the Seven Cities. In fact, there is no reason to suppose that at this time the Spaniards seriously believed them to be on the American mainland, or indeed that they actually still believed in the quaint old medieval legend at all. But they definitely believed in more rich Indian kingdoms to be conquered, and it was curious how many of the rumors drifting down from farther north coincided with their own traditional Seven Cities stereotype. There was the Aztec legend of the Seven Caves somewhere to the north, from which their ancestors had migrated. And the story told by an unnamed Indian slave, of his gold-rich homeland in the north, and of a neighboring land which he had once visited with his father, where there were seven towns, each of about the size of Mexico City, and each with a street of silversmiths.

*Hernando de Soto. Probably
an imaginary likeness.*

There was an uncanny recurrence of the number seven, and the Spaniards, remembering their own ancestral legend, appear to have come to a strong preconception of seven settlements of some kind to be found. Thus the myth of the Seven Cities merged with the myth of Cíbola, which was shortly to make its appearance.

The man selected to make the preliminary check on the Seven Cities was a Franciscan, a native of Nice, known to history as Fray Marcos de Niza. His party included Esteban, the Negro mentioned earlier, who because of his knowledge of the country, volunteered to operate as an advance scout. Esteban had traversed this country in hunger and misery with Cabeza de Vaca, but on his return visit he traveled in style, with an Indian escort. He decked himself out in regal finery of plumes and shells and turquoise, collected a harem of Indian girls, and generally had fun. It was a short life, though a gay one. Arrived at the Zuñi pueblo of Hawikuh, he apparently antagonized the Indians, and they killed him. This was in 1539, but the Zuñi remembered him in folklore for many years afterward.

At the start of the journey, Esteban had made arrangements to relay news of his findings to Fray Marcos by Indian runners, and had set up an odd code involving crosses. If he discovered anything, he was to send back a cross with the courier, the magnitude of the discovery to be indicated by the size of the cross. About the time that Esteban lost his life, his Indian messenger reached Fray Marcos bearing a cross as tall as a man—the agreed-upon signal that he had come upon something equal in importance to the Aztecs' Mexico City. The messenger brought word from Esteban that he had come to the land of Cíbola, with seven large and rich cities, and was pressing on immediately to explore the country.

So arose Cíbola. This was the first recorded mention of the name. Its derivation may have been from the pueblo named Shi-uo-na, from an Aztec word for the buffalo, from Esteban's rich imagination, or from all three. In any case, those concerned with black history may be interested to know that the name Cíbola, which still haunts the imagination, was introduced to the world by a Negro.

What followed has been told too often to need recounting in detail. Fray Marcos's visit to the Zuñi pueblo country, his return to Mexico and report of what he had seen, and the tremendous expeditionary force commanded by Francisco Vásquez de Coronado which set forth in 1540 to comb the country for the rich cities of Cíbola—all of this can be read about in any high-school history text.* They soon found the Cíbola of Fray Marcos's report, which had a certain amount of turquoise but no gleaming treasure of gold and gems. Fray Marcos de Niza was discredited as a witness, and later historians were long to assume that the friar was a liar. The truth seems to be that he was a basically honest reporter, but was carried away by his admiration for the pueblo Indians and their culture (actually they were an eminently gentle people, as compared with the bloodthirsty Aztecs) so that he spoke of them in glorified terms, and the Spaniards

---

* Of marginal interest is the fact, attested to by several contemporary accounts, that the Spaniards of Mexico City regarded it as "good riddance to bad rubbish," since Coronado's force was largely made up of the idle young hooligans of the city—much as the later El Dorado quests were to rid South American cities of their worst troublemakers.

once more interpreted his account in terms of what they wanted to find true.

A few months' search of the Arizona-New Mexico region turned up the Grand Canyon, among other points of interest, but no rich kingdoms. The myth of Cíbola crashed almost as soon as it got off the ground. A few later references in foreign sources indicate a lingering belief in it elsewhere, but the Spaniards who were on the scene quickly abandoned it. Coronado's expedition probably would have returned at once, had it not been for an Indian (referred to as "Turk" for some reason by the explorers), who told them of his homeland, called by a name that the Spaniards rendered as Quivira (pronounced Key-*veer*-a).

As Turk told it, Quivira was well worth a visit. It lay somewhere to the northeast; its people habitually ate from gold dishes; it contained a river 2 leagues wide, in which swam fish as big as horses, and on which traveled sumptuous galleys of forty oars; its king took his daily siesta under a tree hung with little golden bells to lull him to sleep by their jingling. Whether it was Turk or someone else who thought up this story in detail, his imagination is to be commended.

Coronado headed northeast, and spent the better part of a year scouring the country for this land of Quivira. Eventually, Turk admitted under pressure that the whole thing was a lie. The Indians of the Pecos country had put him up to leading the Spaniards on a wild-goose chase, in order to get rid of the Spaniards or to weaken them so that they would be no threat if they came back to the Pecos. So Coronado had him strangled. (His lieutenants had burned Indians at the stake by the scores, but Coronado seems to have been reasonably humanitarian, for a conquistador.)

In spite of this development, Coronado claimed that territory for Spain, under the name of Quivira, and returned to Mexico City, where he got a rather chilly reception.[6] Hopes had run so high for the finding of the Seven Cities that Coronado's failure made him nobody's hero. His report of the land of Quivira was disappointing, but it did put the term into circulation.

Meanwhile, to the eastward, de Soto's expedition was still in progress, and it seems to have missed the Coronado expedition by very few miles. De Soto himself died in 1542, and his lieutenant Luis Moscoso de Alvarado took command. He managed to convince the menacing Indians that de Soto had gone to heaven, as he did now and then, but that he would be back soon.* Thus he bought time to get out of the territory and head west into the present Oklahoma and Texas, since that was unexplored territory where rich kingdoms might lie, and also was in the general direction of Mexico. They picked up several stragglers from Coronado's force, but, finding nothing worthwhile, they returned to the Mississippi River and thus to Mexico. And so ended the actual search for Cíbola and Quivira.

Until more than a decade after Coronado's return, the substance of myth does not actually enter the story. Cíbola and Quivira were not myths, but outright fabrications. The central Great Plains region had to be called something, and Quivira was as good a name as any. Had it been left where Coronado placed it, it could have stayed permanently and legitimately on the map, and there could today be an American state of Quivira. But it was not to stay there.

Before taking up the Quivira myth, it might be well to survey the subsequent careers of the Seven Cities and Cíbola. Geographical concepts in those days were confused, and it is questionable that the Spaniards actually identified their traditional tale of the Seven Cities with any land they seriously hoped to find, though the general idea of "seven cities" apparently had its effect. As stated above, an island of Seven Cities appeared first on the map in 1546, four years after Coronado's expedition. Apparently the association of the Seven Cities with Cíbola and Quivira, like the concept of El Dorado, was a peculiarity of the Spanish-American cultural context. An island of *Sept Cités* was included in the world maps of Ortelius (1571) and Mercator (1587) but later maps dropped it. An area of the Island of San Miguel in the Azores has been known up to modern times as Sete Ciudades, and the origin of the name is a mystery.[7]

But an apparent descendant of the Isle of Seven Cities was to show up once more. In 1639 a group of Franciscans arrived in Lisbon

---

* This may sound funny, but it is not. Like all shamanists, the Indians believed in the medicine man's power to visit the world of spirits and return, and Alvarado was shrewdly trading on this.

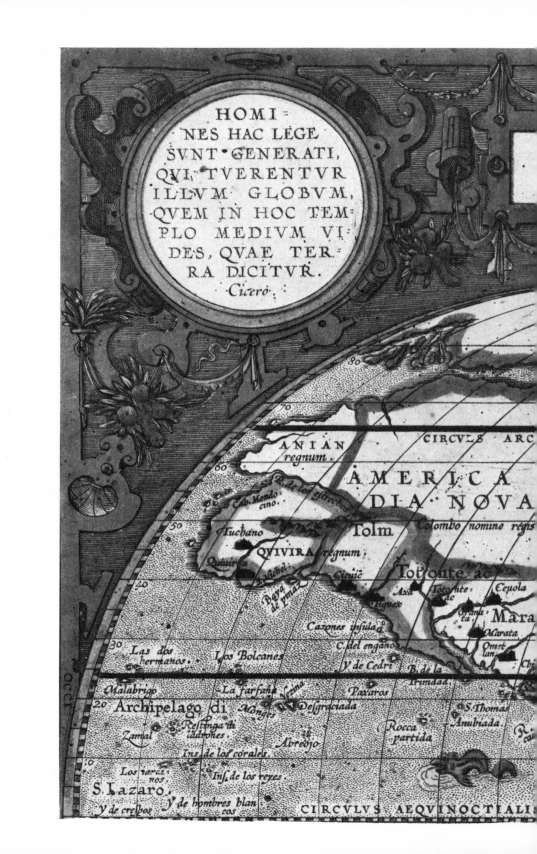

HOMI=
NES HAC LEGE
SVNT·GENERATI,
QVI·TVERENTVR
ILLVM GLOBVM,
QVEM IN HOC TEM=
PLO MEDIVM VI=
DES, QVAE TER=
RA DICITVR.
Cicero

ANIAN
regnum.

CIRCVLS ARC

AMERICA
DIA · NOVA

R. de los Estrechos

Cab. Mendo
cino

80

70

60

Tuchano

50

Tolm.

Colombo nomine regis

Quiuira

QVIVIRA regnum.

Cicuic

Totonte ac

40

Tiguex

Axa

Totonte
ac

Ceuola

Baya
de pmas

Granda

Mara

Cazones insula

Marata

30

Las dos
hermanos.

Los Bolcanes

C. del engaño

Omist
lan.

Y de Cedri

B. de la

Chi

Malabrigo

La farfana

Paxaros

trinidad

20

Archipelago di

Monges

Desgraciada

S.Thomas
Anubiada.

Zamal

Restinga di
ladrones.

Abreojo

Rocca
partida

R.
cae

Ins. de los corales.

10

Los ratci
nos.

Ins. de los reyes.

S.Lazaro

Y de crespos

Y de hombres blan
cos

CIRCVLVS AEQVINOCTIALI

Section of the Ortelius map of 1571, showing Anian, Quivira, Tolm, and other fabulous places mentioned in this chapter.

after a voyage from the Madeiras and made a sworn deposition that they had been blown off course to land on an unknown island. Here they had found an extensive city, with strangely few inhabitants, and no sign of a priest or monk. In the city was an antiquated-looking circular palace with a lighthouse rising above it. They were met by men who spoke Portuguese and called Portugal "God's Chosen Nation," and were presented to the Majestic Ancient, king of the island. In the palace were paintings of battles between Portuguese and Moors, and statues of a long line of kings, and on the palace grounds there was a chapel guarded by lions, containing a statue of the Virgin holding a sword. This island, they said, was about a day's sail from Madeira, but they failed to state in which direction. No specific mention is made of the Seven Cities, but the legendary lineage seems obvious. Apparently, nobody took the story seriously.[8]

As to Cíbola, it was finished as far as the Spaniards were concerned, and had actually had a rather short run in the first place. But the name and the story leaked out, to persist in non-Spanish circles for some time. Ortelius's 1571 map showed a city of "Ceuola" in the country of "Totoneac." As late as 1622, Henry Briggs, professor of geometry at Oxford, spoke of the "large Kingdoms of Cebola and Quivira" as having "great and populous cities of civil people; whose houses are said to be five stories high, and to have within them pillars of Turquesses."[9] Briggs included Cebola on his map, which was published in Purchas his Pilgrimes in 1625. After this, Cíbola dropped off the map. The name of course remains famous today in American history, as the object of Coronado's quest.

So much for the Seven Cities and Cíbola. Quivira, in another form, had a long life ahead.

In 1542, just about the time of Coronado's return, Juan Rodríguez de Cabrillo was sent out from Mexico with two ships to explore the California coast. Cabrillo was a Portuguese in the Spanish service, a captain of crossbowmen and a good soldier, but he had no previous experience of sea voyaging. He sailed north past "California," which then meant the peninsula of Lower California; but he continued to apply the name to the land as he went northward (two centuries later, when the Spaniards settled this territory, they differentiated "Alta California" from "Baja California"). The explorers missed the San Francisco Bay, presumably because of fog, but in November they did catch sight of the Coast Range, with snow on its higher points, and gave it the name of "Snowy Mountains," *Sierras Nevadas*, a name later to be applied to an entirely different range inland. Driven back by storms, they wintered on the present San Miguel Island, north of Santa Catalina, where Cabrillo died.

His second-in-command, Bartolomé Ferrelo, resumed the search in the spring of 1543. He passed the great headland of Cape Mendocino and pushed on as far as southern Oregon, then turned back because he felt it unwise to go farther with his flimsy ships. When he returned to Mexico, Ferrelo made an admirable detailed report on the north coast, that seems to have been influential in the shaping of the new myth of Quivira.

Two clear influences can be found in the report. First, it gave the world the first information about the ferocious bad-weather zone to the north of Cape Mendocino, which for a long time was to keep navigators out of that region and make the cape the farthest landmark on the American west coast to be regarded as actually known, thus leaving the area to the north a legitimate ground for speculation and rumor. Second, the Indians of the present Santa Barbara coast told them of "men like the Spaniards, clothed and bearded, going about on the mainland." The expedition failed to find any such people, so it was later supposed that they must be in the unknown territory to the north. Everything was set for the emergence of another mythical realm, and it promptly emerged.

For some curious reason, the name Quivira, officially established with reference to an inland plains region more than 1000 miles away, was transferred to this incongruous Pacific coast, and why this should have happened is now impossible to say. The first mention of this mythical Quivira is found in a history of the American explorations published in 1552 by Francisco López de Gómara, who is now generally regarded as a most accomplished liar.[10] The Portuguese historian Antonio Galvano in about 1563 made mention of a "Xaquivira," telescoping the two names of Axa and Quivira (of which more later).[11] Apparently Mercator, in 1569, was the first to place it on the map.

In any case, within a couple of decades after Gómara, the concept of Quivira was in full bloom. This Pacific coastal empire had numerous gold mines, naturally; its capital city, also named Quivira, was located on the coast at the mouth of a great river; farther inland and on the shores of this same river was another great city, called Tuchano; there were two more important cities named Axa and Cicuic; and to the southward of Quivira, about the latitude of Cape Mendocino, was another kingdom, that of Tiguex.

They are all there, on Ortelius's map of 1571. He turned Quivira into an ugly bulge on the American west coast, and placed Cape Mendocino on its north-central shore. Quivira is bounded on the south by a river terminating in a "Pinnace Bay," and to the southward is a land of "Tolm," where Cicuic is located. To the southeast of this is the land of "Totoneac," where Axa and Tiguex are placed. Even the rumors of that part of the world were then indefinite enough to make it anyone's guess where a reported place actually was.

Published by Richard Hakluyt in 1586 and drawn from what that careful researcher considered to be impeccable Spanish sources, the following gives some inkling of the wild information circulating with regard to this imaginary realm:

. . . and Francis Vasquez went to Tiguex, which standeth on the banke of a great river. There they had news of Axa and Quivira. There they sayde was a King whose name was Tatarrax, with a long beard, horie headed. . . . They determined to goe thither, with intention to winter in so rich a country as that was reported to be. . . .

Quivira is in fortie degrees; it is a temperate country, and hath very good waters, and much plummes, grasse, mulberries, nuts, melons, and grapes. . . . They apparell themselves with oxe-hides and deered skinnes. They [the explorers] saw shippes on the sea coast, which bare Alcatrarzes or Pellicanes of golde and silver on their prows, and they thought them to be of Cathaya, and China, because shewed our men by signes that they had sayled thirtie dayes.

A bit of commentary is in order. "Francis Vasquez" is Coronado, who never came close to the seacoast in his explorations, and certainly never went on record with such a whopper as this. Gómara is to blame for this yarn. The name "Tiguex" can be explained; it is a distortion of the name of the Tiguas Indians of New Mexico, whom Coronado did visit. The same is true of the name "Totoneac," not mentioned by Hakluyt but used by Ortelius on the map mentioned above, and which is derived from the Totonac Indians. The name of the king, "Tatarrax," teases the mind; could it be derived from "Tatar," in view of the belief, not yet dead at the time, that North America was connected with northern Asia? It is a tempting thought, but impossible to document.

As to the rest, it happens to be true that the California-Oregon region of Quivira is temperate, does have good water and much grass, plums, nuts, and melons, though a bit north of the real grape country; as for mulberries, mention of them may have been inspired by the silk-raising interest of the time, since the region has never been notable for them. It is a fact that Chinese junks have crossed the Pacific and made the American coast in recorded times, but the Chinese vessels mentioned here must be regarded as a pure fabrication, based on the hope for a western route to the Orient.

A quaint world map by Michael Lok, published by Hakluyt along with the one mentioned above, shows the west coast of North America taking a sharp turn to the east at about latitude 47°, and it locates Quivira at this point, with the Sierra Nevada along the coast as the range heads east.

Nineteen years before Hakluyt published this, Sir Francis Drake had visited the north coast of California, christened it New Albion, and found no trace of Quivira. But this made no difference. In 1598 one Edward Wright produced a map on which Quivira retained its old location to the north of Cape Mendocino, with New Albion still farther to the north—and he gave Drake as one of his sources of information.*

---

* The imaginary land of Bensalem in Sir Francis Bacon's utopian *New Atlantis* of 1629 seems to be located on the California redwood coast, following Drake's description, but did not give rise to any geographical myths.[12]

So far as can be determined, there seems only one record of voyagers actually claiming to have visited Quivira. But we have it at second hand only, and its authenticity is dubious.

In 1602, sixty years after Cabrillo, Sebastián Vizcaíno was dispatched to explore the coast from California northward, less in search of Quivira than of the Strait of Anian (Chapter 7). In addition to Vizcaíno's own report, we have one by the Carmelite friar Antonio de la Asunción, written in 1620. He stated therein that King Philip III of Spain, in going through his father's papers, had come across a sworn deposition by "some foreigners" that they had sailed down from the north and reached the city of Quivira. It was situated on the seacoast, by the mouth of a large river, close to Cape Mendocino, "which the ships have sight of in sailing from the Philippines to New Spain." Quivira was "a populous and rich city . . . full of civilized, courteous, and literate people who wore clothes [!], fortified and surrounded by a wall."

Also, according to Friar Antonio, there were "other details . . . in this report worth investigating and justifying exploration"; but he gives none of these details. He later regretfully admitted that the Vizcaíno expedition turned up no trace of Quivira. This actually proved nothing, since Vizcaíno seems to have got only as far north as Point Reyes, and not to have made Mendocino, let alone Quivira.

The mention of ships from the Philippines sighting Cape Mendocino deserves a word. It was early discovered that the most advantageous way to sail from the Philippines to Mexico ("New Spain") was to bear northward till one had the aid of the Japan Current, thus avoiding Central Pacific calms. One would then strike the American mainland in the vicinity of Cape Mendocino, and drift southward to Acapulco, the chief Mexican port of the west coast. And in this connection, the usually truthful Friar Antonio managed to spin quite a tale.

It seemed that the miasmatic fogs in some region of that coastal area gave rise to a dread disease, likely to attack the entire crew of a ship arriving there. The first symptom of what might be called the "Mendocino Syndrome" was that a man's body became agonizingly sore all over. Then his skin broke out in purple spots, his muscles at all the joints hardened into bands two fingers wide and left him paralyzed, and the best he could hope for was a quick death. The friar claimed that this was the cause of most deaths aboard galleons crossing the Pacific from the Philippines, and also that it had taken the lives of more than forty of Cabrillo's men, though there is nothing in Ferrelo's report on the Cabrillo voyage to give a basis to this.[13]

Barred off as it was by such a pestilential zone, Quivira understandably was the object of no more searches. And in actuality, the Pacific coast from Cape Mendocino northward is probably the most difficult strip of coastline on the North American continent, outside the Arctic. There the mild California coast ends, and the trend of the shoreline takes a north-northeasterly direction. From Humboldt Bay to the mouth of the Columbia there is not a decent harbor, the surf is battering, fog and rain constant, and ships find themselves continually in the lee of the prevailing westerly Pacific gale. Without any imaginary diseases, there were reasons enough for mariners to shun that ferocious shore, which was not really explored till the late eighteenth century.

Quivira remained a question mark for over a century. Everybody knew it was there, but nobody claimed to know much about it. The possibility of reaching it by an overland route was occasionally brought up. In 1630 a Franciscan from New Mexico, Alonso de Benavides, sent an urgent appeal to King Philip IV for renewed efforts toward conversion of the Plains Indians, and added as bait that there was a great deal of gold in Quivira. The context makes it sound as if he were referring to the real Quivira of Coronado, but the Spaniards had long before given up all ideas of its being a land of gold, so the friar must have had the mythical West Coast Quivira in mind, perhaps confusing the two.[14] Finally, in 1672, the last real irruption of Quivira into men's practical affairs occurred.

There was a Peruvian-born Spanish adventurer named Diego de Peñalosa, who allegedly had headed an expedition that reached the Mississippi River overland from Santa Fe, and who, as governor of New Mexico, had dealt highhandedly with the Franciscans. According to some reports, the root of the difficulty was Peñalosa's unfavorable reports on the Franciscans' treatment of the Indians. The powerful religious order got him dismissed from his post and recalled to Mexico, where they brought charges against him before the Inquisition—which resulted in Peñalosa's being imprisoned for three years. This left him embittered and vengeful; he went to England and proposed a plan for attacking the feebly defended Texas mining area. But King Charles II had enough problems already, and used Peñalosa as a pawn in his diplomatic dealings with Louis XIV of France.

At the French court, Peñalosa found interested listeners. The result was that when the Comte de Frontenac was sent out as governor of New France in 1672, his orders were to take action toward establishing a French base at the mouth of the Mississippi (to break Spanish control of the Gulf Coast), and also to search out cross-country waterways that might provide a route to Quivira.

Indirectly and in the long run, Peñalosa's proposals resulted in a long-term stepping-up of French investigations of possible transcontinental waterways (Chapter 7). The terminal point of these, it was expected, would be in the kingdom, or at least in the town, of Quivira. It seems, in fact, that after everyone else had ceased to take Quivira seriously, Peñalosa's action led to Quivira's becoming embalmed on French maps as a standard name for the Pacific coastal region that they hoped to reach, wherever it was. The alleged kingdom of Quivira was forgotten, but Quivira was conventionalized on the maps as a town. Its last occurrence that I have been able to trace was perpetrated by Philippe Buache, the French geographer already mentioned circa 1752, on a map representing La Vérendrye's explorations of the American northwest.[15]

The supposed area of Quivira was finally given proper exploration during the 1788–1793 period by two English captains, John Meares and George Vancouver, and by the American Robert Gray (the first American skipper to make the China run). None of them found anything lending the slightest substantiation to the Quivira myth, which by then nobody took seriously anyway.

Then in 1806, Lewis and Clark, near the end of their westward expedition, discovered a mighty river to which they gave the name

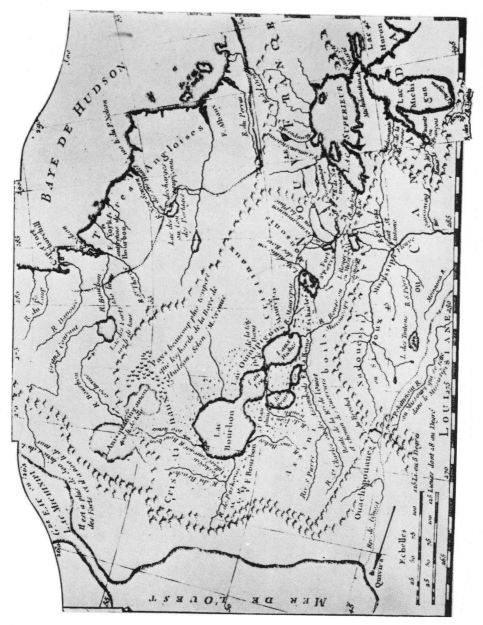

Buache's map of country explored by La Vérendrye, the last to show Quivira (arrow in lower left-hand corner).

of "Oregon," not knowing that fourteen years earlier the sea captain
Robert Gray had discovered its mouth on the Pacific coast, and
given it the name that it bears to this day, after his ship, the *Columbia*.
The name "Oregon" is of unknown derivation, but was in circulation
from the mid-eighteenth century as designating a large river rumored
to exist somewhere in the western part of the continent,* and the explorers apparently assumed that they had found it.

The prior name, Columbia, was eventually made official as
regards the river. But the name Oregon spilled over to be applied to
the region adjacent, which became one of the first territories of the
American Far West to be settled, and thus the fabulous Quivira was
crowded off the map.

---

* Its first recorded mention is in the petition sent in 1765 to King George III by
Robert Rogers, of Rogers' Rangers fame, unsuccessfully requesting subsidy for an
expedition to discover the river "called by the Indians Ouaricon."[16]

CHAPTER 7.

That Elusive Northwest Passage

L ooking at a map of North America, one gets the impression that there are a good many Northwest Passages. The sea to the north of Canada is littered with islands, most of them separated by quite substantial channels, and west of this the way looks clear enough through Beaufort Sea and Bering Strait to the Pacific. Of course, the map is rather deceiving; it gives no indication of the ice-clogged nature of those channels, nor of the ferocious weather conditions prevailing in those parts. There is an actual and (at times) navigable Northwest Passage that skirts the northern mainland coast, from Beaufort Sea through Coronation Gulf, Queen Maude Gulf, Franklin Strait, Peel Sound, Barrow Strait, and Lancaster Strait, into Baffin Bay. Its discovery is usually credited to Sir Robert McClure, in 1853, but he was unable to sail through it because of ice. The first successful traversal of the Passage was made in 1903–1906 by the great latter-day Viking, Roald Amundsen, whose vessel, the 47-ton sloop *Gjoa*, is today preserved in San Francisco's Golden Gate Park, only a few miles from where I am writing this.

But the ringing tale of search for the Northwest Passage would require a book in itself, and has been told before, and excellently well.[1] This is not a history of exploration, and we shall be concerned only tangentially with the voyagers who sought the Passage. The Northwest Passage does exist, but in its days of glory it was a geographical myth, which grew out of earlier myths, and in turn gave rise to others; and thus it must be considered. In fact, the whole concept of a Northwest Passage is clearly the result of wishful thinking.

By the mid-sixteenth century, there were three routes from Europe to the rich Orient: the overland route, controlled by the Turks; the Cape-of-Good-Hope route, controlled by the Portuguese; and the Straits-of-Magellan route, controlled by the Spaniards. Thus it was to remain until 1616, when Schouten rounded the Horn and made known to Europe the existence of a waterway beyond the regions where Spain could keep up effective control.

The Turks of about 1540 still presented an imminent military threat to their immediate neighbors, although they had entered into relatively peaceful relations with the more distant nations of Europe, recognizing the value of foreign trade. But any merchant attempting to bring goods across Turkish territory, or the Persian territory beyond, found himself compelled to pay a tariff at literally every stop, and this expense rose to the point where it could destroy all the profits. It must be pointed out that both the Turkish and Persian rulers used these tolls to maintain caravanserais all along the main routes, where traveling merchants could rest and refresh themselves in safety. But this still did not make the trade artery very lucrative for the alien, especially if he then had to ship his merchandise to some port as distant as London or Amsterdam.

The Spaniards jealously guarded everything they had gained, and the narrow, stormy Straits of Magellan were easy to guard. In 1581 Spain established on the Straits the colony of Porto Felipe for this purpose, but neglected to keep the settlement provisioned, and all the colonists starved, except for one survivor, who was rescued by the English navigator Cavendish in 1587. Though this attempt at setting up a frontier post failed, any foreign vessel venturing the

Straits ran the risk of encountering a well-armed Spanish man-of-war cruising there to keep out intruders.

The great open space south of Africa was obviously easier to sneak through, but it belonged to the Portuguese. In the sixteenth century there was no such concept as "freedom of the seas," and no one questioned Portugal's right to control a certain sea route any more than in the nineteenth century anyone questioned the right of Great Britain to control India. British and Dutch voyagers probing south of the Cape knew that they were on wilful forays, and they went heavily armed and on the lookout for trouble. In *Purchas his Pilgrimes* one may read account after account of early English voyages in which clashes with Portuguese ships are quite nonchalantly recounted as instances of something that everyone knew of—this at a time when England and Portugal were officially at peace.

It was in this context that the belief in a Northwest Passage arose. The English and Dutch, latecomers to the game, found themselves shut out of the race to the Orient, but they would be able to include themselves back in if a route could be found that bypassed the existing claims. The south was shut off, so the route would have to be to the north, and, as a glance at the globe would show, such a route would have the advantage of being much shorter than any of the others.

The Spaniards, even with their control of the Straits of Magellan, took some interest in finding the Northwest Passage, since a shorter route to the Orient would be to their advantage as well. As for the French, who like the English and Dutch were latecomers, their Northwest Passage quest took a different direction, over land.

It is impossible to explain exactly when and how the concept of a Northwest Passage arose. As soon as it was discovered, "America," meaning the present South America, was recognized as a previously unknown continent. The case for North America was less clear. For all anyone knew in the early sixteenth century, it might join up with Asia to the north of the Pacific. There was even the chance that North America might be simply the eastward extension of Asia, making South America only a large peninsula of that vast continent. This would have given Asia a tremendously larger longitudinal spread than the geographical information of the time allowed for, but nobody knew for sure.

Some early maps, notably the famed Waldseemüller map of 1507, showed North America separated from Asia, but this was pure conjecture. Belief in a Northwest Passage was based on faith alone.

The first real impetus toward the search seems to have come from one Robert Thorne, who deserves to be better known in history than he now is. He came from a rich merchant family of Bristol, then the chief maritime port of England, and became mayor of that city; later he lived and did business in Seville, saw the new-found wealth of Spain at first hand, and wanted his country to have its share. In 1527 he wrote a letter containing an audacious proposition to his king, Henry VIII.

The south, he said, was closed off by Spain and Portugal. Consequently, there was nowhere to go but to the north. Thorne claimed to know whereof he spoke because, he said, his father had been with a Bristol voyage that had discovered Newfoundland in 1494, three years before John Cabot.* There were, Thorne urged, three routes to be explored, and one of them certainly must pay off: eastward round the north of Europe, westward round the north of America, and directly north around the world through the polar region. As an added incentive, Thorne pointed out that these cold regions should offer a ready market for woolen fabrics, England's chief export product.

The modern student immediately wonders whether Thorne and his contemporaries were actually unaware of the frigid icebound nature of those high northern latitudes. The only answer is that they were and were not. They knew the traditional repute of the Arctic, but were prepared to disbelieve it.

Medieval geography had been dominated by the theory of climatic zones, first propounded by Hipparchus the Greek in the second century B.C. According to this, climatic conditions all round the world were uniform within a given latitude (allowing, of course, a

---

* There is no other record of this voyage, but it is possible.

little leeway for variations in altitude) and the world could thus be marked off into zones graduating from the uninhabitably hot equatorial to the uninhabitably cold Arctic. Classifications of the nations of the world according to this system were extremely arbitrary and clumsy, placing Scotland and Norway together, for example, because they fell within the same "zone," and ignoring the far more natural and obvious association of Scotland with England. Further, because reports of the weather in two given regions, especially if they were not well known at first hand, made them appear to belong in the same "zone," their position on the map could be distorted to make them fit the pattern.

By Thorne's time, exploration had progressed far enough to invalidate the theory of zones. A given place in America or Asia could be warmer or colder than a place of the same latitude in Europe. The boiling, uncrossable equatorial zone had proved to be a myth (Chapter 2). The frozen, uncrossable Arctic zone might well turn out to be the same.

Robert Thorne expressed his personal opinion that "there is no land uninhabitable, or Sea unnavigable," and offered to lead an expedition to prove his point. It should be noted that Thorne did not specifically emphasize a Northwest Passage, but only mentioned it as one of the possibilities.

Robert Thorne's world map of 1527.

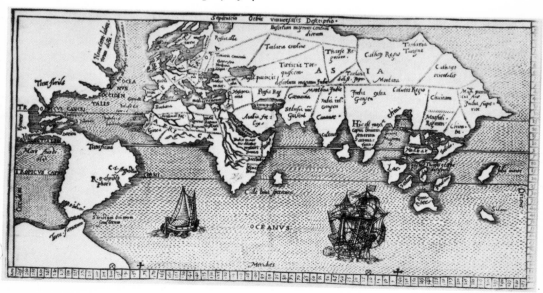

There is no indication that Thorne's proposals had any immediate effect. A few English vessels did probe around a little in the Newfoundland area during the 1530s, but we have no proof that their objective was a Northwest Passage. In the 1570s Thorne's manuscript, accompanied by a fairly good world map, came into the hands of the noted astronomer and mathematician (and occultist) Dr. John Dee, and he apparently passed it on to Richard Hakluyt, who published it in 1582, as promotion for the search for a Northwest Passage.

Meanwhile, Thorne's manuscript circulated and his ideas spread. But their first impulse was toward the east. In 1552 Sir Hugh Willoughby led an expedition in search of a Northeast Passage north of Europe. It came to grief, but the expedition's second-in-command, Richard Chancellor, thus reached Russia by sea, and the result was a rather lucrative trade between England and Russia. The English then did nothing more about the Northeast Passage, and the Dutch later took over the quest, but the disastrous 1596–1597 expedition of Willem Barents seems to have chilled their interest, and they let the project drop. One fruitful result of Barents's voyage was his discovery of Spitsbergen and its rich fishing and whaling grounds, which were to become a valuable factor in the later Dutch prosperity. But the vogue of the Northeast Passage was now over (though Henry Hudson in 1607–1608 did a little halfhearted hunting for it), and the future exploratory impetus was toward the northwest.*

However, three years before Thorne wrote his letter, and apparently unbeknownst to him, an event occurred which would eventually influence concepts of the Northwest Passage.

Not much is known of Giovanni da Verrazano prior to 1523. He was a Florentine sea captain, and he may have engaged in some piracy; he ended up in France, and apparently became a hanger-on of Jean Ango, a rich merchant of Dieppe, who kept open house for poets, artists, and mariners (which seems to have been one of the most "swinging scenes" in sixteenth-century France). He evidently

---

* For the sake of the record, the Northeast Passage past Russia and Siberia was finally navigated in 1878–1879 by the famed Arctic explorer Nordenskjöld in the whaler *Vega*.

became known for advancing his theory that, if given the chance, he could find a northern route, either by sea or overland, to the Orient. In 1524 King Francis I dispatched him on an expedition to give it a try.[2]

He explored the North American coast northward from perhaps the present Cape Fear, in North Carolina, at least to Nova Scotia, (some of his observations will be considered in Chapter 8). The present point is that he reported sighting a place on the eastern North American coast where the continent narrowed to a slender isthmus, to the west of which he could see open ocean, presumably the Pacific.[3]

Verrazano's truthfulness is not in question, and he certainly saw something. It may have been Cape Hatteras, with the wide Pamlico Sound to the west, or it may have been the entrance to Chesapeake Bay, seen under unfavorable conditions. In any case, this fantastic distortion of North America appeared on a map drawn in 1529 by Verrazano's brother Girolamo.[4] Cartier sailed with a copy of this map in 1534, and on his return expressed disappointment at not finding a passage to the western sea. He tried again in 1535, this time up the Saint Lawrence River as far as the unnavigable Lachine Rapids, and set the direction for the future French quest in America.

A copy of this map, allegedly the same one that had belonged to Cartier, came into the hands of Michael Lok, an English merchant whose name will recur in the tale of the Northwest Passage. The map did not show an open passage by sea, but indicated the possibility of waterways across an isthmus, and when Hakluyt published it in 1587 it stirred hopes.[5] The Spaniards had made Panama their chief Pacific port because of the relatively short and easy portage across the isthmus to the eastern seaboard, and this map seemed to offer England the same advantage.

Sir Humphrey Gilbert surveyed the American coast in search of this isthmus in 1583, failed to find it, and so picked the present Saint John's, Newfoundland, as the site to found the first English colony in America. Verrazano had located the isthmus at about 40° N, so it was in that vicinity that Raleigh and John White in 1585 established the "Lost Colony," famed in tale and legend. As late as 1607, hopes of finding this mythical isthmus were a factor in the setting up of the Virginia colony, and Captain John Smith, who knew the interior, wrote sarcastically of Captain Christopher Newport's furnishing a "five peeced Barge, not to beare us to the South sea, till we had borne her over the mountaines."

There is no evidence that the Spaniards, who knew the west coast well, were in any way influenced by the Verrazano map. But by the middle of the century they too were evincing an interest in the Northwest Passage, largely because of a man who now seems to stand forth as history's most successful travel liar, a man who fabricated his way into a centuries-long reputation as a great explorer, and whose pretensions have only in recent years been questioned.[6]

Sebastian Cabot, at the age of twelve, very likely did go along on his father's 1497 voyage to the New World. But his claim to have made a return voyage of his own in 1509 is not backed up by any record, aside from his own story as recorded by Peter Martyr, the

Section of the Verrazano map of 1529, showing the supposed Isthmus, to the north of Florida.

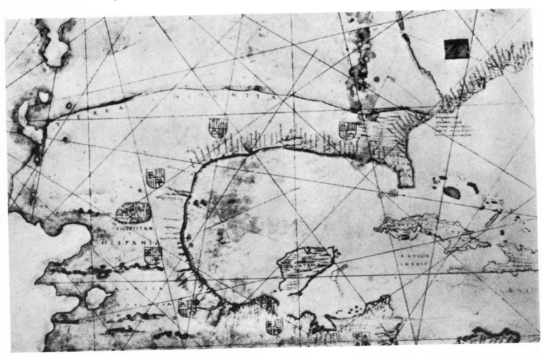

Sebastian Cabot. A nineteenth-century elaboration on a sixteenth-century original.

Spanish chronicler, in 1516. We do know that he traipsed round from one European court to another, working as a cartographer and trading on the fame of his father, whose exploratory accomplishments he thoroughly mixed up with those he claimed for himself. The only voyage he is actually known to have undertaken was in 1526, for the Venetians, in search of the Biblical gold-bearing land of Ophir. He messed it up appallingly, and his navigator had to salvage the situation, but the expedition did survey the Río de la Plata estuary in Argentina.[7] In later life, back in England, Cabot became a man of importance in merchant circles. On his deathbed he claimed to know a sure-fire method for the then-difficult problem of determining longitudes, but said he could not disclose it because it had been specially granted to him by divine revelation.[8]

Such was the man who entered the Spanish service as a cartographer in 1512, and filled everyone's ears with stories of the voyage he had made to the north of the New World three years earlier, on which he had discovered a large inland sea, and found the northern part of North America to be made up of islands. The facts that a large inland sea (Hudson Bay) does exist at about the location where he placed it, and that the Arctic Ocean north of Canada is full of islands, appear to be coincidental. His story may have influenced Thorne, and possibly also Verrazano. The important point, and at the time an influential one, is that he reported waterways by which America could be passed to the north.

But the presence of northern waterways solved only half the problem. If North America were merely an extension of Asia, they indicated only that the great land mass could be navigated to the north. Some sort of division between the two would have to be found if the Northwest Passage were to be a reality. By the 1560s, the existence of such division became a possibility with the emergence of the Strait of Anian, which appears to be an invention entirely of Italian origin.

An Italian, the great Marco Polo, had mentioned a land of "Ania" or "Anian" as lying in the northeastward extremity of Asia. To later Italians, and from their sources the rest of Europe, this seemed to imply that there was a separation between Asia and America. Ironically, it appears that the name "Anian" originally did belong to a strait: the one now called Tatar Strait, between the Asiatic mainland and the Island of Sakhalin, for which the Japanese name is Aniwa.[9]

Another Italian, Jacopo Gastaldi, in a pamphlet published in 1562, made the first mention still preserved of the Strait of Anian; he was quoting from the descriptive text of a map now lost, drawn by the Venetian Mateo Pagano. But no existing map by Pagano shows the strait, and in that same year of 1562 another Venetian, Paolo Forlani, published a map which showed America joined to Asia.

The first map specifically showing a Strait of Anian was drawn by still another Venetian, Zaltieri, in 1566.[10]

Thereafter, for almost two centuries, the Strait of Anian was a fixture on the map. The land of Anian, placed by Marco Polo in Asia, was for no apparent reason moved eastward of the strait and located in the northwest extremity of America (along with Anian, Polo also mentioned a land of "Toloman," which some have conjectured may have been the present Alaska). It was recognized and included, to the north of Quivira, by all the important cartographers of the time—Mercator, Ortelius, etc. Jodocus Hondius, a Dutch cartographer operating in England, published a map along with *Purchas his Pilgrimes* in 1625, on which he located on the northwest American coast an Anian River; as printed, however, the name looks more like "Arian River," and may, in corrupted form, have contributed toward the eighteenth-century belief in a river somewhere in western America named "Oregon."

Another source may have contributed to mid-sixteenth century concepts of a Northwest Passage. The Portuguese historian Antonio Galvano in his *Discoveries of the World* told a tale worth quoting in its entirety.

. . . in the 200 yeere before the Incarnation it is written, that the Romanes sent an armie into India against the great Can [Khan] of Cathaia, which, passing through the Strait of Gibraltar, and running to the northwest, found, right over against the Cape Finisterre, ten islands, wherein was much tinne. And they may be those which were called the Cassiterides,* and being come to fifty degrees of latitude, they found a straight; and passing through it toward the west they arrived in the empire of India, and fought with the king of Cathay, and so came backe againe unto the city of Rome. Which thing howsoever it may seeme either possible or not possible, true or not true, yet so I finde it left to be recorded in the histories of that time.[11]

In a marginal note, Richard Hakluyt comments caustically, "What histories may these be?" And rightly so, for no such story is

---

* The "Tin Islands" of the Phoenician traders, usually supposed to be the Scilly Islands, or the British Isles in general.

extant in Roman annals. But Galvano was a careful and truthful recorder, and he undoubtedly had some documentation for the yarn. There seem in the fifteenth and sixteenth centuries to have been certain spurious documents, now lost, of allegedly classical origin, dealing with fictitious voyages and travels, and Galvano probably based his story on one of these.[12]

These were the sources for the Northwest Passage myth: the Verrazano map, indicating the accessibility of the Pacific; the tales of Sebastian Cabot, indicating that America was circumnavigable to the north; the enthusiasm of Thorne, perhaps influenced by the previous two; the apparently authoritative Italian sources that established a strait of open water between Asia and America; the classic authority lent to the belief by Galvano, in an age when classic authority counted for much.

Add to this the prestige of the Spaniards as explorers, and English credulity and will to believe. By the late sixteenth century, rumors percolating out of Spain regarding the discovery of a Northwest Passage were getting serious attention in England.

An English sailor named Cowles made a sworn statement in 1579 that six years earlier in Lisbon he had heard a Portuguese sailor, whose name was rather improbably given as "Martin Chacke," relate how in 1567 he had discovered a strait to the north of Newfoundland at about latitude 59°, and sailed through to the Pacific. The Portuguese authorities, he alleged, had suppressed the information.[13]

And in 1568 a Spaniard told Sir Humphrey Gilbert about Andro Urdaneta, who had discovered the Northwest Passage from the Pacific side and sailed through as far as Germany. Urdaneta, it seemed, had drawn a map of the Passage, which the Spaniard told Gilbert he had seen. In fact, at about this time, Urdaneta was reporting to King Philip II that a French expedition (unidentified) had discovered the passage at latitude 27° N, at about the area of the Rio Grande.[14]

This same Sir Humphrey Gilbert was to be the most influential propagandist for the existence of a Northwest Passage. In 1576 he published his *Discourse of a discoverie for a new passage to Cataia*, the influence of which spread far beyond England. In this tenden-

Sir Humphrey Gilbert.

tious work he marshaled every bit of evidence he could find. Atlantis, he contended, was none other than America; and according to the highest classical authority Atlantis was known to be an island. It was also a known "fact" that the waters of the ocean flow circularly from east to west, and since there was an open space to the south of America and Africa to permit of this, it followed that there had to be a similar situation to the north. So it appeared that the Northwest Passage was just as good as found.[15]

This triggered the really serious voyaging in search of the Passage: Frobisher in 1576–1578, Davis in 1585–1587, Hudson in 1610–1611, Baffin in 1615–1616. The discovery of Hudson Bay was promising, and for more than a century searches for the Northwest Passage were to concentrate on it. But, as I said before, this story is much too long to be told here.

No name is more memorable in the Northwest Passage saga than that of Michael Lok. This wealthy and much-traveled merchant possessed a copy of the Verrazano map that was published by Hak-

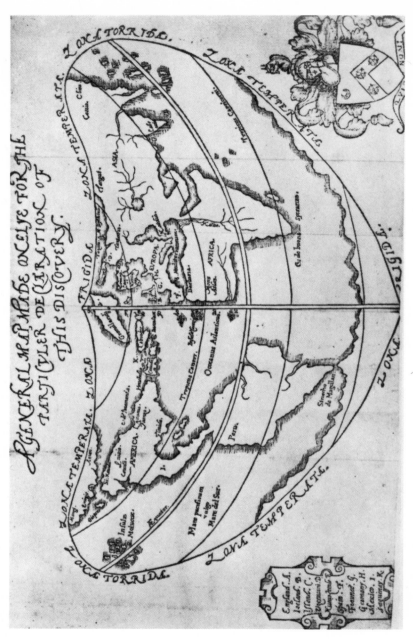

Sir Humphrey Gilbert's world map, showing the supposed North-west Passage.

luyt and touched off the entire English enterprise in that direction. Lok was a principal financial backer of Frobisher's pioneer voyages in search of the Passage; in fact, he bankrupted himself thereby, and later spent some time in debtors' prison.

And it was Michael Lok who met, in Venice in 1595, an old on-the-beach Greek skipper named Apostolos Valerianos, who during his years in the Spanish service had been known as Juan de Fuca. This old salt had a number of tales to tell, but the one that concerns us here is of his having sailed up the west coast of North America in 1592 until, at about 47° N, he came upon a strait, sailed through it, and came out in the Atlantic. And he offered to lead another expedition to prove his story.[16]

Michael Lok, luckless backer of Northwest Passage ventures, thrilled to this word that the Passage did exist and had been found. He lacked the money to bring the old Greek to England, but by correspondence he tried to interest the English merchant companies in backing the voyage. Before anything resulted, Juan de Fuca returned to his home on the island of Cephalonia, and died. Purchas included the story in his *Pilgrimes* for what it was worth, but it seems to have had no immediate impact, and only to have become a factor in the search a century and a half later.

The English and Dutch had both been involved in the search for a Northeast Passage, but seeking the Northwest Passage by sea was to remain primarily an English undertaking, though the Danes also did a little probing in that direction. The Spaniards sent a couple of voyages up the western American coast—the one of Vizcaíno in 1602, which failed to find Quivira, was the last. But they seem to have been trying less to find a Northwest Passage than to verify the existence of the Strait of Anian. The English search went on through the seventeenth century and intermittently into the eighteenth, when the actual Northwest Passage was no longer a commercial necessity —the English and Dutch had been freely trading round the Cape of Good Hope since the 1620s. It was now a point of geographical curiosity in connection with general Arctic exploration. Meanwhile, the French were pursuing a course of their own. Before going into this, however, we might appropriately consider what the maps have to show.

All of the influential maps by important cartographers, from the 1560s on, were unanimous in showing North America with some sort of waterway to the north and a Strait of Anian separating it from Asia. This state of affairs prevailed until the mid-seventeenth century, when fewer attempts were made to map the unknown, and such unexplored regions as the American Arctic were increasingly left blank. A curiosity of this period is to be found on the Nicolas Visscher map of circa 1660. Visscher rounds off eastern Asia in a huge headland and effectively seals off any Northwest Passage by making the coast of Greenland connect up with the west coast of Hudson Bay and leaving the area of northwest North America blank. But he still preserves Anian, as an incomplete bit of coastline drifting just off the northwest littoral, at about the place where Alaska should be. This compromise between caution and tradition is indicative of the state of affairs in geography at the time.

Possibly it was the Verrazano map that kept the notion of cross-country waterways so much to the forefront of French exploratory interest. Numerous students of the subject have noted the fact that the French in North America tended to travel only where they could go by boat, and that La Salle was the only notable cross-country hiker. Too much should not, of course, be made of this. Exploring by boat is doing it the easy way, and the French were lucky in arriving at the region of North America where it was pre-eminently advantageous.

Still, it is worth remembering that the French impetus to explore America grew initially out of a map that made the continent into only a minor obstruction with open sea beyond. And we have plentiful indications that the earliest French *voyageurs* believed that they were on their way to the Orient. There was, for instance, the flamboyant Jean Nicolet, the first white man to reach the Wisconsin region, who toured the wilderness wearing a sumptuous Chinese robe in order to be properly dressed for the search.[17] Earlier, the great Champlain had been seeking a way to China, and this apparently resulted in the optimistic name of "China Rapids" (*la Chine*) being given to the obstacle in the Saint Lawrence that had stopped Cartier; to this day, the rapids, and a neighboring town just south-west of Montreal bear the name of Lachine, pronounced *Lah*-she-en in French-Canadian patois. It seems that geographic concepts of North America as an eastward extension of Asia persisted in France for a century or so after being abandoned elsewhere.

Of course there was more to the French explorations than belief in an ancient concept. The French were attracted also by rumors of rich Indian kingdoms in the interior, but investigation soon exploded these. As they progressed into the Great Lakes region and beyond, they found valuable furs and rich land in abundance, and the China quest receded very far back in their minds. But they never forgot it entirely.

I mentioned in the last chapter the Spanish renegade Peñalosa and how, as a result of his suggestions, the discovery of Quivira became an object of French explorations. Quivira was definitely located in popular belief on the west coast, and Frontenac's instructions while governor of New France included an exhortation to push the search for it.

Nothing much came of it at first. French exploratory enterprise was diverted down the mighty Mississippi—once they had discoverd it. As I mentioned earlier, a stylized Quivira became frozen onto French maps as the hoped-for West Coast terminus, long after every-one else had ceased to believe in it. One man who tried to push the search ahead was the Sieur de Dulhut (whose name is remembered today in the corrupted form of "Duluth"). He attempted to pacify the hostile Sioux of the Minnesota region so that they would no longer block French progress westward; and on a journey that may have taken him as far west as the present North Dakota, he was shown some salt by the Indians and told of a great lake, twenty days' journey farther west, whose water was undrinkable.

Presumably this was a vague rumor of Great Salt Lake, but Dulhut interpreted it wishfully as the western sea. By this time there was sufficient experience of the width of the continent to destroy belief in Verrazano's isthmus, but the western interior was still unknown. It might contain a vast inland sea, an American Mediterranean, debouching into the Pacific. This was supported by concepts, by then traditional, of the New World's containing a counterpart of everything in the Old World. True, no one had come upon the mouth of any such sea along the Pacific coast, but the coast from Cape Mendocino northward was still unknown. Hence the lingering attachment to Quivira, which lay in the critical area. Dulhut made his report in 1679, and it was filed and forgotten. The French in Canada were more immediately concerned with the practical problems of the fur trade, and with English pressures from the east.

One man who took the quest for the western sea very seriously was Pierre Lemoyne, Sieur d'Iberville, the famed first governor of Louisiana, but his duties kept him from doing any exploring. In 1689 Jacques de Noyon opened up the series of lakes and streams known as Rainy River which bypassed the Sioux, so that the French could progress westward. Forty years later, in 1730, a seasoned old fur trader and explorer named Pierre Gaultier de Varennes, Sieur de la Vérendrye, followed by Indian reports till he reached Lake Winnipeg, and obtained a monopoly on the fur trade of this virgin territory by promising to expedite the search for the western sea.

By 1733 he and his sons had reached the country of the now-extinct Mandans, in what is now North Dakota. These people, who appeared to Vérendrye to be white, had a strange culture, strikingly different from those of the surrounding Indian tribes. Vérendrye found among them a stone with undecipherable inscriptions which he sent back to Montreal. Later, in Paris, experts identified the inscriptions as Tataric—which is unbelievable, since the Tatars and Mongols were not seafaring people. But the ancient Turkish-Tataric runic writing is quite similar to the old Scandinavian runes, and this has been cited as evidence by those who believe in the Norse origin of the Mandans.[18] The question is now beyond solution, as this strange artifact has long been lost, though there is no doubt that it really did exist.

Vérendrye apparently was never informed of the Tataric attribution, but in French official circles it stimulated belief that a way to Asia might be in the offing. The belief was strengthened by Vérendrye's report of the Missouri River, which he said flowed west (later he was to admit that it flowed eastward at the point where he saw it, but said that it took a later southerly turn and flowed from there to the Pacific). From a subsequent expedition, in 1738, he brought back from the Indians of the Manitoba region an account of another river to the west. An Indian who said he had traveled down it told him that it led to a land where the climate was warm, where there grew a kind of pepper and a kind of cacao, where there were precious metals, "all kinds of wild beasts, and snakes of a prodigious size," and "white men who have walled towns and forts." Some word of the Spanish settlements and of South America had apparently seeped northward to these Indians.

Two men whom Vérendrye left behind later returned with a version of the previously mentioned Indian tale of the undrinkable lake. Another expedition could not be sent off until 1742, and on this one the explorers were discouraged by reports of hostile tribes to the westward, between them and the sea. They did traverse the Bad Lands country as far as the Black Hills, where one of Vérendrye's sons would have climbed for a hoped-for view of the sea if the caution of the Indian guides, fearful of the tribes of the area, had not prevented this.

This was the last French expedition in search of a waterway to the Pacific. The whole thing seemed fruitless, and those in authority withheld subsidization; and less than two decades later the French empire in America fell to the English, who had never been too strongly influenced by the Verrazano map, and whose quest for the Northwest Passage was not overland but by way of the Arctic.

There is some question as to whether Vérendrye ever came within sight of the Rocky Mountains. But in less than ten years the Frenchmen had reached them, and the discovery of this vast watershed killed all hopes of an overland waterway to the Pacific. This realization is shown on the 1752 map of Philippe Buache, the last one to show Quivira, which clearly shows this mountain range (though much too close to the west coast, possibly through confusion with Spanish reports of the Coast Range) as separating eastward- from westward-flowing river .

In the meantime, a minor geographical myth growing out of the

French cross-country quest was to have its moment on the map. Louis Armand, Baron de Lahontan, spent some time in the Great Lakes region and took part in its exploration, then went back to France and in 1741 published *Mémoires de l'amérique septentrionale*. The fact that Lahontan was an outrageous liar did not prevent the book from going through several editions. In it he told of his discovery of a vast river running into the Mississippi from the west, which he named the Long River (*Rivière Longue*). It was not the Missouri, for he claimed to have explored that river too. As one traveled upstream along the Long River, various Indian tribes were to be met: the Essanapes, characterized by "sweetness and an air of humanity," who were "Pythagoreans" (meaning that they believed in reincarnation); the Gnacsitares, enemies of the Essanapes, who also knew and hated the Spaniards; the long-haired and long-bearded Mozeemleks; and in the mountains where the river had its source, the Tughulauks, also bearded, and skilled coppersmiths. This last tribe was the only one Lahontan did not claim to have visited.[19]

The book was accompanied by a badly drawn map, containing a number of spelling errors, such as "Magara" for Niagara.* And

---

* Another was the rendition of the Wisconsin (*Ouisconsink*) River as Ouariconsint. This has been cited as a possible source for the mythical western Oregon River.[20]

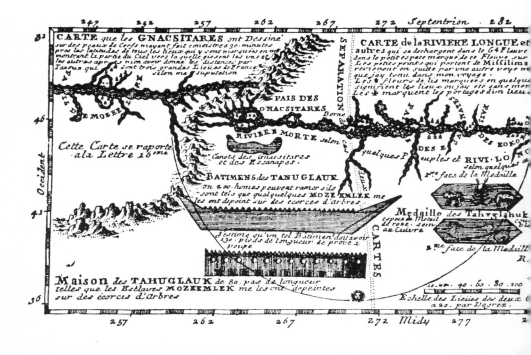

on this map the Long River is shown, stretching far to the westward, thus encouraging ideas of a possible cross-country water route. As far as I can determine, however, this is the only map to show it; Long River does not appear on the Buache map mentioned above.

In the meantime, the Tsar Peter the Great had dispatched the Danish captain Vitus Bering in 1725 to clear up the unanswered question of the Strait of Anian. Peter was dead when, three years later, Bering reported that there was in fact a strait between Asia and America. But his report was considered inconclusive, so he was later sent back to explore further; and although he died on this voyage, in 1741, the report brought back by his expedition was held to settle the matter. It was Captain Cook, on his visit to Alaskan waters in 1776, who named the strait for Bering.

During the seventeenth and eighteenth centuries, a variety of British voyages had probed into the waters northwest of Hudson Bay in search of the Passage. The results were not encouraging, but Bering's verification of the fabled Strait of Anian was promising. Now that ships of every nation moved freely round the Cape of Good Hope and the Horn, the Northwest Passage was no longer of vital importance, but, of course, if it were found to exist after all, it would be a convenience.

The "Rivière Longue" as shown on Lahontan's map.

In 1708, before Bering's explorations, the *Monthly Miscellany*, a London magazine, had published the account of an alleged voyage by an imaginary Spanish admiral named Bartolomeo de Fonte. He was said to have sailed up the west coast of America in 1640, discovered the Northwest Passage, explored it, and come out in Baffin Bay, meeting two Boston ships en route. It is not surprising that the story made no stir when first published, since by this time the British public had developed a distrust of vague travel tales, and (for quite irrelevant political and religious reasons) a special distrust of anything Spanish.[21]

But thirty years later a strange enthusiast, an Irishman named Arthur Dobbs, began stirring up considerable public interest in England by his agitation over the subject of the Northwest Passage. He collected everything he could find dealing with the Hudson Bay region. In addition, he had heard French rumors of the inland western sea, and he bore down hard on the fact that the French knew the North American interior better than the English. His hypothesis was not that the Passage existed to be discovered, but that the nefarious Hudson's Bay Company had already discovered it and was suppressing the information in order to retain its monopoly of the fur trade. Dobbs's propagandizing resulted in public backing for a few unsuccessful voyages.

In 1744 Dobbs published *An Account of the Countries Adjoining to Hudson's Bay*, in which he dredged up all the available data that tended to bolster his claim. He dusted off the old dubious voyage of Juan de Fuca, originally published by Purchas, combined it with the Admiral de Fonte hoax, and claimed that both referred to the same waterway. The Northwest Passage, therefore, had been discovered, and why hadn't we been told? The book occasioned enough stir to lead to the dispatching of an ill-fated expedition to Hudson Bay in 1746; after it failed, Dobbs gave up the cause and retired to North Carolina, where he later served as governor and earned a measure of scientific fame by discovering the Venus's-flytrap.

The Great Probability of a North West Passage appeared in 1768. It bore the signature of Thomas Jefferys, but this is believed to be a pseudonym of Theodore Dragg, an oddball adventurer who sailed as ship's clerk on the 1746 voyage mentioned above, and later prospered as a liquor dealer in the American colonies.[22] The book was based primarily on de Fonte and de Fuca. It is accompanied by a curious map of northern North America which shows two roughly concurrent passages: that of de Fuca as a long narrow channel of open sea, and that of de Fonte (influenced by French conceptions) as a chain of rivers and lakes, the two running side by side in a most implausible way, geographically speaking.

In 1770 Samuel Hearne set out from the trading post of Churchill, on the west coast of Hudson Bay, to cross the Canadian Arctic, and a specific part of his instructions was to search for the alleged passage. He wandered across the bleak northland as far west as Great Slave Lake and then north to the mouth of the Coppermine River, on the Arctic coast. And he found no cross-country channels cutting across his line of march. Then, in 1778, the great Captain

Arthur Dobbs.

Cook explored the western American coast, discovered no passages, and in his report made sarcastic reference to "the pretended strait of Juan de Fuca." It was Captain John Meares who in 1788 explored Puget Sound, which Cook had missed (probably because of fog), and gave its entrance the name of Strait of Juan de Fuca, on the assumption that this was probably what de Fuca had discovered, if anything. The name still stands.

In that same year of 1788, another spurious Northwest Passage story came to light and made its mark. Exactly two hundred years before, in 1588, a Spaniard named Lorenzo Ferrer Maldonado had reported on his voyage from Spain via Iceland through the Northwest Passage, coming out through the Strait of Anian, continuing down the American coast as far as Quivira, then returning the way he had come. The report when dug out of the archives and published came to the attention of our old friend Philippe Buache, who, with his habit of believing anything, had been a strong proponent of the de Fonte story. He read a paper based on the Maldonado report before the Paris Academy of Science in 1790, and this brought it back to the attention of the Spanish authorities. A captain named Alejandro Malaspina was sent out with two vessels in 1791 to check; he thoroughly explored the shores of Alaska north to about 60° and found no strait. His report included a thorough tearing-apart of the Maldonado story, proving it to be a hoax. But Maldonado's account had represented the Northwest Passage as a succession of winding channels running as far as 75° north, which is coincidentally a true description of the real Northwest Passage.[23]

As I have already said, this does not purport to be a complete history of the search for the Northwest Passage. It was not entirely a matter of the exploding of myths. There was a great deal of serious voyaging, which contributed mightily to the expanding knowledge of the Arctic. From the early part of the nineteenth century the North Pole became more of an object of serious quest than the Northwest Passage, though the latter was never forgotten, if only "for the sake of the record." The last expedition seriously and primarily concerned with it was the famous 1845–1847 voyage of Sir John Franklin, which sailed into the Arctic and vanished, and

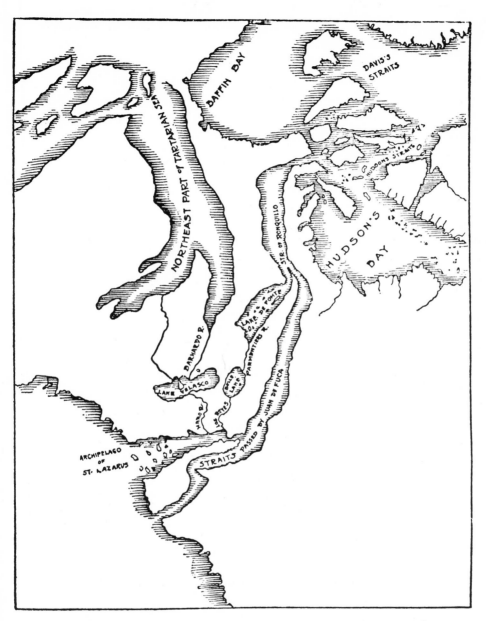

Map of the two alleged Northwest Passages, following de Fuca and de Fonte.

the search for him became a matter of tremendous public concern in early Victorian England.*

The Franklin voyage marked the end of active interest in the Northwest Passage, which was now known to be too frigid to be of any practical use. The opening of the Suez Canal two decades later eliminated the need for it, since it provided a shorter route to the Orient.

But in the wake of the Northwest Passage there arose another myth which was only indirectly connected with it, the myth of the Open Polar Sea. Actually, belief in this fictitious body of water had

---

* Crossword-puzzle addicts such as myself know "Rae" as a three-letter word definable as "Arctic explorer." It may thus be of interest to mention that John Rae was a Hudson's Bay Company physician who explored large stretches of the Canadian Arctic coast, brought back the relics officially accepted as proving the fate of the Franklin expedition, and received the reward offered by the British Admiralty for this.

Sir John Franklin.

originated some two centuries earlier, cropping up first in the account of Joseph Moxon.

Moxon was later to be hydrographer to King Charles II and a mapmaker of renown, but in 1652 he was in exile as a royalist during Cromwell's regime. In an Amsterdam tavern he met a Dutch sailor who spoke of having just returned from the Spitsbergen fishing grounds.* Those present expressed surprise at his being home so early in the season, and the sailor explained that he had merely sailed on a shuttle run to pick up and bring home the fishing fleet's catch. But when they arrived off Spitsbergen, they found that the season's catch was insufficient to make up a full cargo for them. So their captain decided to make use of the delay with a northward voyage to the farthest limits of navigation. They sailed north to the Pole and two degrees beyond, found neither islands nor ice but completely open sea, and the sailor said that the weather was as warm as Amsterdam in summer.

It is hard to tell what to make of this. Moxon said that he believed it, "for [the sailor] seem'd a plain, honest and unaffectatious Person, and one who could have no design upon me." Possibly it was one of those rare ice-free Arctic summers that do occasionally occur, and the voyage did reach an exceptionally high latitude; but the story undoubtedly got embroidered in the telling. The concept of a navigable polar sea arose from the breakdown of the old theories of climatic zones, as discussed in the first part of this chapter, but this apparently was the first instance of anyone's claiming actual experience of such an open sea.

As far back as 1527, Robert Thorne had proposed the direct polar route as one of those that should be investigated. Barents in 1596, and Hudson in 1608, tried for it with no success. But some geographers kept the notion alive with specious reasoning. The fact that the sun shines continuously on the polar regions for six months of each year was stressed; and the fact that for the other six months those regions are without sunlight was conveniently ignored. The

---

* It should be mentioned that Moxon said "Greenland" rather than Spitsbergen. An elucidation of this problem will have to wait until Chapter 9.

fact that ice tends to form only or primarily along the shoreline—a fact well known to anyone with experience of inland lakes in cold climates—was fallaciously applied to the ocean, where numerous other climatic factors obtain. Some explorers' reports of finding unexpected open water beyond the Arctic Circle were given more than their due importance.

But the quest for the Open Polar Sea had more to do with the search for the North Pole than for the Northwest Passage, and it did not become important until the Passage had become only an isolated item in general Arctic exploration. In London during the 1770s there was one Daines Barrington, member of the Royal Society, a good lawyer but a bad amateur scientist, who plugged hard for polar exploration on the grounds of the navigable waterways to be found there. Some of his arguments, erroneous though they are, have a curiosity value: he pointed out that the tropical heat (on the basis of the spotty weather reports then available) tended to be greater at the Tropics of Cancer and Capricorn than at the equator itself; in other words, he claimed that the tropical zone became more temperate toward its middle. One piece of evidence for this was that the Ecuadorian peak of Cotopaxi, situated almost directly on the equator, is snow-capped, while the peak of Tenerife in the Canary Islands, north of the Tropic of Cancer, has no snow even though it is taller than Cotopaxi. And he hazarded the guess that a similar principle might apply to the Arctic—the cold of the Arctic Circle becoming less extreme as one approached the North Pole.

Barrington's ideas were instrumental in persuading the British Admiralty in 1773 to dispatch a well-equipped expedition to investigate the polar sea with two vessels (interestingly named the *Racehorse* and the *Carcass*). One crew member later to be famous was Horatio Nelson, then a young midshipman, who had a dangerous run-in with a polar bear on Spitsbergen. Not far to the north of these islands, the expedition found itself completely blocked by a wall of ice. This more or less killed hopes of an open polar sea, and when Sir William Parry in 1827 made his attempt to reach the Pole from Spitsbergen, he tried it with sleds. But as late as 1818, an exposition of Barrington's ideas was published in New York by one Colonel Beaufoy.

The theory came to life again in the mid-nineteenth century, largely through the influence of the noted Arctic explorer Elisha Kent Kane. In 1852 he mentioned in a report to the American Geographical Society that the eminent Scottish physicist Sir David Brewster had pinpointed two "poles of cold" where the lowest temperatures in the northern hemisphere were to be found, both at 80° N, one in Asia and the other in America. It seemed to follow that if the coldest weather occurred 10 degrees south of the North Pole, then it would be warmer at the Pole itself and there could be open sea in its vicinity.

And Kane apparently proved his point on his next Arctic voyage, which reached the northwesternmost point of Greenland. From atop the looming cliffs of this bleak coast he had sight of open water, with heavy breakers and no ice whatever.

It was not known then, as it is now, that a complexity of causes can at times keep large stretches of Arctic sea completely ice-free temporarily. The Open Polar Sea appeared a reality, and for the next twenty years enjoyed the endorsement of the great German geographer and promoter of exploration, August Petermann, and the first great American oceanographer, Matthew Fontaine Maury. But later voyages failed to find it again, and finally Fridtjof Nansen's three-year voyage of 1893–1896 in the *Fram* disposed forever of the Open Polar Sea.[24]

A decade after the great Norwegian Nansen proved the non-existence of the Open Polar Sea, the great Norwegian Amundsen proved the reality of the Northwest Passage, and its possible navigability. But, if the tale as told is true, it would appear that another vessel had previously come round through the Passage, and under the most macabre conditions imaginable.*

On August 11, 1775, the American whaler *Herald* found herself

---

* I make no claims for the truth of this story. It has appeared in a variety of sensational publications, and I have been unable to trace it beyond them. However, it undoubtedly does have some sort of original documentation, reliable or otherwise.

becalmed near a huge ice field to the west of Greenland. But during the night a gale rose which broke up the ice, and out of it the *Herald*'s crew saw approaching a ghastly ship whose masts and spars were coated with glittering ice. The captain and some of the crew boarded her, and found her name to be the *Octavius*.

In the foc'sle they found each bunk occupied by a dead man, the bodies perfectly preserved by the cold. The captain, likewise dead and frozen, was found seated at the table in his cabin, with the log-book open before him, and lying in the bunk was the body of a woman, presumably the captain's wife. Seated on the cabin floor across from her was a dead sailor with flint and shavings before him, with which he had apparently been about to start a fire when he died. Beside him on the floor, under a sea jacket, was the body of a small boy.

The *Herald*'s captain took the logbook and entrusted it to one of his men. He checked the galley and found no food; when he wanted to check the hold, the crew refused to go down any farther on this charnel vessel. As they returned to the longboat, the man with the *Octavius*'s log dropped it in his haste to get away; the book was brittle with cold and all but the first and last few pages broke loose from their bindings and were lost in the sea. During the following night the *Octavius* drifted out of sight, and nothing more was ever heard of her.

In the logbook there remained three pages at the start, and one at the end. The first pages named the ship's company, including the captain, his wife, and his ten-year-old son, and told of their sailing from England for China on September 10, 1761. They ended with mention of fair weather, and of a sighting of the Canaries on September 19.

The final page bore only one entry, evidently written by one of the crew. It stated that the ship had been trapped in the ice for seventeen days, that the men were suffering terribly from the cold, that the captain's son had died and the captain's wife said that she no longer felt cold (a well-known symptom of approaching death by freezing), that the mate was unsuccessfully trying to get a fire going; and that their approximate location was latitude 75° N, longitude

160° W—or at a position several hundred miles north of Point Barrow, Alaska.

Apparently the captain of the *Octavius* had decided on his return from China to make a try at finding the Northwest Passage instead of using the long way home around the Cape. We can never know, since most of the log is lost. But it appears that the first to traverse the Northwest Passage may have been a fourteen-year voyage by a ship of the dead.[25]

CHAPTER 8.

The Unknown
Northern Land

Mercator on his world map of 1567 and Ortelius, copying him in 1571, balanced off Terra Australis
Incognita (Chapter 2) with a much smaller Terra Septentrionalis Incognita in the north. Unlike the vast graceless
blob that was the Unknown Southern Land, the Unknown
Northern Land appears as a rather handsome and clean-
lined continent, which seems to be spreading its wings
over the multiformed land masses below. Two of its penin-
sulas are placed roughly in the positions of the actual
Spitsbergen and Novaya Zemlya. But this must be put
down to lucky accident, since these island groups were
unknown to Western Europeans until the 1590s.

This Unknown Northern Land is not our concern, however. Its existence was more a matter of artistic symmetry
than geographic myth. Before the end of the century the
voyages of Barents to the east and Davis to the west had
revealed a very different state of affairs in the Arctic, and
the Northern Land seems never to have been generally
believed in, or to have been an object of serious search.

Rather, the title of this chapter refers to another unknown northern land, Norumbega, which for a time haunted the northeast American coast just as Quivira haunted the northwest coast, and in approximately the same latitude. Its first appearance on the map was as a river, but that was only the beginning.

The odd but evocative name of Norumbega has intrigued scholars for the past three centuries, and research into its origin goes back almost that far. Father Sebastian Rasle, the French priest who did heroic missionary work among the Abnaki Indians of Maine and was foully murdered by the English, thought he had found the source in an Abnaki word which he rendered as something like *aranmbegk*. Rasle translated this as "at the water's head"; more recent scholars have favored "at the clay inlet."[1] George R. Stewart mentioned, without further identification, an old map of North America from the 1520s that placed an "Arambe" on the northeast coast, and suggested that this, in corrupted form, was the origin of Norumbega.[2] Whether or not this be true, either *aranmbegk* is the original of Arambe or the coincidence is most striking.

The *Handbook of American Indians* of 1912 quoted a recent expert on the Abnaki language who claimed to have traced it to *nolumbeka*, which he said meant "a succession of falls and still waters," and was applied by these Indians to part of the Penobscot River. Others have been doubtful of this application of the term, and even of its existence. Another, and equally dubious, suggestion was *nalambigik*, "pool of still water."

It will be noted that all the attempts of these Amerindian linguists to fix on something sounding like Norumbega invariably come up with a term applicable only to a small body of water. It is difficult therefore to explain how such a term could have been seized upon by early voyagers and used to designate a considerable area of land. In spite of the fact that Norumbega was a name actually first applied to a river, which suggests that one of the Abnaki derivations could be correct, other explanations for the origin of the word have been sought.

Arthur James Weise in his *Discovery of America*, published in 1884, made the lame suggestion that unidentifiable "first French

Imaginative nineteenth-century depiction of the murder of Father Rasle by the English.

explorers" had entered the mouth of the Hudson (apparently before Verrazano, who commanded the first recorded French voyage to the New World) and given the Palisades the name of *L'Enorme Berge*, "Tremendous Escarpment," and that this became corrupted —quickly enough to place that name in that form on the map by 1529.[3]

Because of the "Nor" in Norumbega, Norse derivations were inevitably suggested and they began cropping up almost as soon as the name itself became established. It began appearing on sixteenth-century maps as *Noruega*, or *Nova Noruega*, and it had much to do with establishing the widely held theory of the time—held by Ortelius and Hugo Grotius among others—that at least some of the American Indians were descendants of Norsemen who had made unrecorded and long-forgotten voyages to America.* In more modern times, a favorite suggestion for the name Norumbega has been *Nordhman Bygdh*, "Norsemen's Settlement." But more of this later.[4]

After his exploratory voyage of 1524 along the North American coast, Giovanni da Verrazano made a written report to the King of France.[5] It was brief and businesslike, concerned chiefly with geographical and climatological data, and with the native peoples he encountered. Nowhere in it is there anything about Norumbega. But in that short document Verrazano did not tell everything that he knew, or believed, or had heard (for instance, he did not mention the isthmus that we considered in Chapter 7). He apparently had much more to tell, and he revealed it in conversations with others, most importantly with his brother Girolamo, a Venetian cartographer, and with another cartographer named Majollo. The latter in 1526 brought out a map of America which credited Verrazano with the discovery of a "Norman Villa" somewhere in the New England region;[6] and Girolamo Verrazano three years later published a map on which the name "Norombega" appears in recognizable form for the first time, as a river in the general area of Maine.[7]

I believe that many investigators have been needlessly led astray

---

* The Norse discovery theory as we know it, based on Leif Ericson's Vinland voyage, was first advanced in 1705, with the publication of the *Historia Vinlandiae Antiquae*, by the Swedish scholar Thormod Torfaeus.

by the similarity of the names "Norombega" and "Norman Villa." The former would appear to have been an Indian name for a river, or an Indian word applying to one, while the latter (if not simply Majollo's mistake for Norumbega) can be otherwise explained, as will be shown. But it appears that the confusion began almost as soon as these maps appeared, so that the Norumbega River quickly came to be located in a considerable area of land bearing the same name.

Perhaps the first appearance of Norumbega on the map as the name of a piece of land was on the Euphrosinius Ulpius globe of 1542. A few years earlier, the first mention of it in this sense had been made by one Pierre Crignon, of Dieppe, in his *Recherches sur les Voyages et Découvertes des Navigateurs Normands*—which, however, could not have exerted much influence at the time, since it was not published till three centuries later. Crignon stated that Verrazano had taken possession of the area for the King of France, and named it New France, but that the natives called it Norumbega.[8]

There is no indication that Jacques Cartier, when he first sailed for the New World in 1534, had any expectation of reaching the land of Norumbega, though he was using Verrazano's map. He sailed up the Saint Lawrence and, near the present site of the city of Quebec, came upon an Indian nation whose name he gave as Hochelaga. On later maps of North America, Hochelaga was to remain as designating a considerable area of the land collectively called New France. Farther upstream, near the present Montreal, he found another Indian nation, whose name he gave as Canada—a name that was not to become important on the maps till more than a century later. In this area he picked up what he believed to be diamonds, but lapidaries back in France later found them to be worthless crystals. This brought "a Canadian diamond" into currency as a slang term for anything bogus, but may also have contributed to the notion of Norumbega as a rich realm worth finding.[9]

On his last voyage, that of 1541–1542, Cartier sailed jointly with Jean François de La Roque, Sieur de Roberval, whom King Francis had appointed Viceroy of New France. The record of this voyage was written by one Jean Alfonce, Cartier's chief navigator. He gave a fix on the "Cape of Norumbegue," which can be easily identified as Cape Cod, and located the "River of Norumbegue" about seventy-five miles to the west. This can only refer to the Narragansett. About forty miles upriver, he said, was the city of Norumbega, "and there is in it a good people, and they have pelts of all kinds of animals."[10] The fur trade had already become the principal attraction of that part of the world. Nevertheless, it was sixty years before the French did anything more about the area of the New World that Verrazano had placed on the map as "New France."

During this time, Norumbega shared map space with New France, or *Nova Francia*. In the geographic concepts of the time, the entire area where Spain held claim, corresponding roughly to our Deep South, was mapped as Florida, and the coast to the north of this, which Verrazano had surveyed, became New France. After the 1580s the situation changed. The English had by then laid claim to an indeterminate area just north of "Florida," which they named Virginia, and it appeared on the maps to separate Florida from *Nova Francia*. This Virginia must not be equated with the present state, or with the site of the Jamestown colony. It applied loosely to all such Atlantic coastal area as England might claim or hold. Then, after the 1620s, the presence of New England further reduced New France on the maps, pushing it back to the area that we now associate with the name.

Within New France, the two most important regional names were (however spelled) Hochelaga and Norumbega. The former tended to be moved farther inland up the Saint Lawrence, but the latter consistently remained on the seacoast. The favored location of it was the Nova Scotia-New Brunswick-Maine area.

And so it appeared on the Zaltieri map of 1566, the Mercator map of 1569, the Ortelius map of 1571, the Wytfliet map of 1597, the Blaeu map of circa 1620, and many others which it would be wearisome to list. The Michael Lok map, published by Hakluyt in 1582, but drawn some time before, restricts Norumbega to the present Nova Scotia, but most of the maps made it lap well over into Maine. The aforesaid Ortelius map presents another curiosity, which later maps were to copy; it extended Cartier's route much too far inland, and placed a misspelled "Chlaga" at about the present site of Chicago. This must be taken as pure coincidence.*

Beginning with Mercator in 1569, Norumbega came to appear on the maps as a place of some importance. Mercator sketched in the capital as a fortified city, bristling with towers. Ortelius, more restrained, used a conventional symbol. Both agreed in placing it some distance inland, up a river in the approximate place of the Bay of Fundy. Jean Alfonce's Cape of Norumbegue apparently had been switched from Cape Cod to Cape Sable, and the city's location altered accordingly.

Voyagers along the North Atlantic coast naturally made their attempts to find Norumbega. The most noteworthy of these was Sir

---

* The name of Chicago actually comes from the Potawatomie *chickagou*, meaning "stink," and referring to the beds of wild onions that formerly grew along the shores of Lake Michigan.[11]

Michael Lok's map of 1582, showing Norumbega as an offshore island.

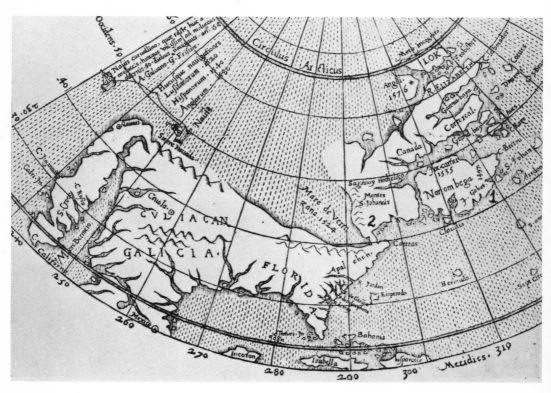

Samuel de Champlain.

Humphrey Gilbert's ill-fated expedition of 1583, which failed to find either Verrazano's isthmus or his Norumbega, and finally settled for founding a British colony in Newfoundland. But the first really systematic effort to track down Norumbega was that of Champlain.

Samuel de Champlain is one of the most engaging figures in the history of American exploration. In his youth he had sailed for the Spaniards, commanding voyages to the West Indies and visiting Panama, and he was apparently the first to suggest a possible Panama Canal. In 1603, having already acquired a reputation as a field geographer, he was commissioned by King Henri IV of France to tackle the area known for so long on the maps as New France, explore it, and try to make it in some way advantageous to its supposed owner. And Champlain took to his task joyously, for he had a mystique of the New World as a sort of new Eden, providing a fresh chance for fallen man—much like the feeling that seems to animate so many people today in their enthusiasm for the space race.

Champlain sailed in 1603, explored the shores of what is now Nova Scotia, and found no Norumbega there. He did set up the colony of Port Royal (now Annapolis Royal, Nova Scotia). And from 1604 through 1607, he carefully combed the coasts southward as far as Cape Cod, in search of Norumbega. As to the results, we can do no better than quote the salty phraseology (as translated and published by Purchas) of Marc Lescarbot, a colorful lawyer and poet, who was the expedition's chronicler.

. . . And there is [on the Maine coast] no remarkable thing (at least that may bee seene in the outside of the Lands) but a River, whereof many have written fables one after another.

I will recite that which is in the last Booke, intituled, The universall Historie of the West Indies, Printed at Douay that last yeere 1607. in the place where hee speaketh of Norumbega: For in reporting this, I shall have also said that which the first have written, from whom they have had it.

Moreover, towards the North (sayth the Authour, after hee has spoken of Virginia) is Norumbega, which is knowne well enough, by reason of a faire Towne, and a great River, though it is not found from whence it hath its name: for the Barbarians doe call it Aguncia [a corruption of "Algonquin"]: At the mouth of this River there is an Iland very fit for fishing. The region that goeth along the Sea, doth abound in fish, and towards New France there is great number of wilde beasts, and is very commodious for hunting; the Inhabitants doe live in the same manner as they of New France.

If this beautiful Towne hath ever been in nature, I would faine knowe who hath pulled it downe: For there is but Cabins heere and there made with pearkes [poles], and covered with barkes of trees, or with skinnes, and both the River and the place inhabited is called Pemptegoet, and not Agguncia. The River (saving the Tide) is scarce as the River on that coast, because there are not Lands sufficient to produce them, by reason of the great River of Canada [the St. Lawrence] which runneth like this coast, and is not fourescore leagues distant from that place in crossing the Lands, which from else-where received many Rivers falling from those parts which are towards Norombega: At the entrie whereof, it is so farre from having but one Iland, that rather the number thereof is almost infinite, for so much as this River enlarging it selfe like the Greeke Lambda Λ, the mouth whereof is all full of Iles, whereof there is one of them lying very farre off (and the formost) in the Sea, which is high and markable above the others [modern Isle au Haut].

But some will say that I equivocate in the situation of Norombega, and that it is not placed where I take it. To this I answer, that the Authour, whose words I have a little before alleaged, is in this my sufficient warrant, who in his Geographicall Mappe, hath placed in the mouth of this River in the 44. degree, and this supposed Towne in the 45. wherein we differ in but one degree, which is a small matter. For the River that I meane is in the 45. degree, and as for any Towne, there is none. Now of necessity it must be this River, because that the same being passed, and that of Kinibeki (which is in the same hight) there is no other River forward, whereof account should be made, till one come to Virginia. I say furthermore, that seeing the Barbarians of Norombega doe live as they of new France, and have abundance of hunting, it must be, that their Province be seated in our new France; for fiftie leagues further to the South-west there is no great game, because the woods are thinner there, and the Inhabitants setled, and in great number than in Norombega.[12]

To clear it up a little: Champlain, after exploring the coast, settled on the Penobscot ("Pemptegoet") as the river reported by Verrazano which had started the whole affair. The "Kinibeki" is of course the Kennebec, and the notable river in "Virginia" which Lescarbot mentioned is undoubtedly the Hudson, whose mouth Verrazano had visited. Apparently, being unwilling simply to dump the traditional name of Norumbega, Champlain on his map of 1612 applied it to the Indian settlement at the mouth of the Penobscot. But now that Norumbega had been reduced to an insignificant Indian village, the learned lost interest in it, and it began to drop off the map.

For some reason, this was not true among the Dutch. Norumbega continued to crop up on Dutch maps throughout the seventeenth century, and even into the eighteenth. It is not clear why. Dutch cartographers were no more conservative or given to copying each other than those of other lands. Perhaps the Dutch disappointment at their New World venture's being wiped out by the English before it properly got going may have fostered a willingness to perpetuate belief in geographical myths.

It should be noted that Champlain explored only as far south as Cape Cod. Had he swung southward of the cape and investigated the Narragansett estuary, where Jean Alfonce had earlier placed Norumbega, it is just possible, as we shall see, that he might have found something.

Champlain had not exactly wiped out Norumbega, but he had

reduced it to insignificance. Within a few years thereafter, Champlain reached the Great Lakes area and subsequent French penetration into the region disposed of the suppositious inland realm of Hochelaga, or Chlaga. Today, Hochelaga is entirely forgotten. Norumbega is not. The name still lurks round the fringes of our American culture, and is one that any person of fairly wide reading is likely to recognize from having come across it somewhere.

The reason for this is that the alleged Norumbega has been propagandized—and as I believe, quite unjustifiably—to buttress the theory of Norse discovery.

Checking back, we find that the Majollo map, on the authority of Verrazano himself, placed a "Norman Villa" somewhere on the coast he had explored, and that the map drawn by the explorer's brother three years later first introduced Norumbega as the name of a river, also on the authority of Verrazano. This map shows the Norman Villa as well.

We can be certain that Verrazano would have kept his own brother straight on the matter, so it appears clear that to the returned voyager "Norman Villa" and "Norumbega" were two quite distinct place-names. The latter is plainly made the name of a river, the one that Champlain eighty years later was to identify as the Penobscot. And we have the Abnaki word *nolumbeka*, which has been questioned but has also been identified as late as the nineteenth century as applying to the Penobscot.

It would appear that in his voyaging Verrazano discovered a river, heard the Indians referring to it with a word that sounded to him like Norumbega, took this for the name of the river, and informed his brother accordingly. The evidence from Indian linguistics is dubious, but there is no real reason not to believe that Champlain's identification of the Norumbega with the Penobscot is correct.

This leaves us with the separate and distinct "Norman Villa" to be considered.

Perhaps at this point it would be worthwhile to assess the present status of the theory of a Norse discovery of America. In a sense, to speak of the Norse as "discovering America" raises a problem in semantics. There was no "America" until 1507, when Martin Waldseemüller introduced the name on his famous map. He applied it only to the present South America, for which there is no serious theory of Norse discovery. And six years later, he changed the name to "Unknown Land," and credited the discovery to Columbus (Chapter 2).

Properly stated, the theory would be that the Norse discovered some part of the continental land mass, with offshore islands, now known as North America. And thus stated, it is not theory but fact. The historical and archaeological evidence admits of no doubt that the Norse did discover and colonize Greenland, and Greenland is as much a part of North America as Cuba or Long Island.

Further, the well-publicized authentication in October 1963 of a Norse site in northern Newfoundland stands as proof that these voyagers did get beyond Greenland.[13] As to Norse venturings onto the continental mainland, they would seem most probable, but so far no incontrovertible evidence for them has turned up.

The only authentic record we have of a Norse attempt to set up a colony in America outside of Greenland is that of Thorfinn Karlsevni, about the years 1007–1008; and the record makes it clear that these would-be settlers were driven out by the Indians. The location of the Karlsevni colony is not clear; it may have been on Newfoundland rather than on the mainland. Leif Ericson's Vinland, on the basis of some slight astronomical evidence, has usually been located in the Cape Cod area, but there is no universal agreement on this, and even northern Newfoundland has been suggested.[14]

There are strong reasons for believing that the Greenland Norse had some dealings with regions farther south. For example, it is known that the Greenlanders built with timber, and it is known that there are not now, and were not then, any forests in Greenland that could have supplied the timber. It seems safe to assume that, rather than importing it from distant Norway, they acquired it from nearby Newfoundland, or perhaps from the coasts of the mainland. And, in the process, they must have had some contact with the Indians.

This is all that is actually known or can be reasonably inferred from the substantial existing evidence. New evidence may well turn up and completely alter the picture, and the search for it is to be commended and encouraged.

But too many students of the matter have been less engaged in examining evidence than in drawing up a brief for a particular theory. And they often have shown a tendency to fall into a dangerous form of apriorism: *a* must be true because it would explain *b*, therefore *b* stands as proof of the truth of *a*. An early Norse settlement in New England would explain the origin of Norumbega, therefore the Norumbega story proves that such a settlement did take place.*

Such theorists always emphasize the possible derivation of Norumbega from *Nordhman Bygdh*, "Norsemen's Settlement," and its association with a "Norman Villa" whose connection seems obvi-

---

* So as not to be a spoilsport, let me add that I personally regard the case presented by Hjalmar Holand and Frederick J. Pohl as cogent and convincing, and most probably true. The point here is simply their faults of logic.

Imaginative nineteenth-century depiction of a clash between Norsemen and Indians.

The Newport Tower.

ous. The Norman Villa is always identified as the famed Round Stone Tower of Newport, Rhode Island, of which one can read in any encyclopedia.

It is not clear whether this tower was built by Governor Benedict Arnold of Rhode Island (an ancestor of the American Revolutionary traitor) during the 1670s, or by the Norse. Both theories can be defended to a certain extent, and there seem to be no alternative ones. Actually, whether the tower is of Norse origin or not, there is reason to believe that it antedates the time of Arnold. In 1632 one Sir Edmund Plowden presented a prospectus for an English colony on Long Island, and mentioned as one of the "commodities" (read, "drawing points") on the site a "round stone Towre" to the northward, which would serve as a good stronghold for a garrison to guard against Indian attacks from that direction.[15] This was not only forty years before Arnold's governorship, but seven years before Newport was settled. Thus, as said before, if Champlain, twenty-five years earlier, had continued his exploration southward and westward past Cape Cod to the Narragansett, he might have discovered something to report.

The usual theory is that the Norse origin of the tower was preserved in the distorted form that "Norseman" or "Norman" took in the Indian language. And in support of this, there is rallied quite an impressive roster of Indian words from the Atlantic seaboard which appear to be of Norse origin.

There is the Nova Scotian tribe called by the French *Souriquois*, in modern spelling Souriké, corresponding to the Norse *sudhr rike*, "southern province." The Souriké called their chiefs *ricmanen*, apparently corresponding to the Norse *rika menn*, "ruling men" (the Norse *rika* is a cognate of the English "rich"). The Souriké *varchim*, "wolf," from the Norse *vargrinn*. Also among the Souriké, there was the word for "two," *tabo* (Norse *tvan*), and the polite phrase after a meal rendered by the French as *epigico iaton edico*, which has been linked to the Norse *vi hafva god aten*, "we have eaten well."[16]

Some of these are plainly rather dubious. More strikingly, there is the northern Algonquins' myth of the evil god who leads the wolves, and whose name of Lok cannot help but suggest Loki. And in 1676, at the end of the so-called King Philip's War, the Indians whom the English put to death included an aged female Narragansett chieftain whose name is given as Magnus. This Scandinavian name means nothing in any Algonquin Indian tongue.[17]

As previously stated, there is reason to assume that the Greenland Norse had contact with the Indians, and that the latter might have picked up a few words from them seems plausible enough. And borrowed words, once established in any language, tend to stay there indefinitely. There is no reason to doubt that some Indian tribes, by the time of Verrazano, and even later, were still using words which they had picked up from the Norsemen.

But the hypothesis that "Norumbega" or "Norman Villa" were examples of this, and thus relics of an earlier Norse settlement, is not necessarily indicated. There is another explanation, from an on-the-spot source.

The aforementioned Marc Lescarbot, the reporter of Champlain's first expedition, told how the French in Nova Scotia in 1606 built two small boats for coastal exploration. Lacking pitch to caulk them, they made do with fir resin, and improvised a still to extract it from the bark of the trees:

Whereof the Savages being astonied, did say in words borrowed from the Basques, Endia chave Normandia, that is to say, that the Normans know many things. Now they call all Frenchmen Normands, except the Basques, because the most part of the fishermen that goe afishing there, be of that Nation.[18]

This seems definite enough. A highly observant Frenchman, who was there, testified that the Basques referred to all other Frenchmen as Normans, and that the Indians had, before any French settlement in the area, picked up the term from them. This seems far more definite than any questionable theorizing about surviving Norse words.

Of course there is this further point. Lescarbot's report was made some eighty years after Verrazano had come upon his so-called Norman Villa somewhere in the New England-Nova Scotia region. Were Basque fishermen visiting the area as early as Verrazano's time?

The indications are that they were fishing in New World waters at least as early as 1500, and possibly even before Columbus.[19] Unfortunately, the medieval and post-medieval Basque seafarers'

The tower at the Abbey Saint Bavo, in Ghent.

records, if any, are now lost. In them there may well have been a record of that feature of the New England coast the Basques chose to call the Norman Villa, and the reason for the name. It may even have been the Newport Tower, which may have been of earlier Norse origin. But the name "Norman," under the circumstances and on the basis of the only substantial evidence available, definitely points to the French rather than the Norse. It may be that the Basques associated a tower of this sort with the north of France and adjoining regions; to this day a small tower of similar design may be seen at the Abbey of Saint Bavo, in Ghent, Belgium.[20]

It thus appears that an Indian word for a river and a Basque name for the French became confused and were treated as a supposed Norse name for an unrecorded settlement. But devotees of the Norse discovery theory need not feel themselves deprived thereby. No case is ever weakened by the elimination or clearing up of a dubious or misleading piece of alleged evidence. That the Norsemen did reach the shores of North America is clear enough—without the assumption that they established a "lost colony" of Norumbega.

The Peregrinations of Greenland

G reenland does, of course, exist and always has. But it does not and never did exist in some of the placements and positions assigned to it on early maps. Further, there is the probability that, for all the reality of the Greenland that we know today, its name originated as the name of a fabulous island.

The names of Iceland and Greenland have always presented problems. How did it come about that a region normally free from ice and snow should be called Iceland, while a grim, infertile Arctic wasteland should be called Greenland? In regard to Iceland, the two most plausible theories are that Floki, the Viking who discovered or rediscovered the island at some time during the 870s, sighted some beached pack-ice on the northern shore (a rare occurrence, but possible), or that the early Norse settlers deliberately gave their new homeland an uninviting name to discourage piratical attackers.

The traditional explanation of the name of Greenland has been that Erik the Red gave his discovery an attractive name to encourage prospective colonists. But this seems rather thin. However dishonest Erik may have been, it is hard to believe that he would have attempted to pull such an arrantly transparent fraud on a group of tough fighting Norsemen among whom he intended to live as their chief. The authority for this source of the name is Ari the Wise, an Icelandic chronicler of the eleventh century, but the earliest copy of his work that is known to us was produced in the thirteenth century, and it is believed to have been added to by other writers who may have contributed this story. In any case, this alleged explanation of "Greenland" has all the earmarks of pure invention, and must be considered highly dubious.

Actually, for the source of the name "Greenland," we may have to go back to Roman antiquity. The author Plutarch, of the first century A.D., is principally remembered for his biographical compilation popularly known as *Plutarch's Lives*. But he also wrote other works, including one titled *The Face in the Moon*, one of those col-

Greenlanders, from the marginal illustrations of William Blaeu's map of the 1620s.

lections of off-beat information which the Romans seem to have loved. And in it he quoted one Demetrius, a Roman civil servant who had spent some years in Britain, as informing him that the Britons knew of an island to the westward, which in their language they called by a name something like Cronos.

This name requires a little comment. It is impossible that it could actually have been Britannic, since the Britons were speakers of the so-called "P-Gaelic" branch of the Celtic language, which substitutes labial for guttural sounds, as against the "Q-Gaelic." As an example, the word for "son" in Q-Gaelic (modern Scottish and Irish) is *mac*; in P-Gaelic (Modern Welsh and Breton) it is *ap*, originally *map*. Thus, in the early Britannic language, the name would have been more like "Pronos."

Professor Arthur Hutson of the University of California (Berkeley) has suggested to me that the most likely original of the name is *Cruidhne*, an early Irish name for the island of Britain, and that this association with an island to the west (Ireland) led to the misapprehension that it was the name of a western island. If so, the original Greenland would have been Britain itself.

This idea of an island named Cronos would have tied in with traditional Greco-Roman religious conceptions, in which Cronus, the dethroned father of Zeus, lay bound in eternal sleep on an island somewhere in the west. It seems that the authority of Plutarch, quoting Demetrius, sufficed to add to Roman geography an island of *Cronia* in the Atlantic.

The rest of the theory is that the early medieval scholars, speakers of Teutonic tongues, substituted a Teutonic suffix for a Latin one, and changed the initial letter in their more guttural speech from a *c* to a *g*—thus Cronia-Cronland-Gronland. The fact that this new form meant "Green-Land" in their language was quite coincidental, and the tradition was established that somewhere in the Atlantic was an island called Greenland. And when Erik the Red discovered a new land, he simply assumed that this was the Greenland of which he had heard, and named it accordingly.[1]

There are indications that the Norse Icelanders knew of the existence of Greenland before the year 982,[2] but it was not until that year that the famed Erik the Red became its first serious investigator. As a young man Erik had come with his father from Norway to Iceland, then the land of opportunity, or so supposed to be. But they arrived to find all the good land taken and the society dominated by old settlers who did not welcome newcomers. Erik's father soon died; Erik himself finally managed to homestead a piece of land, but his neighbors refused to get along with him. The Icelanders of the time had a rough and violent culture, in which every man's best friend was his sword. Twice Erik slew a man in a fight. In each case it appears to have been self-defense, but he had no influential friends, and on both occasions he was sentenced to outlawry—the first time for one year, the second for three.

But on this second occasion he kept his ship, and his retainers remained loyal to him, so he sailed westward to investigate some rumored islands in that direction, possibly Gunnbjorn's Skerries, now vanished. The fruit of his venture was the discovery of the vast isle of Greenland, and the setting up of a nuclear colony there. When his three years were up, he returned to Iceland to recruit more colonists.

For almost a century longer, the knowledge of Greenland seems to have been orally transmitted, via the Icelandic sagas. The first written report of the island, and its introduction to European geographical awareness, dates from about the year 1070.

At that time a German priest known as Adam of Bremen completed his *History of the Diocese of Hamburg* (*Gesta Hammaburgensis Ecclesiae Pontificum*), a title which does not sound particularly exciting until one realizes that the diocese of Hamburg then took in all of Scandinavia and the overseas lands colonized by the Scandinavians, and that the book is a valuable source for early Norse life and exploration.[3] Adam had interviewed King Sweyn II of Denmark for information on these regions, and his mention of Greenland and Vinland constitutes the first authentic reference to America in all of European literature.*

---

* This first reference to America speaks of "an island in that ocean visited by many, which is called Vinland, because vines grow wild there, that yield the best wine. Also, volunteer grain grows there plentifully, and this we know is not a fantasy, because the Danes' accounts prove it true."

Of Greenland, he said: ". . . to the north the ocean flows past the
Orkneys, then endlessly about the circle of the earth, with Hibernia
[now called Ireland], the home of the Scots, on the left, and on the
right the Norwegian skerries, and farther away the islands of Iceland
and Greenland."

Then later, in another passage: "Also, there are many other islands in the wide ocean, of which Greenland is not the least; it lies
farther out, opposite the mountains of Sweden, or Rhiphaean [*sic*]
Mountains. The sailing distance to this island from Norway is said to
be five to seven days, the same as to Iceland. The people there are
bluish-green from the salt water, and this is what gives that region its
name. They live in the same way that the Icelanders do, except that
they are savage and make piratical attacks on seafarers. It is reported
that Christianity has drifted out to them recently."

Here we have a beautiful bit of confusion, which was to leave its
mark in cartography. The first quote definitely places Greenland far
out in the ocean, while the second relates it in some way to the
mountains of Sweden (The "Rhiphaean Mountains" are a myth in
themselves, to be dealt with in Chapter 11; as for Ireland as "the
home of the Scots," see Appendix III. In medieval geography a position "opposite" something usually meant "in the same latitude," and
if this was what Adam of Bremen intended, he was quite correct in
relating what was then known of Greenland to Sweden. But such
loose terminology was wide open to misunderstanding, and it was
apparently these two irreconcilable statements by Adam of Bremen
that gave rise to the late-medieval concept of Greenland as a peninsula of Europe, or as a region connected with Europe by a long
land-bridge.

I am informed that there is, or was before the disastrous floods of
1966, a map in the Pitti Library in Florence dated 1417 which showed
a "Groinlandia" in roughly the right position and connected with
Europe. But I have not been able to see this map, nor to obtain a
facsimile of it. If it exists, it is the earliest known mapping of
Greenland.

Insofar as I have been able to trace cartographical sources, the
earliest placement of Greenland on the map was made ten years after

the Pitti map by the Danish cartographer Claudius Schwartz, for some reason better known to history as Claudius Clavus (Claudius Nail!). Apparently he was influenced by Adam of Bremen, but it seems equally sure that he had other and more modern sources of information. His first map of 1427 shows the east coast of Greenland and cuts off there. The location is right and the trend of the coast-line remarkably accurate; but his Greenland is shown as the western terminus of a long looping land-bridge which swings far north of Iceland to connect up with the North European coast to the east of the White Sea. Numerous maps later were to copy this misconception.

Claudius lived most of his active life in Italy, and had great influence in Mediterranean cartographical circles. He produced another map in 1467, this one showing both coasts of Greenland. Once more the rendering is startlingly accurate as to shape and position, but Greenland is still kept linked to the north coast of Europe.

His attempt to reconcile the two contradictory passages in Adam of Bremen was not universally accepted, however. The famed "Vinland Map" of circa 1440, whose existence was so sensationally revealed in October 1965,[4] shows a properly placed and properly shaped, though rather small, Greenland unconnected with Europe,

Section of the Clavus map of 1427, showing Greenland connected with Europe.

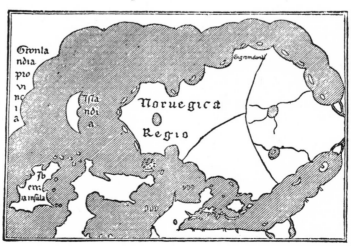

though some think this a later addition. And even earlier, within three years of the appearance of Claudius's first map, the French church-man Guillaume de Filastre brought out a new edition of Ptolemy in 1427, in which he argued that Greenland had to be south of Iceland on the evidence of the name alone, "even though Claudius the Dane described these northern regions and made a map of them, which shows them joined to Europe."[5]

There is no better way to illustrate the Peregrinations of Green-land up to the time of serious voyaging in search of it than by listing its varying appearances on the map through the fifteenth century.

The Genoese World Map of 1447 shows a Greenland connected with Europe, following Claudius Clavus.

The Fra Mauro Map of 1459 (the first European map to show Japan, and a fairly accurate representation of the shape of Africa) shows Green-land as a western promontory of northern Scandinavia.

A map accompanying the 1467 edition of Ptolemy copies Clavus, but appears to be the first influenced by him that does not show Greenland connected with Europe.

The Catalan Map of circa 1480 (previously cited in Chapter 4) shows an oblong "Illa Verde" (literal translation of "Green Land") in the latitude of Ireland, and associated with the island of Breasil.

The Nicholas Donis Map of 1482 shows a roughly correct Greenland unconnected with Europe, but duplicates it with another island of "Engronelant." This confusion between two names for the same island will recur.

An anonymous map of about this same time shows "Gronlanda" in approximately the proper place, but duplicates it with "Engroneland" as an island to the north of Norway; and to the north of this places "Pillappelanth" (Lapland), the "last habitable land."

The Martin Behaim Globe of 1492 once more makes Greenland an Arctic peninsula north of Norway.

The Johann Ruysch Map of circa 1495 places a small "Gruenlant" west-southwest of Iceland ("Islant").

Juan de la Cosa on his map of 1500 makes Greenland one of a con-geries of small islands to the north of Iceland.

It is impossible to draw any sort of pattern out of such chaos. The truth seems to be that fifteenth-century geographers simply did not

Map showing "Engroneland" to the north of the "island" of "Norbegia," and to the north of it the land of "Pillappelanth."

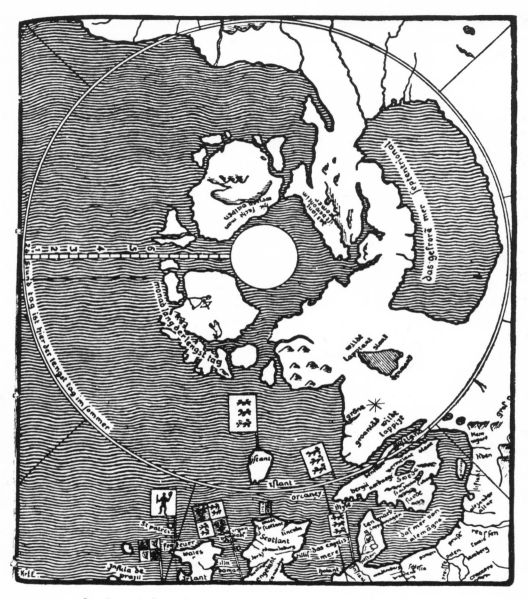

Section of the Behaim globe of 1492, showing "Groenland"' as a peninsula of Europe, to the north of Scandinavia, which is shown as an island; and westward, islands resembling the entrance to the Gulf of Saint Lawrence.

know where Greenland was or what it was, that their sources of information were confusing and contradictory, and that it was merely a question of which one a cartographer chose to follow. The Norse colony in Greenland fizzled out by the middle of the century; the last record of contact is a papal letter of 1418 stating that church services were still being held.[6] With the state of communications at the time, it is understandable that to the dominant cartographical circles of the Mediterranean area, Greenland could within fifty years' time become a vaguely remembered Somewhere on the edge of Nowhere.

But Greenland though lost was not forgotten. At least two Popes —Nicholas V in 1448 and Alexander VI in 1492[7]—expressed their concern over this farthest outpost of Christendom.* It was inevitable that voyages would be sent out for its rediscovery, and that the Danish-Norwegian kingdom, which had provided the first Greenland settlers, would be prominent in the quest.

The first of these for which we have any record is one of the most shadowy exploratory voyages of all time, known only from scrappy references here and there long after the event, and chiefly from allusions on sixteenth-century maps.[8] It is not clear whether the voyage took place in 1472 or 1476, and it is not clear who its commanders were. Most modern historians identify them as Didrick Pining and Johannes Pothorst, two Norwegian skippers of renown; but most of the references on old maps attribute the voyage to one Johannes Scolvus, whom the Dutch geographer Cornelius Wytfliet in 1597 even referred to as a Pole.[9]

This much at least is established. The Portuguese were then in the midst of their great era of exploration which was to lead them to India round the southern tip of Africa, but they were interested in northern routes as well. Henry the Navigator had maintained a policy of cultivating close relations with the Danes in order to draw on

---

* Nicholas V referred to Greenland as "an island north of Norway," and Hjalmar Holand has suggested this as the source for the error of believing Greenland to be connected with Europe. I cannot agree. The error appears in the Clavus map of 1424, preceding the Pope's letter by some twenty years; and the latter was undoubtedly influenced by Adam of Bremen.

their greater experience of the northern seas, and the voyage seems to have been largely inspired by the Portuguese. More than one Dane had been involved in the Portuguese exploration of African shores,[10] and in exchange this Arctic voyage of the 1470s took along two Portuguese observers, João Vaz Corte-Real and Alvaro Martines Homen.

Exactly where this expedition went is likewise unclear. That they visited Greenland is certain; that they passed on and touched at other areas of Arctic America is highly probable. The Gemma Frisius globe of 1537 places to the north of the Gulf of Saint Lawrence the land of the *Quij* people, and attributes their discovery to Johannes Scolvus. A suggested explanation of *Quij* (pronounced Kwee) is that it is a version of the name of the Cree Indians who at that time seem to have lived much farther east than at present.[11]

On his return to Portugal, Corte-Real requested and got from King Alfonso V a grant to the lands he had discovered. But he did nothing further about it. He was growing old, and he accepted instead a less arduous appointment as governor of the Azores. There he met an imaginative young German geographer from Bohemia, known to us as Martin Behaim (Martin of Bohemia), who married a relative of his wife, and who apparently learned much from him. Behaim's famous globe of 1492 continues the error of making Greenland a peninsula of Arctic Europe, but to the west of this places some islands which look strikingly like those around the mouth of the Gulf of Saint Lawrence.[12]

In 1493 a certain Dr. Monetarius of Nuremberg, a friend of Behaim's, wrote to King João of Portugal a letter in which he mentioned that "some years before" an expedition sent out by the Duke of Moscow* had discovered Greenland, and that a considerable colony of Russians were still there.[13] This can only refer to Spitsbergen, which the Russians apparently reached as early as 1435, and where they set up a colony near the present Bell Sound.[14] Spitsbergen is to

---

* The ruler of Russia was thus known until Ivan IV ("The Terrible") had himself crowned as Tsar of Russia in 1547.

crop up later in the gnarled history of Greenland, to complicate it still further.

João Vaz Corte-Real's claim to the lands he had discovered remained in the family, and as the Spaniards began exploring and exploiting the West Indies and adjacent areas, Corte-Real's sons got royal backing to do something about this Portuguese claim to the New World before it was too late. Pope Alexander VI's famed Line of Demarcation of 1493, dividing all the discoverable world between Spain and Portugal, definitely placed Greenland in the Spanish sector. Even the revision of this arrangement by the Treaty of Tordesillas a year later would have awarded all of the habitable and desirable parts to Spain. But this was not realized at the time. And besides, the finding of longitudes was a very uncertain procedure at that date, so that there could be an arguable case for placing Greenland east of the line.

Corte-Real's three sons sank the entire family fortune into rediscovering the land their father had visited. The youngest son, Gaspar, in 1500 commanded a voyage which had no luck, and then in 1501 another which cost his life but from which two of his ships returned with news of the rediscovery of Greenland and of the *Tierra do Llabrador*, which explains that northern American region's having a Portuguese name.* Gaspar Corte-Real must be given the credit for the actual rediscovery of Greenland. His elder brother Miguel sailed in 1502 to take effective possession of those lands, but nothing more was ever heard of him.

The Corte-Real discovery had quick geographical impact. Maps now dropped the old suppositious Greenland north of Norway, and moved it back to its proper position in the west Atlantic. The Cantino map of 1502 places it on the eastern (Portuguese) side of the Line of Demarcation, and makes it too small and too far south, but at least shows awareness of the latest knowledge.

---

* *Llabrador* in old Portuguese literally meant "laborer," but was also the term for the sort of second-rank nobility known in Spanish as "hidalgo" and in English as "gentleman." There are several theories as to why this name should have been applied to this territory, but its Corte-Real origin is certain.

The further history of the Peregrinations of Greenland is mainly cartographical, so we may as well at this point give a quick windup of the voyagings that searched it out. The Corte-Real voyage had largely taken it away from the Danes and turned it over to Portugal, but the Portuguese failed to follow up, and Greenland remained no one's land. King Christian II of Denmark projected a voyage to Greenland in 1513, but circumstances prevented its taking place; and the same was true in 1522, when King Frederick I entertained a like project. In 1578 Frederick II did send an expedition commanded by one Magnus Henningsen, who sighted the coast but did not land. It was about this same time that Martin Frobisher, as mentioned in Chapter 3, landed on southern Greenland, mistook it for Friesland, and took possession of it as West England.

From this time on, Greenland was an area quite well known to the world. The various English expeditions in search of a Northwest Passage combed its coasts at least up to 75° N. During the early seventeenth century the Danes sent out several voyages, four of them piloted by James Hall, an Englishman, who in 1612 was to be pilot to the great William Baffin and to be killed in a petty skirmish with the Greenland Eskimos. Throughout the seventeenth and eighteenth centuries, Greenland was familiar ground to whalers and sealers of all nations. It was the 1721 voyage of the famed missionary Hans Egede that re-established the Danish claim to Greenland. Egede went out with the idea of rediscovering the remnants of the lost and by now half-fabulous Norse colony and preaching to them Christianity of the Protestant sort, but, failing to find them, he remained to preach to the Eskimos. And it was the voyage of Wilhelm Graah, of the Danish Navy, in 1832, that turned up the first discovered relics of the old Norse colonists, and clinched the Danish claim, which has stood ever since.

The exploratory data has thus been summarized. The cartographical data is not so simple.

Greenland had been made part of Europe, and now briefly it was to be shown as part of Asia. As earlier noted, South America came to be known and recognized as a new land in the years immediately after Columbus's discovery, but North America was regarded as quite possibly an eastward extension of the Old World. Such was the concept behind the famed Contarini map of 1506. The Isthmus of Panama attaches South America to Asia; there is no North American continent, but a tremendous elongated peninsula sticks out like a sore thumb into the longitudes where this continent should be, and its eastern terminal points are identical with the names of the Corte-Real discoveries—Greenland and Labrador.

Section of the Contarini map of 1506, showing Greenland as a peninsula of what was then supposed to be a part of Asia.

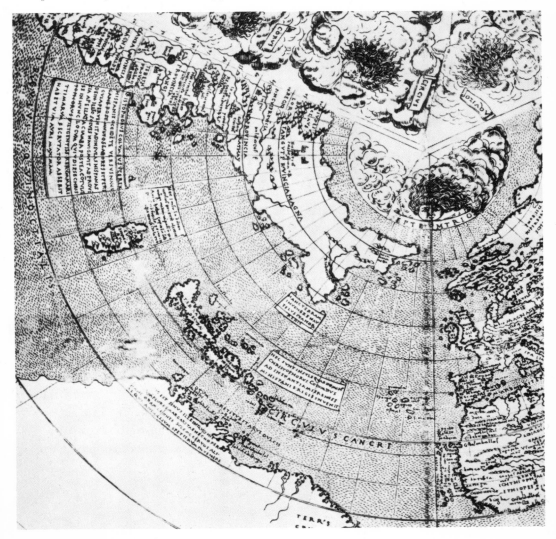

But this was a freakish instance. Displacements and disassociations of Greenland usually involved one of two errors: duplication or revival of that land-bridge.

The duplication is easily explained. After the Corte-Real discovery had restored Greenland to the maps as a known reality rather than a romantic article of faith, it became common practice for cartographers to translate "Green Land" (Groenland, or Gronland, or Engroenland, or however spelled) into the language in which they worked. This placed a vaguely known Green Island (in whatever language) on the maps, and it quickly became dissociated from the real Greenland.

The Coppo map of 1528 places an Isola Verde in about the correct position. But as Greenland became better known, and its Nordic name more standard, cartographers came to make the mistake mentioned in Chapter 3, of assuming two islands to fit the duplicated names.

There would be little point served by listing them all here. Throughout the sixteenth century and well into the seventeenth, maps showing an awareness of the real Greenland would also include a "Green Island" (*Isla Verde*, or *Insula Viridis*) somewhere in American waters, usually in the North Atlantic, proving the association of the name with that region.

But not all of the Green Islands were a result of this mistake. In 1503 Rodrigo Bastidas sailed from Seville to the West Indies and discovered a small island near Guadeloupe which he named Isla Verde, and it is shown on Peter Martyr's map of 1511. Obviously here the name had reference to the vegetation, and no confusion with Greenland is involved.[15]

The imaginary North Atlantic Green Island was to have a long life, but in the meantime a lesser duplication of Greenland had occurred. In the late sixteenth century, maps began showing Greenland flanked to the westward by a much-smaller island of Grocland.

The standard placing of this island to the west of Greenland seems to indicate some early awareness of Baffin Island. The name Grocland undoubtedly originated from the spelling of Greenland as Groëland, with a tilde, the same stylized abbreviation that seems to have caused Nicolò Zeno to read Sinclair as Zichmni, as mentioned in Chapter 3. It is easy to see how the tilde could be overlooked, and the *e* read as a *c*, and how the aforesaid technique of including enough islands to match the names could have been applied.

But I have come no closer than any previous student to clearing up the question of what map was first responsible for the Grocland error and precisely what caused Grocland to vanish from the map. The earliest map that I know to show Grocland is the Mercator of 1569, the latest the Mathias Quadus map of 1608. The Hessel Gerritsz map of 1612, illustrating Henry Hudson's discoveries, shows a quite good Greenland with land to the west, but no Grocland. Actually, Grocland had a relatively short run on the maps, but since it occurred in time to be included in the great classics of early cartography, it attained a greater fame than it actually merited.

A couple of curiosities of this time deserve mention. Ortelius in 1571 reduced the mighty Greenland to a virtual squiggle, dwarfed by the mythical isle of Estotiland to its westward, and he placed his Grocland more to the north than the west, just beneath his imaginary Unknown Northern Continent (Chapter 6).

The Michael Lok map published by Hakluyt in 1582 shows a small Greenland just north of the mythical Friesland, and to the west of this, in the approximate position of Baffin Island, a much larger area designated as "Jac. Scolvus Groctland." This attribution is interesting. Michael Lok was a man of much learning and much travel, with a lively interest in geography, and he was undoubtedly familiar with all the best sources of his time. He may well have taken this from some report, now lost or not yet rediscovered, of the aforesaid Danish expedition of the 1470s—which, whoever actually headed it, was traditionally supposed to have been commanded by one Scolvus (whose name, however, is usually given as Johannes, not Jacobus). This may prove that this expedition penetrated to areas of North America beyond Greenland, but corroborative proof is lacking.

Meanwhile, among the Danes themselves, some more misconceptions were being recorded. The Royal Library at Copenhagen preserves a map drawn by Sigurdr Stefansson, an Icelander, in 1590, and

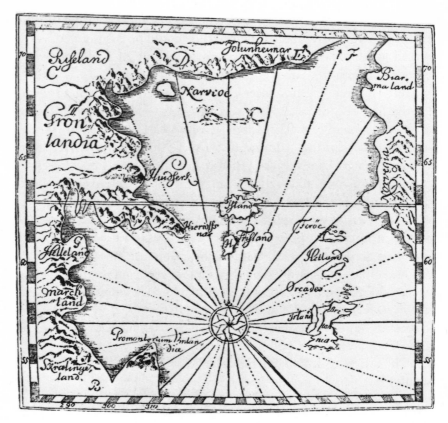

Section of the Stefansson map of 1590, showing Greenland as a peninsula of North America, unconnected to Europe.

apparently intended to illustrate old accounts or Norse discoveries in America. Greenland here appears in roughly the right shape and area, but as a vast peninsula of the American continent. Having already been part of Europe and Asia, it now becomes part of North America. All of the other place-names are taken from the Norse sagas of Leif Ericson's discovery: Hvitserk and Herjulfsness in Greenland; and southward down the coast Helluland, Markland, *Promontorium Winlandiae*, and Skraelingeland.

But even more remarkable is the map drawn in 1605 by Johannes Resen, Rector of the Royal Danish University. It also makes Greenland a peninsula of North America, and duplicates all of Stefansson's place-names and coastal features, but it adds a couple out of more modern sources. Friesland and Estotiland are given from the Zeno Narrative (Estotiland being made equivalent with the Helluland of Stefansson), and south of Vinland is an inlet apparently supposed to be the Gulf of Saint Lawrence and labeled *Portus Jacobi Carterii Anno 1525* (Port of Jacques Cartier, Year of 1525 [should be 1535]). The easy explanation would be that Resen simply copied Stefansson with a few embellishments of his own; but in a marginal notation Resen stated that his map was several hundred years old (*ante aliquot centenos annos*). Possibly he worked from an original dating from the time of actual Norse contacts with North America. Some day another lucky discovery, like that of the famed "Vinland Map," may bear this out. But as of now we do not know Resen's source.

In 1596 the Dutch navigator Willem Barents, sailing in search of a Northeast Passage to the Orient, sighted the coasts of a land which he named Spitsbergen, and believed to be a part of Greenland. Barents himself did not survive the voyage, but members of his party

Section of the Resen map of 1605.

brought back the report, and another displacement of Greenland occurred.

As mentioned earlier, a Russian discovery and colonization of Spitsbergen had been reported in Europe a hundred years before Barents's time, and attributed as "Greenland." But since at that time Greenland was generally supposed to be a part of northern Europe, adjacent to Russia, this had no impact on geographical concepts then.

From the 1520s on, European maps had almost universally shown a Greenland separated from Europe. There was no actual evidence of a land-bridge between the two; and the climate of opinion preferred to assume open seas to the north, which might allow of a Northeast or Northwest Passage. The map accompanying the Zeno Narrative in 1558 stands as an exception to this, for it shows Greenland as a vastly elongated peninsula of Europe. But it appears probable that Nicolò Zeno II copied this feature from the age-rotted map which he had to reconstruct, and which no doubt reflected the conceptions of its time.* A Greenland connected with Europe was, so far as we know, first mapped by Claudius Clavus in 1424, but the idea most likely was established earlier than that, or he would not have mapped it so.

Arctic voyagings north of Europe had by Barents's time disposed of the theory of this land-bridge, but the possibility still remained that Greenland might extend eastward far enough to make Spitsbergen a part of it, and that the old land-bridge might thus have some basis in fact. Purchas in his *Pilgrimes* records voyage after voyage to "Greenland," meaning Spitsbergen,[16] as well as several voyages to the Greenland we now know. The two were regarded as one land.

Once the existence of the rich whaling, sealing, and fishing grounds off Spitsbergen became known, it appeared as a prize worth grabbing. The Dutch had first claim by reason of discovery and

---

* This to me is one of the most compelling reasons for accepting the Zeno Narrative as genuine. Had Nicolò II been perpetrating a hoax he would (living as he did in Venice, an important center of cartography) have used more modern maps as his basis, and not have passed on geographical concepts which were by that time obsolete and "no longer on the map."

naming. An English expedition in 1613 took possession of a part of Spitsbergen and named it King James His Newland, but the claim could never be made to stick. Additionally some of the English began making the baseless assertion that the archipelago had actually been discovered in 1553, long before Barents, by Sir Hugh Willoughby on his voyage to discover a Northeast Passage past Russia, and many English insisted doggedly on calling it "Willoughby Land." But for the most part they called it Greenland.[17]

Rival English and Dutch claims led to some tricky diplomatic maneuvering, but as the Dutch gradually established effective control of the harbors the English claim was allowed to lapse. By the 1640s the Dutch were in complete control of the Spitsbergen waters, and exploiting them to fullest advantage. Extensive works for salting fish and rendering blubber were set up on the shore, and there came into being the remarkable Arctic town of *Smeerenburg* ("Blubberville"), which provided lodgings, taverns, and other entertainments for the workers and was during the short summer season a wild, wide-open frontier town where money flowed like schnapps. Then during the long winter it would be deserted, except for a few caretakers, until spring brought the fleets back again.[18]

Maps of the seventeenth century generally showed Spitsbergen as gradually trending westerly toward Greenland. The two were supposed to be one, but it was not customary to make a hypothetical drawing of the unknown connecting coastline.

Mention has been made in Chapter 6 of the hydrographer Joseph Moxon and his meeting during the 1650s with a Dutch sailor just returned from the "Greenland" fishing grounds, who claimed to have sailed past the North Pole; and mention has also been made of the fact that Moxon's "Greenland" meant Spitsbergen. The reader will now understand how this misidentification came about. On a map published in 1675, Joseph Moxon showed the actual Greenland as Groenlandia, and Spitsbergen as Greenland. The area between, and beyond toward Europe, is vaguely designated, but looks like a sketchy attempt at showing the old discredited land-bridge, which hardly accords with Moxon's acceptance of the Dutch sailor's tale of sailing past "Greenland" to the North Pole. But so it appears, and the lettering of the name "Greenland" is made to straggle across the map almost to "Nova Zembla" [*sic*].*

These identifications of Spitsbergen with Greenland implied a long eastward extension of the Greenland coast. One map of the same period commits an equivalent error to the west. The Nicolas Visscher map, mentioned in Chapter 6, causes the west coast of Greenland to curve westward at about 78° N, past the northern end of Baffin Island, and then to loop southward, to hook up with the western shores of Hudson Bay. If this were true, as we have seen, it would have eliminated any possibility of a Northwest Passage.

By the 1670s the Spitsbergen fishing and whaling grounds petered out from overexploitation. The Dutch frequented these waters less and less, and Spitsbergen was no one's land for two-and-a-half centuries, until Norway made its claim effective in 1925, but of this more later. Meanwhile, a Dutch skipper named Willem de Vlamingh, in search of new whaling grounds, sailed north clear round Spitsbergen. This disposed of any ideas of Spitsbergen as connected with Greenland. Vlamingh incidentally sailed north to 82° 10', the highest northern latitude to be reached by any European until 1827, when William Parry's expedition in search of the North Pole reached a latitude of 82° 45'.

By the early eighteenth century, the differentiation between Spitsbergen and Greenland was clear, and Greenland, though its coastlines were as yet imperfectly known, assumed something like its proper shape on the map. But Greenland still had a few moves to make.

There was still the mythical Green Island, originating as a duplication of Greenland, which remained on the maps in the North Atlantic, and usually in American waters, all through the eighteenth

---

* The name of this island is correctly Novaya Zemlya (Russian, "new land"). The erroneous Latinized form "Nova Zembla" raises the question of where was the original Zembla for which it was named? There is a story that during the 1920s a group of Italian observers managed to get admitted to a closed League of Nations session by representing themselves as delegates from "Zembla."

century and well into the nineteenth. By the mid-1800s it had dwindled to a suppositious Green Rock.

As previously mentioned, the American explorer Elisha Kent Kane reached the north coast of Greenland in 1854, and reported open sea beyond. The German geographer August Petermann was one of the chief upholders of the Open Polar Sea hypothesis, largely based on Kane's report. But, rather inconsistently, Petermann also promulgated during the 1860s the theory that the still-unexplored northern end of Greenland might extend northwestward, clear past the North Pole, to terminate in a headland just north of Point Barrow, Alaska. The only maps to show Greenland thus were those of Petermann's drawing, but the notion was not finally laid to rest till 1900, when Peary's explorations made the true northern end of Greenland known.[19]

In fact, Greenland was not fully and properly in place until the twentieth century. Even then, it still veered around a little. Writing in 1920, the Scottish explorer Rudmose Brown stated that whalers of his country still referred to Spitsbergen as Greenland.[20]

The Green Rock mentioned above also faded from the maps. But its actual nonexistence was never made clear. William H. Babcock, the authority on mythical Atlantic islands, went so far as to check with the United States Hydrographic Office as to whether they had any knowledge of it. Their reply indicated disbelief, but did mention (on the authority of one "Captain Tulloch of New Hampshire") the story of one Captain Coombs, skipper of the *Pallas* out of Bath, Maine, who reported sighting Green Rock. According to him, it was a large rock covered with green moss, which at first sighting he took for the bottom of a capsized ship.* The depth of the sea adjoining was sounded as 1500 fathoms.[21]

Since not every inch of the Atlantic has been combed, it is possible that something describable as a Green Rock does exist, coincidentally with the mythical one. But its existence seems to remain unproved.

---

* Babcock's account gives no bearings for the rock, and no date for either the voyage or the Hydrographic Office's letter. His book was published in 1922.

Finally, two more or less contemporary displacements of Greenland remain to be mentioned.

In the year 1194 a voyage out of Iceland discovered land somewhere to the northward, and named it Svalbard. Most likely this was some part of the east coast of Greenland, or possibly the formidable craggy island now called Jan Mayen.[22] But from the 1890s, seven centuries after the discovery, the government of Norway officially insisted that Svalbard was Spitsbergen, as reason for laying a claim on the basis of original Norse discovery. This identification is highly doubtful, to put it mildly. But in 1925 the League of Nations ratified Norway's claim to Spitsbergen, and since that time this arctic archipelago has had the official name of Svalbard—a name that apparently began as applying to a part of Greenland.

And while writing the first draft of this chapter, I first heard the report of the explorer David Humphreys' surveying expedition in Greenland in 1966, that proved that existing maps of Greenland are too large by some 300,000 square miles. Has this finally stabilized Greenland, or is it just the latest of its peregrinations? Time will give the answer, undoubtedly. But it does appear that, even in the age of space, the age of romance in the geography of our earth is still not over.

CHAPTER 10.

The Maybe of Mayda

Some places are no longer on the map because physically they no longer exist, at least above water. There is no solid historical or geographical evidence for the existence of Atlantis or Lemuria or any other of the lost continents beloved of cultists (which is not to say that they did not exist). But it is true that a good many islands, and strips of coastline, and at least one city,* which were once on the map, now lie at the bottom of the sea.

This study is not concerned with them, except peripherally. But it should be mentioned that between the category of vanished islands and that of fabulous islands there lies a shadowy category of dubious vanished islands.[1] The difference is brought out by comparing the instances of two South Pacific cases, those of Tuanaki and Sarah Ann Island.

Tuanaki comprised a group of three small islands in the Cook archipelago, within two days' sail of the Island of Mangaia. They were inhabited by a Polynesian people as skilled in seafaring as any of their brothers throughout the Pacific. In 1916 the Polynesian Society of Honolulu

---

* Port Royal, once capital of Jamaica and a notorious pirate hangout, sank in an earthquake in 1692, the only authentic historical case of a submerged city.

Nineteenth-century German engraving of the birth of a volcanic island.

published the account of a sailor who had visited Tuanaki in 1842, and spent six days there. The people, according to this witness, were peaceful and friendly, loved to dance and sing, and knew nothing of war. But two years later, in 1844, a group of English missionaries were dispatched to Tuanaki, and their schooner combed the entire area of sea without finding the islands.

Some time within that two years, the isles of Tuanaki sank, or blew up, or were in some manner destroyed. And since the island people were expert seamen, and no islanders survived to bring the news, the destruction must have occurred with great suddenness. The only Tuanakians known to have been alive after 1842 were a few who had earlier emigrated to Rarotonga, and some of them are said to have lived until the twentieth century.[2]

Compare this with the case of Sarah Ann Island, long shown on the maps at about 175° W, and just north of the equator. In 1932 astronomers became interested in this island as an advantageous site from which to view the impending total eclipse of the sun. American Navy vessels were dispatched to search for it, and found nothing. The island was removed from the maps, and the astronomical observations made instead from the nearby Canton and Enderbury Islands, which as a result of this international venture have since been under joint United States-British ownership.[3]

The difference should now be clear. There is no reasonable doubt that Tuanaki did exist, and did cease to exist within a time span that can be roughly pinpointed. As against this, there is no clear evidence that Sarah Ann Island ever did exist, and no real indication of when or how it got onto the map. To the question, "Did it sink?" the answer is, "Probably—if it did exist." In Chapter 5 we have already dealt with a few more of such doubtful cases.

This has been by way of leading up to the point that there is one island, no longer on the map, which has until recently been regarded by geographers as purely mythical. It now appears, however, that the island was real, and may have sunk.

The Island of Mayda was the last survivor of the mythical isles that once dotted maps of the North Atlantic. A Rand McNally map was still showing it as late as 1906. Some might maintain that this long existence of Mayda on the maps constitutes an argument for its actual existence, but the point will not hold. We have already encountered the mythical Brazil Rock which lingered, from pure inertia, after belief in the Island of Breasil had faded; and also the remnant of a misplaced Greenland which survived as Green Rock, its mythicality unaffected by the possibility that there might actually exist something to which the name could literally apply.

We have also seen something of the conservatism of cartographers, and their bad habit of copying each other. In the sixteenth and seventeenth centuries, it was always possible that some new feature on the map owed its existence to some unrecorded sailor's report. By the nineteenth century, this was no longer true. Cartographers based their maps on the reports of officially organized expeditions, not on random rumor from those who claimed to have been there. And we seem to have no record of anyone's claiming actually to have landed on Mayda.

A far more cogent argument is that the island, which finally came to be known as Mayda, underwent several changes of name on the maps over the centuries. This is much more likely to be true of an actual island than of a traditional one, for in the latter case retention of the name forms part of the tradition.

But, if the name changed, how do we know that we are dealing with the same island? From its location, for one thing. On medieval maps, as on modern ones, the effort was made to place islands and other physical features in the proper place—as nearly as possible. And, for another, from its shape. The form of the island varied from a stylized crescent, with horns pointing north, on medieval maps, to a rough circle with a prominent indentation on its northern side, on maps of the early modern period.

So, whatever it is called, when we meet with an island of this form in the Atlantic to the west of southern Brittany, and southwest of Ireland, we can be assured that it is Mayda.

Its first appearance on any map still extant was on the one drawn in 1367 by the Pizigani brothers. On this it is called *Brazir*, obviously indicating some sort of association with Breasil. But the two are not identical, for this same map (already discussed in Chapter 4) shows Breasil as well, located to the west of Ireland and referred to, apparently, as "Harmful." There is obviously some duplication involved here, and available sources give no explanation for it. In any case, what later became Mayda first appeared on the map as a confusion with Breasil, but indicated as a separate island, and that island was there to stay for a long time. On later maps, it was to appear in some association with Breasil.

On the Pizigani map, the island appears to be a place to avoid. Three Breton ships (identifiable as such by their barred ensigns, the device of the port of Nantes) are shown in the vicinity, and one of them is in dire distress. It is half submerged, stern first, by some sort of octopoid sea monster, and a dragon flies over it with a man in its mouth. The map bears an inscription, written close to the island, which would probably explain this association with sea monsters, if only it could be read. It is faded and blurred into illegibility, but a reference to dragons can be made out, as well as two others possibly referring to Arabs.

The island next appears on the Catalan map of 1375, where it is called Mam. And from the fourteenth century to the sixteenth it usually bore the name of Mam or Man. The conjecture has been made that this island was discovered, or imagined, first by Irish seamen, who named it for the Isle of Man in the Irish Sea, but there seems to be no evidence to support this. Other guesses, likewise unsubstantiated, have derived the name from a variety of Arabic words. The point is of interest, but not crucial, since the later name of Mayda is equally unexplained.

Not all fourteenth- and fifteenth-century maps used the name Mam or Man, and the other names used are similarly beyond explanation. The Pinelli map of 1384 makes it something that looks like *Jonzele*, but should probably be read *I.Onzele*, in view of the tendency of medieval cartographers to prefix an abbreviatory *I* or *Y to* the name of an island.* The great Andrea Bianco map of 1448 calls it Bentusla. Some maps showed it but did not call it anything, which would seem likely only in the case of an island that was not only real but very well known, at least to sailors.

This island, however named, came to have a fixed association with Breasil. The latter was shown to the west of Ireland, the former roughly due south of it and to the west of Brittany. Wherever the one went on the map, the other followed. Some maps placed them close to shore, others well out in the Atlantic. A couple of maps of the 1380s brought the two islands closer together than was warranted by any precedent, but later cartographers restored them to their traditional position.

The next development of any significance came with Martin Waldseemüller's 1513 edition of Ptolemy. On one of the maps accompanying it he represented the island, not in its conventional cres-

---

* It could signify English *island*, German *Insel*, French *île*, Italian *isola*, Spanish *isla*, Portuguese *ilha*, Latin *insula*, or Gaelic *innis*.

cent shape, but as a roughly drawn circle with a conspicuous dent in its northern littoral, and he gave it the name of Asmaidas, the first occurrence of the name in something recognizably like the form it was to assume. Waldseemüller was a very important, and very assiduous and well-informed, geographer. Was he working on the basis of some new information received, or some old information then recently uncovered? Unfortunately, we no longer have any way to tell.

An anonymous Portuguese map of about 1520 makes it Mayd, and the Prunes map of 1553 seems to be the first to use the spelling of "Mayda," which later became standard. But with only two or three exceptions, from the early sixteenth century on, cartographers agreed in calling the island Mayda, Maida, Maidas, or some equally recognizable variation. However, they did not agree on its location. Some kept it close to Europe, and others moved it westward to the American side of the Atlantic.

This latter fact has led some students, notably William H. Babcock, to speculate that belief in the island of Mayda (by whatever name) originated in some pre-Columbian knowledge of some part of

Section of a map of 1513, showing (1) Mayda as "asmaidas," and (2) Breasil as "obrassil."

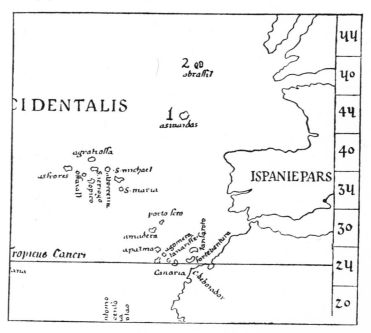

the New World; that its position close to Europe on old maps was due to the cartographers' ignorance; and that when America became known, the island was moved back to its proper place. Of course, almost every North Atlantic geographical myth has been suggested as reflecting some pre-Columbian knowledge of America, and some of the attributions are quite possibly correct. But in the case of Mayda, as we shall see, there is another equally probable explanation.

On the Nicolay map of 1560, the island is placed in the latitude of northern Newfoundland and given the strange name of *I man orbolunda*. The reversion to the earlier name of Man is obvious, the word *orbolunda* less so. It would appear to mean, in bad late Latin, "orb of the moon." If this is correct, it may constitute some sort of reference to the crescent shape which the island had been given on so many earlier (and hence traditional) maps.

The two greatest of sixteenth-century cartographers, Mercator and Ortelius, did not show Mayda at all. But in the position traditionally assigned to it—west of Brittany and south of Breasil—they did show a fair-sized crescent-shaped island to which they gave the name of Vlaenderen. This easily recognizable version of "Flanders" raises some interesting points, in view of the fact that both Mercator and Ortelius were Flemish. Was the naming merely a matter of some sort of national pride? Did some unrecorded Flemish skipper discover the island—or rediscover it, after it had come to be supposed to lie in American waters—and give it a name which these cartographers picked up from him and saw fit to perpetuate on their maps? The latter supposition is not likely, since the name Vlaenderen never caught on, and was used only by Mercator and Ortelius, while Mayda under that name survived on the map to live merrily for more than three centuries to follow.

All through the seventeenth and eighteenth centuries, virtually every map showing the Atlantic Ocean included Mayda, south of Iceland and west of Brittany. During the nineteenth century, some maps did and others did not, and as the century passed more and more came to drop it. Its inclusion on the Rand McNally map of 1906 was most likely done in a spirit of "Let's put it in, just to be sure."

We have seen that Mayda was atypical of mythical or fabulous islands in a number of respects: its changes of name, its taken-for-granted character on some maps, its lack of any literary or legendary sources to explain either its names or its appearance. We have noted, too, the standard crescent shape, or indented-circle shape, maintained for it on the maps. This in itself is not too significant; it was the practice of medieval cartographers to stylize Atlantic islands as circles, rectangles, clover leaves, and the like. Still, Mayda has shown characteristics more in keeping with a real island than an imaginary one. And this leads us to the modern evidence.

On August 22, 1948, the freighter *American Scientist*, bound for London from New Orleans, was in latitude 46° 23′ N, longitude 37° 20′ W, or roughly below the southern tip of Greenland, and *due west of southern Brittany*. The charts showed a depth of 2400 fathoms, but for reasons best known to himself, the captain of the *American Scientist* gave orders to check the depth with sonar, and got a reading of only 20 fathoms.

The ship circled the area twice, with sonar readings being carefully checked and noted, and the second check bore out the first. There was an unnoted rise of land not too far below the surface at that point, about 28 miles in diameter, and varying in depth from 15 to 35 fathoms. Beyond this, readings indicated a drop to the usual mid-Atlantic deep.

The *American Scientist* radioed a report of her findings, which was picked up by another American freighter, the *Southland*, following the same course two days behind. On reaching the area, the skipper of the *Southland* ran a sonar check on the *American Scientist* report, and found it substantially true. The *Southland* got readings of 29 to 35 fathoms, but did verify the existence of the underwater land, and found it to have on its north side an indentation which might have been a bay, where the depth was 90 fathoms.

So, it appears that something does exist, though now a bit below water, in a location west of Brittany which could fit Mayda. It should be remembered that medieval navigators knew how to figure latitude quite well, though longitude was a problem. Their placement of the island in the latitude of southern Brittany is quite plausible, and

Rockall, the only actual island in the North Atlantic area where so many nonexistent islands were placed by early geographers.

their estimate of how far west it was would have been a matter of dead reckoning, which cartographers might have preferred to underestimate, thus bringing it too close to the European coast.*

An island about 28 miles across, in the mid-Atlantic, uninhabited

---

* This rather startling information may be found in the United States Hydrographic Office's *Notices to Mariners*, Nos. 32 and 42.[4]

and desolate, without resources, perhaps an above-water projection of one of the tremendous submarine peaks known to exist in that area,* of interest to nobody but worth recording as a navigational hazard, placed on the map from the report of some venturesome medieval skipper who discovered it in course of his probing into the dark Atlantic—we are hardly in the world of fantasy in imagining this. And that some suboceanic disturbance might have caused it to sink, not to depths unthinkable but just enough that it would no longer be seen and that ships could safely sail over it—this also seems not too fantastic for belief. There may actually have existed the supposedly fabulous island of Mayda. Just maybe.

---

* One such still exists above water: the peak of Rockall, in about latitude 58° N, longitude 14° W, or about 400 miles west of the Hebridean island of Lewis.

C H A P T E R   1 1 .

Three Special Cases

Three more areas of one-time importance remain to be considered. We shall take them in chronological order, since they date, respectively, from classical Greece, the Age of Exploration, and the last century.

Rhipaean Mountains

Everyone surely knows the legend of Jason. Everyone has read of the voyage of the *Argo* in search of the Golden Fleece, of how Jason with his crew of fifty heroes reached the land of Colchis; of how, with the aid of the king's sorceress daughter, Medea, he slew the dragon guarding the Golden Fleece, and then sailed away with the fleece and the girl.[1]

Modern scholars believe that Jason did exist and did voyage, and that Jason's was the first early Greek voyage into unknown waters of which any record remains.[2] And it is plain that the story of Jason was regarded as fact by the Greeks, and that it took a powerful hold on their imagination.

Just when Jason lived and sailed is anyone's guess, but

apparently it was before the time of Homer,* for in the incident of the Clashing Rocks (which slammed together to smash any ship passing between) in the *Odyssey*, it was stated that only one ship had ever successfully sailed between them, and that it was "the *Argo*, which all men remember." However, Homer said nothing of the Golden Fleece or the direction of Jason's voyage. The poet Hesiod, of approximately Homer's time, also did not mention the fleece, but did bring Medea into the story for the first time on record.

The association of Jason's voyage with the Golden Fleece and the land of Colchis is first found in the poet Mimnermus of Colophon, of the seventh century B.C. There is little point in listing all the obscure Greek poets who treated of the legend, and added to it. Suffice to say that all three of the great Greek dramatists—Aeschylus, Sophocles, and Euripides—wrote plays bearing on some aspect of the Jason legend, the best known today being Euripides' *Medea*.

The Jason legend as we now generally know it—complete with Amazons, harpies, fire-breathing bulls, and a ship's crew consisting of all the famed heroes of Greek myth—first emerges in the *Argonautica* of about the second century B.C., written by Apollonius of Rhodes, a grammarian who was later to become the head librarian of Alexandria. He attempted to do it in the style of the great Homeric epics, and his conscious archaism did not work; it can be compared with the bad pseudo-Biblical English affected by some authors of more modern times. This led to a rather nasty feud between Apollonius and his teacher, one Callimachus, who did not approve of such butchery of the Greek language.

A generation or so later, another Greek grammarian, Apollodorus, turned out a version of Apollonius's *Argonautica* in prose —of a more acceptable variety than Apollonius's poetry—and the Jason myth had taken its form for the ages. But in the hypercivilized Alexandrian world, and in the Roman world which was largely to draw its literary culture from Alexandrian sources, this was not enough. Old legends became of interest only for their possibilities of imaginative embroidery.

---

* Or at least it was so regarded in the sixth century B.C., when the Homeric epics were edited into the form in which we now have them.

Apollonius had added to the story the detail that Medea, to avert her father's pursuit of herself and Jason, killed her brother, cut him in pieces, and strewed them over the sea, thus forcing the king to slow down and collect his son for burial. Because of this fratricide, Jason's return voyage was slowed, and a wandering through all sorts of regions of wonder (*suivant* the *Odyssey*) was indicated.

By this time the Black Sea, traditional site of Jason's voyagings, was well known to the Greeks. The land of Colchis was standardly identified as the Caucasus, and the legend of the Golden Fleece was regarded by geographers as stemming from the Caucasian natives' practice, continued until modern times, of placing sheep's skins in the mountain streams to collect alluvial gold.[3] Insofar as the Jason story related to actual geography, the Greeks had by now placed it in its proper spot. What has to be considered, from Apollonius onward, is pure poetic fantasizing.

According to Apollonius, for example, this was the *Argo*'s homeward route: out of the Black Sea via a nonexistent channel which brought it across the Balkan peninsula into the Adriatic, then up the Po and into another channel to sail (across the Alps!) into the lakes of Gaul ("of marvelous size"), down the Rhone and around Italy (revisiting en route the sites of Ulysses' adventures), south to Africa, west to the Hesperides, then east again to Crete, and finally back to Greece.

This fantastic hash has nothing to do with geography. The learned of the time—and Apollonius, head librarian of Alexandria, was certainly learned—knew the face of the earth better than this. They certainly knew that there were no channels of open water cutting off the Balkan peninsula and the Italian peninsula from the mainland. To call this rearrangement "poetic license" may seem inadequate to the modern reader, but the sensibility of the times was quite different from our own, and in a way difficult for us to recapture, since it permitted any sort of tampering with the known world in order to produce a good story.*

---

* Or perhaps not so different at that. We today enjoy J. R. R. Tolkien's magnificent histories of Middle Earth, without worrying about the fact that they cannot be fitted into what we know of history and geography.

Several centuries later, these late Greek fantasies merged with the late Roman poetry, a product of that culture's decadence that found value only in stunts and displays of technical virtuosity. Those poets not exercised in mere word games usually applied their efforts to milking some new and amusing possibilities out of traditional classic material.

This is the background that produced the mad *Argonautica* of "Pseudo-Orpheus" (meaning somebody or other who used the pen name of Orpheus) of the fourth century A.D. The author was apparently trying to do just one more variation on Jason without violating the facts of geography that everyone knew. So instead of making that channel out of the Black Sea run eastward across the well-known Balkan peninsula, he ran it northward across the present Russia, a territory little known to Romans. After ten days' voyage north up this channel, Jason and his crew came out in the Cronian Sea, which apparently means the vaguely known sea to the north of Europe, and then sailed round past Ireland on their return to Greece. And in the course of this voyage, before emerging from the channel into the sea, Jason discovered the Rhipaean Mountains.

A location in northern Europe would be definitely indicated, if the story were to be taken seriously. And in medieval Europe, it was taken seriously. We have already noticed, in Chapter 9, Adam of Bremen's placement of Greenland "opposite the mountains of Sweden, or Rhiphaean Mountains." It appears thus that in the early Middle Ages the mountains of Scandinavia were identified with the fabled Rhipaeans. But as time passed, and the Hanseatic traders made Norway and Sweden better known, and it came to be found that the mountains of the area had no native name anything like that, geographers came to move the Rhipaeans farther eastward, into the unfamiliar cold northern region then inhabited only by a few nomadic tribes, and today constituting northern Russia.

Clement Adams, writing about 1555 of the earliest English contacts with the half-fabulous land of "Muscovy," had this to say on the subject:

Touching the Riphean [*sic*] mountains, whereupon the Snow lyeth continually, and where hence it was thought in times past that Tanais the river [the Don] did spring, and that the rest of the wonders of nature, which the Grecians fained and invented of old, were there to be seene: our men which lately came from thence, neither saw them, nor yet brought home any perfect relation of them, although they had remained there for the space of three months, and had gotten in that time some intelligence of the language of Muscovie.[4]

Adams then went on to describe the countryside of northern Russia, on the returned Englishmen's accounts, as flat and with few hills, which is an entirely correct description.

The question will arise: Could the idea of the Rhipaean Mountains have had its source in some early report of the Urals? The answer is: Most likely not. True, some vague knowledge of the Urals may in medieval times have helped keep belief in the Rhipaeans alive. But the late Greco-Roman author of the *Argonautica*, even assuming that he knew anything of the Urals, was not concerned with geography. His intent rather was to project the voyagings of Jason into a region sufficiently unknown to permit of its use as a locale for fantastic invention.

The Rhipaean Mountains present one instance of a geographical myth born of pure literary caprice. Early English contacts with Russia were chiefly by way of the northern coast, where these mountains were supposed to be, and English reports were largely responsible for discrediting them. Nevertheless, some conservative cartographers, copying each other, kept the Rhipaean Mountains on a few maps as late as the early 1700s.

California

As I sit typing these lines, in my cottage beneath the trees, under a glowing California sun, it would seem to me that no place on earth could be less mythical, and more a solid part of the here and now, than California. Still, there was once the myth of the Island of California, and, before that, California existed as a fabulous island.

For a beginning, we must go back approximately nine hundred years, to the time in which the *Chanson de Roland* was put together in the form in which we have it now. The mighty deeds of Charlemagne's heroic warrior Roland in battle with the Saracens of Spain* in the late ninth century had been remembered for some two centuries in songs of war and glory. But late in the eleventh century, a knightly poet of Provence, about whom nothing is actually known except that his name is supposed to have been Théroulde or Turoldus, reworked the traditional material into epic form, in a manner more in keeping with the sensibility of his time. This meant dressing up the simple tales of combat and valor with all sorts of chivalric stylizations and fantastic embroideries.

One example of this catering to the taste of the times was a passing mention of an imaginary land of Califerne, beyond the Indies, where griffins and Amazons were to be found.[5] The name Califerne may be a coined word; if it is supposed to have a Latin derivation, it would mean "hot furnace," the relevance of which is not quite clear. The *Chanson de Roland* apparently did not give rise to any serious belief in the existence of such a country.

It was used once again, also as a fictional device, in the *Deeds of Esplandian*, an overblown romance of knights and fair ladies, by an unknown author, published in Spain about 1497 (being, incidentally, a prime example of the ridiculous tale of chivalry that Cervantes later satirized in *Don Quixote*). Here, the name California assumed its modern form for the first time. California is represented as to the "right hand" (the east) of the Indies, and once more as the home of griffins and Amazons, only this time the Amazons are black.[6]

This silly novel had a great vogue in Spain, and apparently made everyone familiar with the name California. In 1532 Cortes sent out an expedition which crossed Mexico to the Pacific coast and discovered a long barren peninsula lying farther westward. Exactly why they named this peninsula California is not known—it may have been some sort of "in-group" joke—but the source of the name is clear. In any case, the name stuck, and as the Spaniards pushed farther up the western American coast the name moved with them.

California's career as fable was not quite over. As late as about

---

* Actually, Roland was killed in battle with the Basques, but the *Chanson* is chiefly concerned with warfare with the Moors.

1550, the Portuguese author Vasco de Lobeira was to copy old sources and attribute griffins and black Amazons to the "island" of California. But this was fiction, not geography. By Lobeira's time, California was shown quite correctly on the maps as a peninsula of Western North America, and so it appeared on the maps throughout

Section of the Castillo map of 1541, showing the Gulf of California in an approximately correct manner.

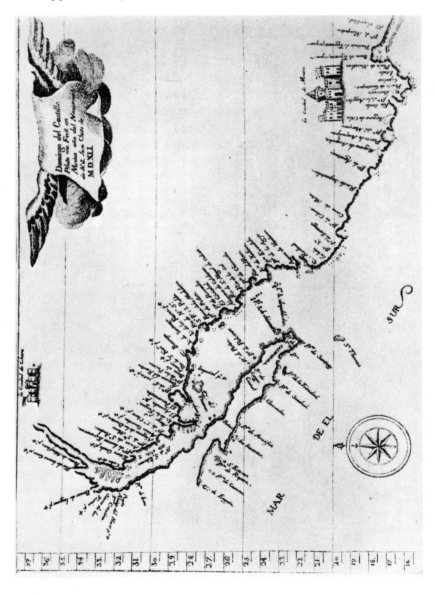

the sixteenth century. Then something happened. Let me quote from Herman Moll's *System of Geography* of 1709.

CALIFORNIA, or NEW-ALBION, is in the South Sea, on the back of *New-Mexico*, and it was long dubious whether a Peninsula or an Island, but at last the Spaniards sail'd quite round, and made a Map of it, which shews it to extend from 24 to 36 Degrees of North Latitude, lying North-west and South-east, being above 500 leagues in length, the breadth near 150 leagues, in 40 Degrees Latitude, for somewhat to the Southward it grows narrower, and continues tapering off all the way to the end. The Streight which parts it from the Continent is all along 30, 40, or 50 Leagues over, and even more in many Places, but every where shoal, and many small scattering Islands in it, which renders the Passage very dangerous, and together with the vehement Cold of the Northern part hinder'd the full Discovery of it for many Years; for the Discoveries have found it colder in 50 Degrees of North Latitude in *America* than in 60 in *Europe*, and so proportionably. All the Island is inhabited by abundance of *Indian* Nations, who either go naked, or at best use only some small covering of Mats, or Skins. Their way of living, and Superstitions much the same, as has been said, of other Northern *Americans*, besides that, to say the Truth, the Inland of it has never been discover'd, nor have any made so long a stay upon the Coasts as to know much of it. To this Day the Spaniards have made no Conquests in it that we have heard of. . . . This makes it evident that the Island is not worth their trouble, tho' so large. . . . This is as much as need be said of California till better known, and for the small Islands about it, the Name of them may suffice, there being nothing in them remarkable.

Even today, this much of Moll's account remains true: that Californians tend to wear no more clothes than necessary; that their way of life and superstitions are much like those of other North Americans; that those who have not stayed long on these coasts are likely not to know much of it; and that, contrary to common belief, it can get uncomfortably cold in northern California. As to there being "nothing remarkable" in the offshore islands, this would appear to be no longer true; except for Santa Catalina, they are now United States Government property, and unauthorized personnel are not allowed to land there.

More seriously, and referring to the peninsula of Baja California, which was what Moll had in mind, its desolate interior scarcely is worth anyone's while. And it is also true that it was another fifty years before the Spanish began taking a serious interest in more than the coastal areas of California.

But Baja California is not and has never been an island. Moll's description has been selected for its vividness, but any geography of the period circa 1630–1710 reads essentially the same. And any map of this same period would show the Island of California as a vast sprawling monstrosity off the west coast of North America, extending from the Tropic of Cancer to approximately latitude 45° N. But earlier maps, as I said before, made California a peninsula.

The whole trouble resulted from the report of Sebastián Vizcaíno, after his voyage of 1602–1603. He mentioned sailing into the Gulf of California, exploring it, and then sailing out—but he failed to mention that he had sailed back by the way he had come. Some

Section of the Henry Briggs map of 1625, the first to show California as an island.

unknown, presumably Spanish, cartographer jumped to the conclusion that Vizcaíno had held a steady course and sailed out of the north end of the Gulf, and that therefore California was an island. The first map known to us that shows California as an island is the one published by Henry Briggs in 1625. He attributed his information to an earlier Spanish map captured by the Dutch, which is now lost.[7]

It was an Austrian Jesuit of scientific bent, named Franz Kuhn and known to history as Padre Kino, who disposed of the idea of California as an island. As a missionary in the present area of northern Sonora and southern Arizona, he traversed the country extensively, and established beyond any doubt that there was no strait separating Baja California from the mainland. But his findings did not become known in Europe till after his death in 1711, and even after that, for a few years, the conservatism of cartographers kept the Island of California on the map. But by the 1720s, Baja California was once more being mapped correctly.[8]

Crocker Land

In 1818 Commander John Ross of the Royal Navy headed an Arctic expedition, to the westward of Greenland, in search of the Northwest Passage. Among the concrete results of this voyage were the rediscovery and re-exploration of the east coast of Baffin Island, and the naming of it for its first explorer, Captain William Baffin, who had surveyed its coast to its full extent in 1616.

To the north of the island, Baffin had found a channel of open water, which he named Lancaster Sound. Ross confirmed the discovery, and made the name official on the maps. Lancaster Sound appeared the most promising lead to a Northwest Passage, and Ross pressed his search westerly through it—but for one day only. Later, back in London, Ross reported that Lancaster Sound did not afford a waterway past the island, but was closed off to the west by a span of land linking Baffin Island with Devon Island to the north. A notable feature of this newly found land was an impressive chain of mountains, which he had named the Croker Mountains, in honor of a secretary in the Admiralty.

It seemed hard to doubt the word of an officer of the experience and probity of John Ross. The hitch was that no other member of the expedition could see these mountains, and to a man they denied that there were any. All agreed that there had been open water and clear sailing ahead, that they had felt themselves on the verge of discovering something, and had been eager to push on. Ross, they charged, had lost his nerve, and concocted a flimsy excuse to turn back.

In official circles Ross was held in too high an esteem for this charge to be believed, and it was concluded that he had been the victim of some sort of optical illusion. But the rumor that Ross had

Padre Kino's map, showing Baja California correctly as a peninsula.

turned yellow spread rapidly in London, and did the Admiralty no good, so another expedition was dispatched in 1819 to clear up the matter. It appeared that John Ross's eyesight was not to be trusted, so command was given this time to William Parry, who had been Ross's lieutenant on the expedition of the year before.

Parry retraced Ross's course, and sailed toward his reported Croker Mountains. It appears from his account that tension mounted agonizingly as they neared the alleged site of the range; all hands crowded to the best vantage points that they could find. Finally Parry checked his longitude, and found that he had sailed farther westward than Ross. There were no mountains in sight, so the Croker Mountains were written off as a myth.[9]

It would take us too far afield to describe in detail how Parry's expedition wintered in the ice, and of how Parry, expecting this, had stocked his two ships with what seemed indicated: musical instruments, theatrical props so that the men could stage plays, a little press for printing a ship's newspaper. The following spring, the expedition explored the coasts of Melville Island, then returned home with the news that there were no Croker Mountains.

The name "Crocker Land" chosen as title for this section of the chapter is an amalgam of two Arctic myths, both having more to do

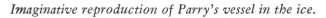

Imaginative reproduction of Parry's vessel in the ice.

with optics than with geography *per se*. Although the Croker Mountains never appeared on any map, so far as I know (they were wiped out almost as soon as reported), and although there is no real reason to believe that they have anything to do, except coincidentally, with Peary's Crocker Land, which was discovered some ninety years later and over 1000 miles away, there may be a remote connection worth exploring.

In 1906, on his next-to-the-last push toward the North Pole, Robert E. Peary, in a latitude of 86° N, caught sight through his glasses of a distant land beyond the pack ice. Visibility was good, and he could distinctly see the towering peaks against the sky, in a region to the northwest of Ellesmere Land. He gave his discovery the name of Crocker Land. Why he selected this name is not clear. Peary seldom explained the names he bestowed, so the reason he picked this particular name is not known. Although it seems unlikely that Ross's "Croker" had any direct bearing on his "Crocker," Peary was a man well versed in the literature of the Arctic, and he was fully aware of what Ross had reported. The sighting of a range of unknown mountains may have brought the name to his mind by some process of subliminal association. There is no question of Peary's supposing that he had rediscovered Ross's mountains.

Peary made no attempt to investigate his discovery. His objective was the North Pole, not some unimportant icebound island. On this voyage he came within 175 miles of the Pole, and on his next attempt in 1909 he made it.

Crocker Land appeared, in vaguely indicated form, on a few maps of the early twentieth century, but not for long. Donald B. Macmillan in 1914 headed an expedition in search of it, sailed to the area indicated by Peary, and found nothing but ice. Two hundred miles further westward he did sight a distant range of mountains, but found that they retreated as he advanced.

He, and Peary before him, had seen a mirage, of the so-called looming type, in which the objects reflected are optically brought up from below the horizon to be seen as if at a great distance. It is doubtful that this is the explanation for Ross's mountains, because a genuine mirage would have been visible to others besides Ross him-

A nineteenth-century's artist's conception of an arctic mirage, such as might have deceived Peary.

self, and his crew members said that they could see nothing. Most likely the Admiralty was right in assuming that it was a defect in Ross's own vision. But the Crocker Land of Peary was a mirage, in the literal sense.[10]

This dropped Crocker Land from the map, but did not quite close the question. Mirages are reflections of solid objects, and this one too had to have a real-life original. The 1925–1926 aerial Arctic explorations of Richard E. Byrd and Floyd Bennett had as one of their objectives the search for Crocker Land, in which they were unsuccessful. As late as 1936, William H. Hobbs, in his biography of Peary, mapped a possible position for Crocker Land, should it exist.[11] Even today—despite atomic submarines, jets, and the Great Circle route—all the subpolar areas are not perfectly known, and somewhere among them the original of Crocker Land may still be awaiting discovery.

But it now can never be identified with certainty. Both Peary's and Macmillan's accounts are too vague and general, and neither man took photographs, and there are a lot of mountainous areas in the islands that fringe the Pole. We simply do not know what Crocker Land is supposed to look like, but it may be there.

Epilogue

It seems somehow fitting to close the account with these three last instances, since they illustrate the three most common origins for geographical myths: sheer fantasy, misinterpretation or exaggeration of factual reports, and mistakes made by all-too-human explorers. There is also a fourth reason, caused by erroneous conceptions of the physical world, as in the cases of the Northwest Passage and Terra Australis Incognita. If the reader looks closely, he will find that every case treated herein can be traced to one of these causes, or to a combination of them.

Thus, El Dorado arose from exaggeration of an actual Indian custom, plus fantasy in the form of the lies told by the Tupinambas. Friesland arose from misreading of a badly damaged old document and an old map. The Seven-Cities-Cíbola-Quivira myth arose from pure fancy: first the wishful thinking of medieval Spaniards under Moslem rule, then the beautiful yarn of Esteban, then the calculated lie of the Indian called "Turk," then the "creative lying" of Gómara.

The Northwest Passage as a concept originated in a wrong idea of the nature of the world, but as an object of quest was kept going by such explorers' errors as Verrazano's "isthmus" and by such misunderstandings as the transferral of Anian to the American coast. Norumbega evidently had its origin in the misapplication of the name of a river to an entire territory. The Greenland-Europe land-bridge arose out of a misinterpretation of the writings of Adam of Bremen—although we must understand the difficulty of making any logical interpretation of Adam's confused material.

Then, too, it must be mentioned that along with the mythical there is the doubtful—Mayda, the Auroras, Dougherty Island—where the distinction is not always clear. In most cases, however, the mythical is not hard to recognize. The reader has the idea, and can make his own interpretations. And there is no point in running through the entire roster. Of greater interest is the situation as it exists today. Are the factors that in the past placed nonexistent regions on the map still operating?

Well, lies are still told, and sometimes believed, and could influence geography for a time. But the distinction between truth and fiction is now more marked than it once was. There is little chance today that an imaginary island will stray out of a novel and onto the map.

People can still misinterpret what they read. But geography is now in the hands of scholars who use established, rigorous methods, and they are much less likely to repeat each other's mistakes. In cartography, as mentioned before, doubtful locations are still given, just to be safe, which means that a few myths may be still haunting the map.

Explorers are still capable of making mistakes. But, in this age of teamwork, we are not usually dependent upon one man's report for geographical data, and of course modern methods and modern instruments have done away with the situation in which John Ross's own bad eyesight could create an entire new range of mountains.

As for erroneous concepts of the world, it may sound rash and dogmatic, but it can be stated that they are no longer prevalent—at least in any form likely to influence geography. However open to criticism modern science may be in some of its reaches, it does seem to have a clear and accurate picture of the surface of the world we live on, to the extent that the said world has been explored. And as to its habitable portions, the exploration is practically complete; or at least complete enough to make it certain that there are no Quiviras, no Norumbegas, no Unknown Continents waiting to be found.

However, most of the globe's surface is not habitable, or at least not to humans, or at least only under very special and costly conditions. Most of our world is ocean. And it would be a rash man indeed who would state that there is nothing more to discover in the great ocean.

Vast stretches of the ocean are still unknown—and I speak here only of surface phenomena, not of the depths. Ships, and airline traffic as well, keep to established routes. The days of loose sea-wandering are pretty well over, and there are stretches of ocean measurable in thousands of miles which are hardly visited once in a decade. It is literally true that there are oceanic regions, especially in the high latitude and in the Pacific, that were better known a century and a half ago, in the days of the whalers and sealers, than they are today. These sea tracts may still contain undiscovered islands, and they may still spawn mythical ones.

In fact, as to some of the minor isolated islands that maps place in the Pacific and sub-Antarctic regions, one searches in vain for a record of anyone's having visited them recently, as verification that they do exist.

So, this word to the romantically minded: The time of the quest into the blue is not yet past. And this word to the scientifically minded: The time is now past when myth of the crude sort is likely to be of any constitutive importance in geography.

Appendices

These constitute selections of little-known material having a bearing on the subject matter of this book. Possibly some of them could have been incorporated in the text, but this arrangement seemed simpler for the reader as well as for the author. There is a great deal more of such material, from around the fringes of historical geography, that would have been equally interesting, but is not directly germane to the present study. Perhaps next time . . . but meanwhile, the interested reader is referred to the rather numerous books cited in my endnotes, which will no doubt lead him on to others of equal interest.

Places "No Longer on the Map"

Here is a brief sampling, in no particular order, of places that for political reasons are "no longer on the map," though the areas the names once designated still exist.

NEW FRANCE, as everyone knows, was conquered by the British under General Wolfe in 1759. By the Treaty of Paris of 1763, France ceded the territory to Great Britain.

In 1922 SIBERIA was incorporated into the Russian Soviet Federated Socialist Republic, largest of the republics making up the USSR. However, in the Soviet Union as elsewhere, Siberia (*Sibirsk*) continues in use as a popular unofficial name for the territory.

BELGIAN CONGO had formerly been recognized (1885–1908) by international agreement as Congo Free State (it was during this period, as of about 1902, that Belgian abuse of the natives brought on an international scandal). In 1908 Belgium, already the dominant force in the so-called Free State, annexed the area, making it officially Belgian Congo. After its stormy attainment of independence in 1960, the former Belgian Congo became The Congo. This was confusing, since its neighbor to the northwest, until then part of French Equatorial Africa (no longer on the map) gained independence as Congo Republic. But the confusion ceased to exist in 1971, when The Congo, formerly Belgian Congo, changed its name to Zaire.

BALUCHISTAN, a former British protectorate west of India, has since 1948 been part of Pakistan.

COURLAND or KURLAND was from the mid-sixteenth century a semi-independent duchy subject to Poland, but the final partition of Poland in 1796 turned it over to Russia. After World War I it became independent as Latvia, which in 1940 was reincorporated into the Soviet Union.

HISPANIOLA was the Spanish name for the island of Haiti. After the decline of Spanish power, and the independence of SANTO DOMINGO (now the Dominican Republic) in 1843, the original Indian name of Haiti was restored to the island.

The name of SIAM in 1938 was officially changed to Thailand.

DAKOTA TERRITORY in 1889 was divided into North and South Dakota, which were admitted to statehood.

CHOSEN was the name of Korea during the period (1910-1945) of its occupation by Japan.

BURGUNDY was a more or less independent duchy until 1477, when it became a province of France. Following the French Revolution it was divided into a number of *départements*. The name Burgundy continues to be used loosely for the area producing the wine of that name.

THE VICEROYALTY OF NEW GRANADA, in the days of Spanish America, comprised the present Colombia, Venezuela, Ecuador, and part of Brazil. After Bolívar's victories it became independent, and was variously named and divided throughout the nineteenth century.

WESTERN RESERVE was a strip of territory south of Lake Erie and west of Pennsylvania, to which Connecticut laid claim according to the terms of her colonial charter, and refused in 1786 to cede to the Federal government. Open warfare between Connecticut and Pennsylvania almost resulted (it should be realized that in the early days of this country the various states regarded themselves as sovereign nations, and the United States only as a voluntary association, like the United Nations today), but in 1800 Connecticut gave up her claims to Western Reserve. It is now part of the state of Ohio.

The official name of PERSIA since 1935 has been Iran, historically the name of the plateau occupied by that kingdom.

THE ORANGE FREE STATE, result of the Great Trek of the South African Boers in 1842, was annexed by Great Britain in 1900. It has returned to the map—more recently, as one of the states comprising the Union of South Africa (the other U.S.A.).

By the Treaty of Saint Germain in 1919 and the Treaty of Trianon in 1920, THE EMPIRE OF AUSTRIA-HUNGARY, or DUAL MONARCHY (the latter a rather self-contradictory term in Latin) ceased to exist. It was divided into the modern states of Austria, Hungary, and Czechoslovakia, with some of its territory going to Poland, Yugoslavia, and Rumania.

The southern part of China around Canton was not conquered by

Genghis Khan, and comprised the independent kingdom of MENG-TSE until subjugated by Kublai Khan in 1277. It was reported by Marco Polo, and for long after appeared on European maps as *Manji, Mangi,* or *Mancy.*

EAST PRUSSIA was set up by the Treaty of Versailles as an outlying enclave of Germany, separated from it by the Polish Corridor. The German conquest of Poland in 1939 temporarily restored it to the *Vaterland,* but territorial seizure by the Russian Army in 1945 ended by incorporating most of it into Poland and the rest into the Soviet Union.

TANGANYIKA on attaining independence in 1962 changed its name to Tanzania.

The capital of China was historically named Peking, but in 1928 the name was changed to PEIPING. After the establishment of the Chinese People's Republic in 1949 the old name of Peking was revived, but American diplomatic and journalistic sources doggedly insisted on calling it "Peiping" up until recent years.

The three Guianas are traditionally mapped as "British, Dutch, and French," probably for the sake of symmetry; but the official name of DUTCH GUIANA is Surinam, and in recent years this has come to be recognized on most maps. Since 1966 BRITISH GUIANA has been the independent country of Guyana.

MADAGASCAR was a misnomer in the first place, being Marco Polo's mistaken version ("Madeigascar") of the East African port of Mogadisco. The name was given by the Portuguese Diego Dias to the large island east of Africa which he discovered in 1500. Since gaining independence from France in 1960, the island has had the name of Malagasy Republic.

The breakup of Genghis Khan's empire left the KHANATE OF THE GOLDEN HORDE in control of southern Russia, which control they maintained for about two centuries until Russia began coming into its own. Thereafter, the Mongol power dwindled to the KHANATE OF THE CRIM TATARS (not "Tartar"), a decreasingly important state on the north shores of the Black Sea, best known to history through the report of one Martin Bronovski, a Polish diplomat who visited them during the 1560s. In 1774 Russia recognized the independence of the Tatars of the Crimea, but nine years later Russia annexed the Crimea, and the KHANATE came to an end.

THE KINGDOM OF THE TWO SICILIES, or KINGDOM OF NAPLES AND SICILY, founded by the Norse adventurer Robert de Guiscard in the eleventh century, lost its existence when Garibaldi unified Italy in 1861.

Hawaii, by all early accounts, had a name renderable more like OWYHEE, and it is thus shown on early maps.

THE HOLY ROMAN EMPIRE (which, as we all know, Voltaire characterized as "neither holy, nor Roman, nor an empire") in medieval times theoretically included all of Christendom; and even more theoretically, the entire world, as subject to God's viceroy, the Pope. In practice, its boundaries varied, taking in such territory as a particular emperor could control, and seldom extending much beyond Germany, Austria, and northern Italy. Any European Catholic sovereign was theoretically eligible for the position, but the electors who chose the emperors were chiefly German princes, so that most of the emperors were Germanic. The last of them was Franz II, crowned in 1792, who in 1804 proclaimed himself Emperor of Austria and in 1806 abdicated as Holy Roman Emperor. Thenceforth there were no more takers for the position, and the hoary old anachronism came to an end.

The town of TIPPERARY, North Dakota, is likewise no longer on the map. As a boy, I grew up near that town, situated within a couple of miles of the Canadian border. But it became deserted, and was torn down during the 1930s, and so is no longer on the map. Please pardon this bit of nostalgia. It's a long way back to Tipperary.

APPENDIX II.

Sunken Islands near Iceland

The possible sunken island of Buss, and the evidence for its actuality, have already been discussed in Chapter 3.

Gunnbjorn's Skerries, a group of small islands between Iceland and Greenland, were discovered about the year 876 by one Gunnbjorn Ulfson, who probably also sighted the coast of Greenland, to make him its Norse discoverer. They later became a regular halting point on voyages to Greenland, and an unsuccessful attempt was made to set up a colony there about 970. Apparently there was also a later successful attempt, since a document of 1391 tells us that there were then eighteen farms in the islands. But the islands are no longer there. The Dutch cartographer Ruysch, on his 1507 map, adds a note that in 1456 Gunnbjorn's Skerries were *totaliter combusta*. There seems no doubt that these islands did exist, and whether they sank or "completely burned up," that they did disappear.

During a cataclysmic earthquake in Iceland in 1783, a craggy new island was thrown up in the sea nearby. It was named Nyoe ("New Island"), and claimed in the name of King Christian VII of Denmark; but in a few years' time it sank, leaving a reef of rocks near the surface.

The most famous of Icelandic sunken islands is the one that caused the final extinction of the great auk. Geirfuglaskir ("Gare-Fowl Skerry") near Iceland was the last nesting place of these majestic birds, the great auks or gare-fowl; it was a rugged volcanic skerry ringed with sheer cliffs and inaccessible to men on all its sea-sides, and atop it the birds could nest in safety. But in 1830 the island sank. The auks then moved to the nearby isle of Eldey, likewise craggy and precipitous, but with one shore where men could land. In 1844 came the day when Jon Brandsson and Sigurdr Islefsson—two names which live in infamy—killed the only two great auks they managed to find, which happened to be the last ones on earth.

APPENDIX III.

Evidences of Irish Colonization in America

Saint Brendan's alleged seven-year voyage of discovery in the sixth century, if it occurred, just possibly might have touched on the American continent. Geoffrey Ashe (*Land to the West*) does not believe so, nor do I; but the great Alexander von Humboldt did.

The Icelandic *Heimskringla* relates that about 980 one Ari Marsson was blown across the Atlantic to a country variously called "Greater Ireland" and "White Man's Land," where he was converted to Christianity and baptized (Christianity was not preached in Iceland till around the year 1000). This name of "Greater Ireland" also occurs in the *Flateyahrbok*, in loose association with Vinland, and apparently used as an identification of the area where Leif Ericson made his landfall (though

Ashe believes that Greater Ireland can be identified as Greenland, so this may be a confusion that arose later). The eleventh-century Arab geographer Idrisi also located an "Ireland the Great" (*Irlandah al-Kabirah*) in the western Atlantic.

A certain Feargal, an Irish priest in Germany during the eighth century, got in trouble with the ecclesiastical authorities for maintaining that the world contained other inhabited lands. He cleared himself by satisfying the authorities that the Irish had regular dealings with a land across the Atlantic, and this show of erudition led to his appointment as bishop of Salzburg.

As stated previously in Chapter 3, sites of houses excavated in Greenland have been found to be of medieval Irish, rather than Norse, ground plan. It seems probable that Irish monks, ousted from Iceland by the Norsemen, fled to Greenland, which would well suit their predilection for remote desolate scenes. Some have maintained that Greenland Eskimo tradition, insofar as it can be dated, places the coming of the whites two centuries too early (the eighth century instead of the tenth), possibly referring to an earlier arrival of the Irish, who could have died out (being celibate monks) before the Norse came.

Here on our continent, there is a strange congeries of stone structures near North Salem, New Hampshire, which have never been satisfactorily explained. They resemble a cluster of huts, walls, drains, and a great stone slab which apparently was used as a wine press, all done in unmortared rubblework and identified by some archaeologists as undistinguishable from early Irish stone construction. However, similar stonework has been found in the Channel Isles; and the fact that the Pattee family, from the Isle of Jersey, farmed the land in question a hundred years ago—if we take into consideration the New England farmer's perennial problem of disposing of rocks—has led many to consider the matter solved. But similar, less extensive, stone constructions are also found near Upton, Massachusetts, and in Elephant Hill Valley, Vermont; all of them unexplainable by any such theory of Channel Islands influence. The archaeologist Roland Wells Robbins checked out all three sites and found nothing to indicate that they were of earlier than colonial date. However, Frank Glynn (previously mentioned in Chapter 3 as discoverer of the Sinclair arms) subsequently went through the North Salem site in more detail, and found shards of definitely primitive pottery and bricks of a sort often found in early Mediterranean ruins but never in colonial New England.

Whether these sites are Irish or not, the subject remains open. Geoffrey Ashe, the best recent student of the matter, has proposed an alternative theory of a European Bronze Age emigration to America.

Upholders of the Irish discovery theory generally bring in the "Estotiland" story from the Zeno Narrative because in an aprioristic way it can be used to bolster the hypothesis. They simply derive "Estotiland" from "Escotiland"—literally "Scot-Land," but to be construed as Ireland. In Latin the word "Scot" (*Scotus*) meant Irish, and must always be understood thus; the people of the present Scotland were known to the Romans as *Caledoni*. During the late fourth century Niall, the great Irish king, opened hostilities against the Romans in Britain, attacking largely by sea but also by overland invasions from the north, which brought these Irish "Scots" into association with the land north of Britain, and allied them with the Pechs (*Picti*) from the north of the island; this is the reason for the association of "Picts and Scots" that has confused so many generations of schoolboys. The result was a long-standing uncertainty as to which island a "Scot" was actually from; as late as the tenth century an important theologian had to be identified as Johannes Scotus Erigena ("John, the Scot, born in Ireland"), though later he came to be known simply as Johannes Scotus.

"Escotiland," these people maintain, was the remnant of an unrecorded Irish colony in America, still preserving a butchered form of the name of the old country. Frequently they make an issue of the fact that a Nova Scotia, or "New Scotland" coincidentally still exists in this same area. If this Escotiland hypothesis has any basis, it may just possibly be that the Zenos' Estotiland was in the vicinity of the present North Salem, New Hampshire.

APPENDIX IV.

Example of Climatic Zone System of Geography

The accompanying map illustrates the arrangement of geographical locations in terms of climatic zones, as prepared by Ibn Khaldun, the great late-fourteenth-century Arab geographer and historian, who is regarded,

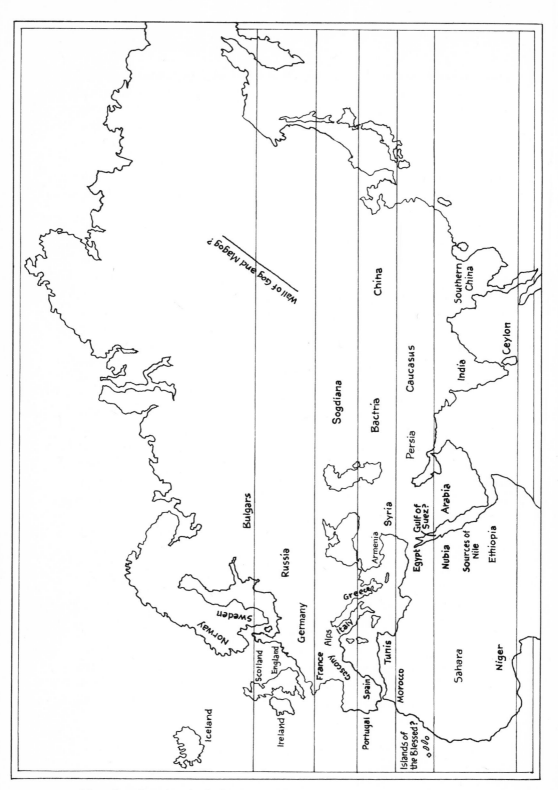

Map showing the Arab theory of climatic zones.

among his other distinctions, as the founder of sociology. Other examples could also be used, but one should serve for purposes of illustration.

It will be noted that the zones vary considerably in width, based as they are on reported climatic conditions and not intended to fit with a system of equidistant degrees of latitude (though the Arabs were quite familiar with this system as well). By medieval standards, the zone system was felt to have more descriptive value. It should be noted that only the supposedly inhabitable parts of the world are covered. To the north and the south respectively were the frozen Arctic and the burning equatorial, so Ibn Khaldun's system actually entails two additional zones, undescribable because unknown.

Within the zones, Ibn Khaldun located the constitutive regions in general quite accurately. Not all of his place names are given here; only enough to illustrate the system involved. There is little point in trying to locate the lands of the Khazars, Bashkirs, or Kipchaks; they were the temporary habitats of nomadic Central Asian peoples. The interested reader is referred to any good historical atlas. The Bulgars at that time had a domain that can be located, in east central Russia, and not to be confused with the modern nation of Bulgaria.

Some of the identifications are doubtful. "Gascony" apparently means the Basque country, and "Southern China" seems to be Malaya. The "Islands of the Blessed" are generally assumed to be the Canaries. The true sources of the Nile are well south of the equator, but medieval geographers made various guesses as to their location, always placing them in the inhabitable zone north of the equator so as to make their discovery possible (it may also be that Ibn Khaldun knew something of the sources of the Blue Nile, in Ethiopia and thus north of the equator).

"The Caucasus" must not be confused with the mountain range now so called. Ibn Khaldun, following Strabo, applied the name to the entire mountain massif that bisects central Asia—the modern Caucasus, the Elburz, Hindu Kush, Pamirs, Himalayas, and Tien Shans. The "Caucasus" here should probably be understood as meaning the Himalayas, and is so placed.

Two dubious locations are here indicated by question marks and underlining. The "Gulf of Suez" may have meant the Red Sea; if not, Ibn Khaldun placed it far too much to the south. The "Wall of Gog and Magog" is here mapped on the assumption that it is supposed to be the Great Wall of China, but if so it is badly misplaced, since Ibn

Khaldun located it in the northernmost zone. But the identification is open to doubt. Medieval geographical rumor placed a number of walls and iron gates here and there in central Asia, and it is anyone's guess which of these Ibn Khaldun had in mind, though the Chinese Wall was probably the origin of the whole legend.

APPENDIX V.

Possible Equatorial Crossings in Pre-Portuguese Times

Herodotus records that the Pharaoh Necho, about 600 B.C., sent out a force of Phoenician seamen to see if Africa could be circumnavigated. They sailed southward from the Red Sea down the east coast of Africa, and twice during their voyage stopped and went ashore to plant grain, living off the country till the grain ripened, then harvesting the crop to provision themselves, and sailed on. After a three-year voyage they entered the Mediterranean via the Strait of Gibraltar, allegedly having proved the possibility of sailing round Africa. "They claimed," says Herodotus, "that during their voyage they had the sun on the right hand, which some may believe, but I do not." But this is the detail that makes the account believable to a modern reader, since while south of the equator they would have seen the sun to the northward (the "right hand").

The historian Diodorus of Sicily (*Siculus*) tells of one Iambulos, a Greek skipper in the India trade, who sailed out of the regular trade lanes and discovered a large island, where he stayed seven years. It has been speculated that this island may have been Madagascar. Some details of his account seem to bear this out: giant birds and animals "very different from all others, and so strange as to be unbelievable" (the giant bird *Aepyornix*, now extinct, was then probably still around in Madagascar; and the "very strange animals" sound like an incoherent reaction to the lemurs). Iambulos described the people of the island as beautiful, light-skinned, with very little hair, and skilled in handcrafts and music; and this fits the Malagasy people well enough. Even more convincing is his description of their alphabet of twenty-eight sounds but using only seven characters, each of which could be written four ways. This tallies with the pre-Hindu alphabet of the Malays, which the Malagasy emigrants would have brought with them. The only difficulty is that this account is from the second century A.D., while most archaeologists place the Malagasy invasion of the island about two centuries later. Some have suggested Sumatra, whence the Malagasy came, as Iambulos's island; but this leaves the giant birds and strange animals unexplained, except on the supposition that they were mere travelers' yarns. The subject is an open one.

Ptolemy records the adventures of another Greek Indiaman named Diogenes, who was blown off course to the coast of Africa. He landed, traveled inland, and discovered the true source of the Nile. If this Diogenes actually did discover the lakes visited so much later by Speke and Burton, his landfall must have been on the coast of Tanganyika (now Tanzania), well below the equator. But the account is vague and open to doubt. In any cast, it was Diogenes as quoted by Ptolemy who placed the Mountains of the Moon (*Montes Lunae*) on the African map. There they were to remain until well into the nineteenth century, and in more modern times the name has often been applied to the Ruwenzori range.

Despite the medieval European belief in the uncrossability of the equator, there is also one possible case on record from that period. Beazley in *The Dawn of Modern Geography* cites an anonymous alleged bishop, writing circa 1330 about his travels in Persia and elsewhere, who claimed to have traveled so far south that he not only lost sight of the North Star (which occurs at about 5° north of the equator) but could view the southern stars 24° high in the sky. If true, this would have brought him close to the Tropic of Capricorn. He also said that "some merchants" had traveled about 30 degrees farther south still, which if true would have brought them about to the latitude of New Zealand. To call these voyagings doubtful would be putting it mildly. But the document itself is authentic, and seems to indicate some belief in late-medieval circles that the equator could be crossed.

APPENDIX VI.

Classical Quotations Taken as Referring to America

As mentioned in Chapter 2, these quotations are best understood as poetic invention or extrapolation from the geographical concepts of the time.

Hanno, the Carthaginian navigator of about 500 B.C., who explored the west coast of Africa, told of a voyage which sailed westward from the Pillars of Hercules (Gibraltar), and discovered land.

Aristotle suggested that there was land across the Atlantic, that its distance from Africa was not great, and that elephants were common to both shores.

Theopompus of Chios, a contemporary of Aristotle, spoke of a land beyond the Atlantic with large animals and populous cities, one with over a million people. The inhabitants of this land, in his version, were twice as tall and lived twice as long as Europeans, and had so much gold that they attached no value to it.

Cicero spoke of a land across the Atlantic, so large that its inhabitants regarded Europe as a small island.

Horace made poetic mention of large islands far away in the Atlantic, where the Romans might find refuge in the bad times to come.

Seneca in his *Medusa* made the alleged prophecy; "After many years the time shall come that the ocean will loosen the bounds with which it confines the earth, and the great continent will be thrown open. Tethis [the sea goddess] will uncover new worlds, and Thule shall no longer be the farthest land."

Pope Gregory the Great said, in the sixth century, that anyone who crossed the Atlantic would discover unknown lands.

Cosmos Indicopleustes, a Byzantine sea captain and geographer of about the time of Pope Gregory, and best remembered as formulator of an elaborate theory that the earth was flat, indicated his belief in another continent west of the Atlantic, which he considered to have been the original home of man.

A number of medieval scholars and philosophers believed in a trans-atlantic world and in the possibility of reaching it. Among them may be mentioned Albertus Magnus, Vincent of Beauvais, John of Salisbury, and Roger Bacon.

Dante in Canto XXVI of the *Inferno,* speaks of "the world devoid of people that lies beyond the setting sun."

The reader will see that the only one of these with any factual value is the Hanno report, which may have been based on an actual voyage of discovery. But the land involved need not be America, since it is assumed by many historians that the Carthaginians did discover the Azores; the thirty days' sail may have been an exaggeration, or have been due to calms or contrary winds. All the rest of these citations are plainly statements of faith in the prevailing geographical concepts, or imaginative embroideries on them.

There is also the "Pseudo-Aristotelian" book *Of Unheard-of Wonders* (i.e., the book was traditionally ascribed to Aristotle but is now regarded as not his work), in which mention is made of a Carthaginian discovery, about 590 B.C., of a large Atlantic island. Conditions on that island, it was said, were so salubrious that mass emigration from Carthage ensued, until the authorities had to forbid it in order to prevent depopulation of the city. It is hard to know what to make of this. It may have been the voyage mentioned by Hanno, or it may have been merely a blown-up rumor recorded by the Greeks. The Carthaginian records were destroyed, along with Carthage, by the Romans; but no other annals of any other Mediterranean nation confirm any such memorable exodus from the important city of Carthage. We do know that a good many Carthaginians did settle in a large Atlantic island, namely Britain (the whole ocean to the west of Europe was then regarded as one, without our present divisions into North Sea, Irish Sea, etc.); so the most likely explanation seems to be that the story was an exaggeration of this. Certainly there is not the slightest evidence of any such massive Carthaginian incursion into America.

APPENDIX VII.

Bouvet Island

Bouvet Island, some 1300 miles south-southwest of Capetown, has been called the remotest spot on earth. Over 1000 miles separate it from the nearest land in any direction. It is thus extremely ironical that its discoverer, Bouvet, should have taken it for a headland of the southern continent.

Captain Cook searched for it unsuccessfully in 1772, and made another attempt on his way back from the Antarctic in 1775; and Captain Furneaux of the Royal Navy tried in 1776, with no better luck. Following this the island was regarded as nonexistent. Cook suggested that Bouvet had been deceived by a large iceberg. The island was rediscovered in 1808 by one of the Enderby Brothers' whaling skippers, James Lindsay, but geographers discounted his report.

In his *Narrative of Four Voyages*, published in 1832, the American sealing captain Benjamin Morrell claimed not only to have rediscovered, but also to have landed on, "Bouvette's Island" in 1824. This book (now an underground classic of sea lore) was so generally untrustworthy as to earn Morrell the sobriquet of "the biggest liar in the Pacific," and his claim to have visited an island that everyone knew didn't exist seemed merely to put the cap on it. To a modern reader Morrell's account seems questionable enough, particularly since he makes it appear that he sailed directly to the island and had no trouble finding it—though it must be admitted that his description of the island, even highly colored as it is, is correct enough.

It was another Enderby whaling captain, George Norris, in command of the brig *Sprightly*, who actually deserves credit for the rediscovery. In December 1825 he came upon a towering glaciated volcanic twin-peak which he named "Liverpool Island," apparently on the assumption that he had discovered something other than the supposedly nonexistent Bouvet Island. While exploring the waters roundabout, as he later claimed, he came upon three jutting rocks which he named the Chimneys, as well as a low-lying island smaller than Bouvet, which he named Thompson Island.

Thus was born a minor geographical myth. Thompson Island has never been conclusively proved nonexistent, but no subsequent searcher has ever been able to find it; barring a dubious report by a whaler in 1893, who made several alleged sketches of it. This did not prevent its turning up on maps, including a Hammond world map as recently as 1954. It may be appropriate to mention that Harold T. Wilkins, in his book *Pirate Treasure*, has called attention to the uncanny frequency with which the name "Thompson" seems to crop up in doubtful tales of the sea.

James Ross, the Antarctic explorer (and nephew of John Ross of the "Croker Mountains" myth) made a futile search for Bouvet in 1843; and a Lieutenant Moore of the Royal Navy, sent out by the Admiralty in 1845 to fix the location of Bouvet Island, had no better luck. It would appear that neither of them knew of Norris's rediscovery, but this sudden official interest in the island would seem to stem from the fact that Norris had taken possession of it for Great Britain. Despite these fiascos, the Admiralty in 1853 was sufficiently convinced that the island existed as to include it in the charts—along with Thompson Island and a "Lindsay Island" dubbed in to cover James Lindsay's reported discovery in 1808. Lindsay Island is still there, on a 1907 Rand McNally map in my possession, but has been dropped since.

The first accurate fix on Bouvet Island was made in 1898 by the German oceanographic vessel *Valdivia*, which also took soundings of over 1200 fathoms at the reported site of Thompson Island.

In 1927 the Norwegian government sent Captain Harald Horntvedt, commanding the whaler *Norvegia*, to the Antarctic on an expedition described as "partly scientific and partly commercial." Horntvedt landed on Bouvet, and, in defiance of the century-old British claim, took possession for Norway. When the United Kingdom contested this claim, Norway proposed to take it up with the League of Nations. But in the end Great Britain gave in gracefully, and Bouvet is now one of Norway's few overseas possessions.

Why Norway was so anxious to secure this seemingly useless island was never made clear. The best guess seems to be that Horntvedt had discovered the long-sought breeding grounds of the sperm whale to be in the vicinity (before World War II, the whaling industry, now dominated by the Greeks, Japanese, and Russians, was almost a Norwegian monopoly).

Norwegian airplanes were sent out, under top-secret conditions, to survey the area. In 1930 a well-equipped Norwegian expedition set out for Bouvet, announcing intentions of staying for a year; but shortly later they were in Capetown en route back to Norway, and those interviewed would only say, "We have received strictest orders to say nothing about our work." And there the matter rests.

During World War II, some action between British and German naval vessels took place in the waters near Bouvet, none of it of any crucial historical importance. Today, Bouvet is occasionally visited by whalers, and the Norwegian government maintains a shelter there for possible victims of shipwreck. And in recent years, Bouvet Island has only been of public interest as the setting for the South African author Geoffrey Jenkins' super-thriller, *A Grue of Ice*.

Surely no island of this sort—remote, uninhabited, without resources, and on the face of it of no value—can have had so strange and romantic a history. Bouvet Island is a striking case history out of the dim region that separates the fabulous from the real. If it could happen to Bouvet, perhaps it could happen to Dougherty. . . . Time may tell.

Notes

CHAPTER 1. *El Dorado: Man and Myth*

The primary sources for this chapter have been Adolph Bandelier, *The Gilded Man* (New York, 1893) and Father John A. Zahm, *The Quest for El Dorado* (New York, 1917). Other sources:

1. Vittorio Lanternari, *Religions of the Oppressed* (New York, 1963), pp. 173–74.
2. R. A. Skelton, *Explorers' Maps* (London and New York, 1958), p. 88.
3. These legends of deformed races have been covered many times and by many scholars. For a good modern popular study, see Chapter 3 of L. Sprague De Camp and Willy Ley, *Lands Beyond* (New York, 1952).
4. Skelton, *op. cit.*, p. 90.

CHAPTER 2. *Terra Australis Quasi Cognita*

The primary sources for this chapter have been Finn Ronne, *Antarctic Conquest* (New York, 1949) and L. Sprague De Camp and Willy Ley, *Lands Beyond* (New York, 1952). Other sources:

1. R. A. Skelton, *Explorers' Maps* (London and New York, 1958), p. 68.
2. W. W. Jarvis, *The World in Maps* (New York, 1937), p. 190.
3. Skelton, *op. cit.*, p. 21.
4. Walter Woodburn Hyde, *Ancient Greek Mariners* (New York, 1947), p. 307.
5. Marjorie Barnard, *A History of Australia* (New York, 1963), p. 21.
6. For a good modern description, see Charles J. Finger, *Valiant Vagabonds* (New York, 1936), pp. 55–56.
7. Skelton, *op. cit.*, p. 245.

8. Herbert Wendt, *It Began in Babel*, translated from the German by James Kirkup (New York, 1961), p. 309.
9. L. P. Kirwan, *A History of Polar Exploration* (New York, 1960), Chapter 8.
10. John Fiske, *Myths and Myth Makers* (Boston, 1896), p. 28*n*.

CHAPTER 3. *The Very Strange Case of Friesland*

1. Translated into English, with introduction, by Richard Henry Major, as *The Voyages of the Venetian Brothers Nicolo and Antonio Zeno in the Northern Seas* (London: Hakluyt Society, 1873). The narrative as given in this chapter is based on Major's translation.
2. Major, *op. cit.*; Frederick L. Lucas, *The Annals of the Voyages of the Brothers Niccolò and Antonio Zeno . . .* (London, 1898); William H. Babcock, *Legendary Islands of the Atlantic* (New York, 1922); Frederick J. Pohl, *Atlantic Crossings Before Columbus* (New York, 1961).
3. As in Peter de Roo, *History of America Before Columbus* (Philadelphia, 1900), Vol. 2, pp. 263–64.
4. Pohl, *op. cit.*, p. 240.
5. Vilhjalmur Stefansson, *Greenland* (Garden City, 1942), pp. 104–105.
6. Farley Mowat, *Westviking* (Boston, 1965), pp. 48–52.
7. Major, *op. cit.*, pp. lxxii–lxxxvi.
8. Pohl, *op. cit.*, pp. 248–57.
9. Roland Wells Robbins and Evan Jones, *Hidden America* (New York, 1959), pp. 145–47; also photograph.
10. Charles M. Boland, *They All Discovered America* (Garden City, 1961), p. 335; quoting from *Massachusetts Archaeological Society Bulletin*, Vol. 21, no. 2, January 1960.
11. Babcock, *op. cit.*, pp. 140–41.
12. Major, *op. cit.*, p. xviii.
13. In *The Omnibus Book of Travelers' Tales*, edited by Milton Waldman (New York, 1932), p. 427. This book, despite its commercial title, is a valuable collection of source material in modern translation.
14. Samuel Purchas, *Hakluytus Posthumus, or Purchas his Pilgrimes* (Glasgow and New York, 1905 ed.), Vol. 14, p. 341.
15. Mowat, *op. cit.*, p. 370.
16. Babcock, *op. cit.*, pp. 130–31.
17. De Roo, *op. cit.*, pp. 486–88; also John Bartlet Brebner, *Explorers of North America* (New York, 1933), pp. 106–107.
18. Babcock, *op. cit.*, pp. 174–78.
19. Purchas, *op. cit.*
20. Ernest S. Dodge, *Northwest by Sea* (New York, 1961), p. 187.
21. Babcock, *op. cit.*
22. *Ibid.*
23. Dodge, *op. cit.*, pp. 228, 245.

CHAPTER 4. *Two Irish Questions: Saint Brendan and Breasil*

This chapter is based primarily on William H. Babcock, *Legendary Islands of the Atlantic* (New York, 1922), Chapters 3 and 4; and, for the voyaging of Saint Brendan, Sir C. Raymond Beazley, *The Dawn of Modern Geography* (London, 1897), Vol. 1, pp. 230–40. Other sources:

1. A modern edition of the *Book of Lismore* is available (Dublin, 1950), as also of the *Imrama* (Dublin, 1941).
2. Charles Edwardes, *Rides and Studies in the Canary Islands* (London, 1888), p. 62.
3. Geoffrey Ashe, *Land to the West* (New York, 1962), Chapters 1–3.
4. *Ibid.*, p. 133.
5. Beazley, *op. cit.*, Vol. 3, pp. 441–42.
6. Ashe, *op. cit.*, p. 294.
7. *The Book of the Knowledge of all the Kingdoms, Lands, and Lordships that are in the World, and the Arms and Devices of Each Land and Lordship, or of the Kings and Lords Who Possess Them. By a Spanish Franciscan,* translated by Sir Clements Markham (London, 1912), p. 29. This was, among other distinctions, the first book on record to attempt to show the flags of all nations.
8. Edwardes, *op. cit.*, p. 61; also Margaret d'Este, *In the Canaries With a Camera* (London, 1909), p. 60. Both of them very informative books despite their unfortunate touristy titles.
9. Lewis Spence, *The Problem of Atlantis* (London, 1924), p. 85. The subject of the book is equivocal, and it could stand a good deal more documentation; but the author was a world-famous folklorist, and even with its faults the book is a valuable repository of Atlantic lore.
10. Mario Pei, *The Story of Language* (Philadelphia, 1949), p. 51.
11. *Book of the Knowledge. . . .* (as Note 7 above), p. 29.
12. Samuel Eliot Morison, *Admiral of the Ocean Sea* (Boston, 1942), pp. 140–41.
13. Bryan Little, *The City and County of Bristol* (London, 1954), pp. 89–91.
14. John Bartlet Brebner, *Explorers of North America* (New York, 1933), p. 108.
15. Clark B. Firestone, *The Coasts of Illusion* (New York, 1924), p. 256.
16. Hugh Marwick, *The Orkneys* (London, 1951), pp. 110–11.
17. Seumas McManus, *The Story of the Irish Race* (New York, 1921), p. 100.
18. *Ibid.*, p. 101.
19. Spence, *op. cit.*, p. 88.
20. Curtis Macdougall, *Hoaxes* (New York, 1940), pp. 293–94.

CHAPTER 5. *Various Islands, Some of Them Devilish*

1. This section is mainly based on William H. Babcock, *Legendary Islands of the Atlantic* (New York, 1922), Chapter 10.

2. Samuel Eliot Morison, *Admiral of the Ocean Sea* (Boston, 1942), Chapter 6.

3. Lieutenant Commander Rupert T. Gould, *Oddities* (London, 1928), pp. 233–47.

4. Babcock, *op. cit.*, pp. 181–84.

5. Philip Gosse, *The Pirates' Who's Who* (Boston, 1924), pp. 273–76.

6. J. Macmillan Brown, *The Riddle of the Pacific* (London, 1924), p. 56; Karl Baarslag, *Islands of Adventure* (New York, 1940), pp. 4–5; Lewis Spence, *The Problem of Lemuria* (London, 1932), p. 22.

7. As in Spence, *op. cit.* A book on so dubious a subject may seem an unsuitable source, but Lewis Spence's erudition is unquestionable and his reputation in other areas firmly established.

8. The primary source here is Gould, *op. cit.*, pp. 225–33.

9. *Ibid.*, pp. 198–203.

10. Benjamin Morrell, *A Narrative of Four Voyages....* (New York, 1832), p. 250. This recondite classic of sea lore badly needs to be made available in a new edition.

11. Babcock, *op. cit.*, pp. 180–81.

12. Reverend H. C. Adams, *Travellers' Tales* (New York, 1927 ed.), pp. 121–24.

13. Gould, *op. cit.*, pp. 203–208.

14. The interested reader can find Incorporado in Babcock, *op. cit.*, and Podesta in Baarslag, *op. cit.* As for Saint John of Lisbon, I have been able to trace it only to the *Occult Review* for November 1921; hardly a proper source for this purpose.

This section was based primarily on Babcock, *op. cit.*, Chapters 10 and 12. Other sources:

15. Rachel Carson, *The Sea Around Us* (New York, 1951), p. 83.

16. For the Steinheimer treasure, see J. Frank Dobie, *Coronado's Children* (Garden City, 1930), pp. 121–24. A good discussion of the Cocos Island myth can be found in Harold T. Wilkins, *Pirate Treasure* (New York, 1937), pp. 271–96.

17. Antonio Galvano, *Discoveries of the World* (London, 1862), p. 31.

18. Holmes Welch, *The Parting of the Way* (Boston, 1957), pp. 91–97.

19. Guy C. Rothery, *Amazons in Antiquity and Modern Times* (London, 1910), pp. 81–82.

20. *Book of the Knowledge....* (as cited in Chapter 4, Note 7), p. 28.

21. Nils Adolf Erik Nordenskjold, *Periplus* (Stockholm, 1897), pl. 20.

22. Farley Mowat, *Westviking* (Boston, 1965), pp. 466–72.

23. *Ibid., passim.*

CHAPTER 6.   *From Seven Cities to None*

The accounts of Spanish exploration are based upon *Spanish Explorations in the Southwest*, edited by Herbert Eugene Bolton (New York, 1946 ed.), a very valuable and readily available collection of source materials in modern translation, in which the interested reader can find the original accounts of Cabeza de Vaca, Fray Marcos, Coronado, Cabrillo, de Soto, etc. Also useful was commentary in John Bartlet Brebner, *Explorers of North America* (New York, 1933). Other sources:

1. William H. Babcock, *Legendary Islands of the Atlantic* (New York, 1922), Chapter 5.
2. Walter F. Walker, *The Azores* (London, 1886), p. 11.
3. Babcock, *op. cit.*, pp. 144–45.
4. Peter de Roo, *History of America Before Columbus* (Philadelphia, 1900), Vol. 2, p. 503.
5. Brebner, *op. cit.*, p. 108.
6. Roland Wells Robbins and Evan Jones, *Hidden America* (New York, 1959), pp. 245–46, includes the story of a stone allegedly found at Lyons, Kansas, on which was chiseled "Augusto el Tiers / 1541 / Toma / Per España / Quiver / [F]rancisco." This stone is no longer believed to be authentic, since "Quiver" is a common misspelling with modern writers but a form never found in the old Spanish inscriptions or literature. (Letter to the author from Horace Jones, editor of the Lyons *Daily News*, April 1971.)
7. Babcock, *op. cit.*, p. 78.
8. William H. Koebel, *Madeira Old and New* (London, 1909), pp. 33–35.
9. Brebner, *op. cit.*, pp. 200–201.
10. Alfred Powers, *Redwood Country* (New York, 1949), p. 22.
11. Antonio Galvano, *Discoveries of the World* (London: Hakluyt Society, 1862), p. 227.
12. Powers, *op. cit.*, p. 23.
13. *Ibid.*, pp. 23–25.
14. Brebner, *op. cit.*, p. 323.
15. R. A. Skelton, *Explorers' Maps* (London and New York, 1958), p. 266.
16. George R. Stewart, *Names on the Land* (New York, 1957 ed.), pp. 153–54.

CHAPTER 7.   *That Elusive Northwest Passage*

1. Particularly well-told by Ernest S. Dodge in *Northwest by Sea* (New York, 1961), a primary source for this chapter. Accounts of French explorations were based largely on John Bartlet Brebner, *Explorers of North America* (New York, 1933).
2. Harold Lamb, *New Found World* (Garden City, 1955), pp. 111–12.
3. R. A. Skelton, *Explorers' Maps* (London and New York, 1958), p. 92.
4. It is not mentioned in any extant version of Verrazano's actual report, which the reader may find in *The Omnibus Book of Travelers' Tales*, edited by Milton Waldman (New York, 1932).
5. Skelton, *op. cit.*
6. Lamb, *op. cit.*, pp. 125–27.

7. *Ibid.*
8. Lloyd A. Brown, *The Story of Maps* (Boston, 1949), p. 208.
9. Leo Bagrow, *History of Cartography*, translated from the German by R. A. Skelton (Cambridge, 1964), p. 200.
10. Bagrow, *op. cit.*, pp. 135–36; also Skelton, *op. cit.*, p. 117.
11. Antonio Galvano, *Discoveries of the World* (London, 1862), p. 49.
12. For one such which may have influenced Columbus, see Samuel Eliot Morison, *Admiral of the Ocean Sea* (Boston, 1942), pp. 137–38.
13. Samuel Purchas, *Hakluytus Posthumus, or Purchas his Pilgrimes* (Glasgow and New York, 1905), Vol. 14, p. 414.
14. Dodge, *op. cit.*, p. 67.
15. Brebner, *op. cit.*, p. 200.
16. Purchas, *op. cit.*, Vol. 14, pp. 415–21; also Percy G. Adams, *Travelers and Travel Liars* (Berkeley, 1962), pp. 133–37.
17. Meridel Le Sueur, *North Star Country* (New York, 1945), p. 45.
18. Hjalmar Holand, *America 1355–1364* (New York, 1946), pp. 237–38.
19. Adams, *op. cit.*, pp. 54–57.
20. George R. Stewart, *Names on the Land* (New York, 1958 ed.), pp. 153–54.
21. Skelton, *op. cit.*, pp. 130–31.
22. Dodge, *op. cit.*, pp. 211–14.
23. *Ibid.*, pp. 183–84.
24. A good discussion of the Open Polar Sea can be found in John K. Wright, *Human Nature in Geography* (New York, 1966), Chapter 6.
25. The story is given here as in Vincent Gaddis, *Invisible Horizons* (Philadelphia, 1965), pp. 105–108.

CHAPTER 8. *The Unknown Northern Land*

1. A good coverage of the suggested Indian etymologies of the name Norumbega can be found in Hjalmar Holand, *Explorations in America Before Columbus* (New York, 1956), pp. 252–53. I am not in agreement with all of Holand's conclusions, but his book was extremely useful in the preparing of this chapter.
2. George R. Stewart, *Names on the Land* (New York, 1958 ed.), p. 36.
3. Holand, *op. cit.*
4. Peter de Roo, *History of America Before Columbus* (Philadelphia, 1900), Vol. 2, p. 301.
5. *The Omnibus Book of Travelers' Tales*, edited by Milton Waldman (New York, 1932).
6. Holand, *op. cit.*, p. 256.
7. R. A. Skelton, *Explorers' Maps* (London and New York, 1958), p. 92.
8. Holand, *op. cit.*, p. 254.
9. John Bartlet Brebner, *Explorers of North America* (New York, 1933), pp. 132–33.

10. Holand, *op. cit.*, pp. 254–55.
11. Stewart, *op. cit.*, p. 86.
12. Samuel Purchas, *Hakluytus Posthumus, or Purchas his Pilgrimes* (Glasgow and New York, 1905), Vol. 18, pp. 243–44.
13. See the *Science Digest*, February 1964; *Science Newsletter*, Nov. 16, 1963; *National Geographic Magazine*, November 1963.
14. As in Farley Mowat, *Westviking* (Boston, 1965), *passim*.
15. Frederick J. Pohl, *Atlantic Crossings Before Columbus* (New York, 1961), pp. 183–84.
16. De Roo, *op. cit.*, Vol. 2, pp. 318–19.
17. Holand, *op. cit.*, pp. 246–47.
18. Purchas, *op. cit.*, pp. 277–78.
19. De Roo, *op. cit.*, pp. 486–87.
20. Holand, *op. cit.*, pp. 219–20.

CHAPTER 9.   *The Peregrinations of Greenland*

1. As nearly as I can determine, this theory was first advanced by Peter de Roo in *History of America Before Columbus* (Philadelphia, 1900), Vol. 2, pp. 64–65; it has since been accepted by other students, such as Geoffrey Ashe in *Land to the West* (New York, 1962), pp. 176–82, and Farley Mowat in *Westviking* (Boston, 1965), p. 6. However, I believe that I have been the first to grapple with the Gaelic linguistic problem involved. De Roo was a diligent scholar, and very knowledgeable about obscure Latin documents. His two-volume study suffers from a clumsy system of documentation and from the author's quasi-religious preconceptions, and many of the conclusions drawn are now untenable. But it is a valuable and unjustly neglected treasury of data not now easily available, and I have cited it rather frequently in the present work.
2. De Roo, *op. cit.*, Vol. 2, pp. 142–43.
3. The translation here is my own, based on the 1948 Copenhagen edition of the Latin text. Interested readers are referred to the modern English translation by Francis J. Tschan, *History of the Archbishops of Hamburg-Bremen* (New York, 1959).
4. *Time*, October 15, 1965; *Newsweek*, October 18, 1965; *Science Newsletter*, October 23, 1965; or any metropolitan newspaper of about October 4–11, 1965.
5. Leo Bagrow, *History of Cartography*, translated from the German by R. A. Skelton (Cambridge, 1964), pp. 77–79.
6. De Roo, *op. cit.*, Vol. 2, p. 448.
7. Hjalmar Holand, *Explorations in America Before Columbus* (New York, 1956), pp. 303, 305; also Leonard Outhwaite, *The Atlantic* (New York, 1957), p. 120.
8. A good study of this voyage can be found in Holand, *op. cit.*, Chapter 26.
9. *Ibid.*, p. 298 (reference to "Johannes Scolvus Pilonus").

10. For an account of a Portuguese voyage commanded by a Dane, see Gomes Eannes de Azurara, *The Chronicle of the Discovery and Conquest of Guinea*, translated from the Portuguese by C. Raymond Beazley and Edgar Prestage (London, 1896), Vol. 2, pp. 280–86.
11. Holand, *op. cit.*, p. 298.
12. For this suggested identification, see Holand, *op. cit.*, pp. 303–304.
13. *Ibid.*, p. 299.
14. R. N. Rudmose Brown, *Spitsbergen* (London, 1920), pp. 19–20.
15. Antonio Galvano, *Discoveries of the World* (London, 1862), p. 49.
16. See the voyages of Jonas Poole in Samuel Purchas, *Hakluytus Posthumus, or Purchas his Pilgrimes* (Glasgow and New York, 1905), Vol. 14.
17. Brown, *op. cit.*, pp. 21, 78–79.
18. *Ibid.*, pp. 70–72.
19. John K. Wright, *Human Nature in Geography* (New York, 1966), pp. 91, 109–10.
20. Brown, *op. cit.*, p. 79.
21. William H. Babcock, *Legendary Islands of the Atlantic* (New York, 1922), p. 100.
22. Vilkjalmur Stefansson, *Greenland* (Garden City, 1942), p. 232.

CHAPTER 10.   *The Maybe of Mayda*

This chapter is based primarily on Chapter 6 of William H. Babcock, *Legendary Islands of the Atlantic* (New York, 1922). Other sources:

1. A good concise rundown on vanished islands can be found in Karl Baarslag, *Islands of Adventure* (New York, 1940), Chapter 15.
2. J. Macmillan Brown, *The Riddle of the Pacific* (London, 1924), pp. 55–56.
3. Lewis Spence, *The Problem of Lemuria* (London, 1932), pp. 161–62, quoting from the London *Sunday Times*, July 31, 1932.
4. As nearly as I can determine, the identification of this land with Mayda was first made in Vincent Gaddis, *Invisible Horizons* (Philadelphia, 1965), pp. 29–30. Gaddis's book is sensational and not a good source, but the two Hydrographic Office notices, cited by him, are authentic.

CHAPTER 11.   *Three Special Cases*

1. Except when otherwise indicated, this section of the chapter is based on Walter Woodburn Hyde, *Ancient Greek Mariners* (New York, 1947), Chapter 3.
2. As Lionel Casson in *The Ancient Mariners* (New York, 1959), pp. 58–65.
3. *The Geography of Strabo*, translated by Horace Leonard Jones (London, 1917), Vol. 5, p. 215.
4. Samuel Purchas, *Hakluytus Posthumus, or Purchas his Pilgrimes* (Glasgow and New York, 1905), Vol. 11, p. 620.

5. Mario Pei, *The Story of Language* (Philadelphia, 1949), p. 48.

6. Alfred Powers, *Redwood Country* (New York, 1949), p. 229; also George R. Stewart, *Names on the Land* (New York, 1958 ed.), pp. 14–15.

7. R. A. Skelton, *Explorers' Maps* (London and New York, 1958), p. 271.

8. *Ibid.*, p. 265.

9. L. P. Kirwan, *History of Polar Exploration* (New York, 1960), pp. 83–86.

10. William H. Hobbs, *Peary* (New York, 1936), pp. 289–99; also Theo Loebsack, *Our Atmosphere*, translated from the German by E. and D. Redwald (New York, 1959), pp. 50–51.

11. Hobbs, *op. cit.*, p. 279.

Index

THE WORLD

SCALE 1:120,000,000

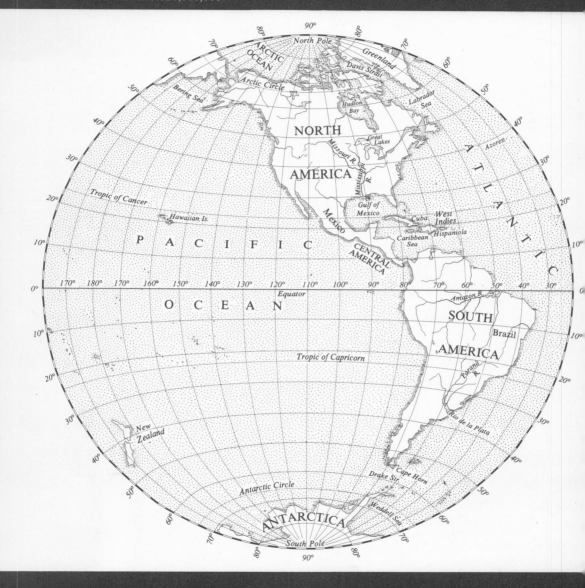